Enterprise Augmented Reality Projects

Build real-world, large-scale AR solutions for various industries

Jorge R. López Benito
Enara Artetxe González

BIRMINGHAM - MUMBAI

Enterprise Augmented Reality Projects

Commissioning Editor: Pavan Ramchandani
Acquisition Editor: Ashitosh Gupta
Content Development Editor: Aamir Ahmed
Senior Editor: Hayden Edwards
Technical Editor: Jane Dsouza
Copy Editor: Safis Editing
Project Coordinator: Manthan Patel
Proofreader: Safis Editing
Indexer: Rekha Nair
Production Designer: Joshua Misquitta

First published: December 2019

Production reference: 1201219

Published by Packt Publishing Ltd.
Livery Place
35 Livery Street
Birmingham
B3 2PB, UK.

ISBN 978-1-78980-740-0

www.packt.com

To my family, Ama, Aita, Ibai, Carlos, and Luka. Eskerrik asko. Beti.

– Enara Artetxe González

To my parents, my mother Isabel and my father Luis, for their on-going support and endless encouragement. And to my better half Ana, for always being there and helping me to overcome any challenges I face.

– Jorge R. López Benito

`Packt.com`

Subscribe to our online digital library for full access to over 7,000 books and videos, as well as industry leading tools to help you plan your personal development and advance your career. For more information, please visit our website.

Why subscribe?

- Spend less time learning and more time coding with practical eBooks and Videos from over 4,000 industry professionals

- Improve your learning with Skill Plans built especially for you

- Get a free eBook or video every month

- Fully searchable for easy access to vital information

- Copy and paste, print, and bookmark content

Did you know that Packt offers eBook versions of every book published, with PDF and ePub files available? You can upgrade to the eBook version at `www.packt.com` and as a print book customer, you are entitled to a discount on the eBook copy. Get in touch with us at `customercare@packtpub.com` for more details.

At `www.packt.com`, you can also read a collection of free technical articles, sign up for a range of free newsletters, and receive exclusive discounts and offers on Packt books and eBooks.

Contributors

About the authors

Jorge R. López Benito is a tech entrepreneur passionate about emerging and exponential technologies with more than 10 years of experience in researching and building **Augmented Reality** (**AR**), **Virtual Reality** (**VR**), and **Artificial Intelligence** (**AI**) products. In 2010, he became the co-founder and CEO of CreativiTIC, which focused on the research of disruptive technologies, new business models, and market innovation trends. He has been involved in several R&D projects throughout his career, including FP7 and H2020 European projects, and because of that, he was named as a Key Innovator in AR & Deep Learning Technologies by the European Commission; whom he also supports as an independent expert on interactive technologies to explore emerging trends and identify opportunities for impact across the industries, and also as a Jury Member at the European Innovation Council (EIC) Accelerator.

https://www.linkedin.com/in/jrlopezbenito/

Enara Artetxe González is the co-founder and CTO of CreativiTIC, a company dedicated to **Mixed Reality** (**MR**) technologies. With a bachelor's degree in telecommunications engineering, she has been working with **Augmented Reality** (**AR**) and **Virtual Reality** (**VR**) technologies for more than 10 years, developing innovative solutions for desktop, mobile, web, and **head-mounted display** (**HMD**) platforms in fields such as industry, healthcare, and education. She has participated in several R&D projects including FP7 and H2020 European research projects, and because of that, she was named as a Key Innovator in AR & Deep Learning Technologies by the European Commission. She actively supports vocational actions to involve girls in science and technology through STEAM methodologies.

https://www.linkedin.com/in/eartetxe/

About the reviewer

Ken Crawford is an AR developer and researcher based in the United States with a focus on AR glasses used in enterprise and manufacturing settings. He currently works for an engineering company where he is involved with testing AR software for remote assistance, employee training, and developing the organization's technical capabilities to implement and effectively use AR throughout its operations.

Prior to his engineering position, Ken had an AR start-up called Ear Compass, from 2015 to 2017, that looked to leverage the spatial awareness of the Microsoft HoloLens platform for the visually impaired.

Ken holds a doctorate and a master's degree from Northern Illinois University. He was formerly a combat engineer with the US Marine Corps.

Packt is searching for authors like you

If you're interested in becoming an author for Packt, please visit `authors.packtpub.com` and apply today. We have worked with thousands of developers and tech professionals, just like you, to help them share their insight with the global tech community. You can make a general application, apply for a specific hot topic that we are recruiting an author for, or submit your own idea.

Acknowledgments

We would like to acknowledge the amazing staff and editorial team at Packt Publishing: without their talent and dedication, this book would not have turned out to be such a valuable asset. First, we would like to thank Ashitosh Gupta for contacting us and giving us the opportunity of writing about a subject, Augmented Reality, that we love. We also want to thank our editors Aamir Ahmed, Jane D'souza, and Hayden Edwards for their many insightful comments and guiding us through the process of writing. Thanks for your efforts and helpfulness.

A special mention goes to our good friend Aitor Sansebastián for encouraging us to carry out this project out. We would also like to thank all those who've supporting us in this journey since we founded our company, the ones who have been there from the beginning, and those who joined us along the way. You know who you are :)

"I would especially like to thank the two women who have accompanied me along the process of this book. First, to Enara Artetxe, the co-author of this book and a professional colleague, who I consider the best "ninja developer" in augmented reality. Without her, this book could not have been possible. And second, to my better half Ana Laín, for her daily support in every aspect of my life and for helping me to overcome any challenges I encountered." - Jorge R. López Benito

"A special thanks goes to my cat Keiko; without her constant jumping on my keyboard, threatening to write the book herself, or the endless hours of sitting in my lap, leaving me without anything to do but coding and writing, the process of writing this book wouldn't have been the same :)" - Enara Artetxe González

Last but not least, a big THANK YOU to you all, our readers, for investing your time in reading our book. We hope you have learned and enjoyed as much as we have.

Table of Contents

Preface

Augmented reality (**AR**) is an amazing technology that dates back to the 1990s and was mostly unknown to the general public until the appearance of Google Glass and the release of the AR-based game Pokemon Go. Although, initially, it was mainly used in marketing to get the *wow effect*, it has since proved to be a natural interface for the user in many other fields, such as tourism, industry, medicine, and education. Its versatility of features (based on image or physical world recognition, GPS location, and more) and target devices (Android/iOS mobile devices, computer, web, and **Head Mounted Displays** (**HMD**)) makes it the perfect complement for different sectors and implementations such as industrial guides, live art experiences, and training tools.

Enterprise Augmented Reality Projects aims to take you on a journey of developing and building applications with AR using the best-known frameworks on the market. In this book, we'll explore the aspects of developing AR-based applications for six different enterprise sectors (manufacturing, training, marketing, retail, automation, and tourism) in detail, starting from the market needs and choosing the most suitable tool in each case. Each chapter will cover a new use of AR by using a different framework or target device.

The first chapter will be an introduction to AR so that you will have a good understanding of its uses and potential before starting to code. Next, we'll introduce you to Unity, an amazing 3D tool that will simplify the task of integrating AR frameworks and manipulating 3D objects and scenes in many of the chapters. Then, we'll work with Android Studio and ARCore to create our first augmented project for prototyping. Afterward, we will explore both WebAR with the Google Web Component `<model-viewer>`, and the emerging AR authoring tool, Augmented Class!, for education. Next, we will start working with Unity to integrate the AR framework, EasyAR, to create an AR catalog for a marketing experience. We will then continue with the Vuforia framework and use it retail. Furthermore, we will use Vuforia combined with AR glasses to create a step-by-step guide for an automation process. We will then end the book with ARKit, developed, in this case, inside Xcode, to implement an augmented dimensional portal for tourism.

Who this book is for

Enterprise Augmented Reality Projects is aimed at enthusiasts of emerging and interactive technologies interested in building AR applications for any field step by step, and learning about the latest tools to develop them. No prior AR experience is required. Some object-oriented programming skills would be helpful.

What this book covers

Chapter 1, *Introduction to AR and How it Fits the Enterprise*, starts off the book by introducing AR and its uses. It covers the origins of the technology, types of AR that can be developed, the frameworks you will be using through the book, and the main uses of AR in different enterprise sectors.

Chapter 2, *Introduction to Unity for AR Development*, is an introduction to the real-time 3D development platform Unity, where you will learn the nomenclature and uses of the main elements. You will also learn how to create a first script in C# to see the potential of this tool.

Chapter 3, *AR for Manufacturing with ARCore*, introduces the ARCore technology and how to implement its surface detection features. You will create a prototype viewer for Android using Android Studio and the Sceneform plugin, which will help us to easily integrate 3D models in our project.

Chapter 4, *AR for Training with WebAR and Augmented Class!*, explores two different tools in a common project for training purposes. With WebAR, you will learn how to develop a simple web app that includes the `<model-viewer>` web component, which will be used to launch AR from an ARCore-supporting mobile device. Augmented Class! is an authoring tool for Android that's used to easily create interactive educational AR projects.

Chapter 5, *AR for Marketing with EasyAR*, introduces you to using Unity to develop AR projects with the EasyAR framework. You will learn how to develop an augmented catalog based on image tracking and how to create interfaces in Unity and link them to scripts and objects in the scene.

Chapter 6, *AR for Retail with Vuforia*, teaches you how to use Vuforia's ground detection features inside Unity to place 3D objects over flat surfaces and move/rotate/scale them, with the possibility of adding ARCore on top of Vuforia. All the while, you will work further with Unity and its components to reinforce previous concepts.

Chapter 7, *AR for Automation with Vuforia and AR Glasses*, continues developing with the Vuforia framework but oriented in this case to building on AR glasses. You will learn about the similarities and differences between mobile and glasses-oriented apps while creating an augmented guide for an automation process.

Chapter 8, *AR for Tourism with ARKit*, developed over Xcode and aimed at iOS devices. In this chapter, you will create an augmented portal anchored to the real world that will transport the user to a hidden virtual world. To do this, you will also learn how to work with the SceneKit framework to create 3D scenes and display 3D models.

To get the most out of this book

To get the most of this book, no prior AR or Unity experience is required as they will be covered in detail. Similarly, prior understanding of Android Studio and Xcode would be helpful, but is not required. Object-oriented programming skills would be helpful as we will be using Java, C#, and Swift for our projects. However, if you follow the steps in the book and copy and paste the code, you will be able to build all the projects from scratch.

Every chapter will contain the installation instructions and information you will need to implement each project.

VS: Although VS2019 is out, we are using 2017 as it comes integrated with Unity and will ensure it works directly without further configuration.

JDK: Any version of JDK 8 and above from the new OpenJDK should be functional but specifying that to avoid errors, the version 8 works.

Download the example code files

You can download the example code files for this book from your account at `www.packt.com`. If you purchased this book elsewhere, you can visit `www.packtpub.com/support` and register to have the files emailed directly to you.

You can download the code files by following these steps:

1. Log in or register at `www.packt.com`.
2. Select the **Support** tab.
3. Click on **Code Downloads**.
4. Enter the name of the book in the **Search** box and follow the onscreen instructions.

Once the file is downloaded, please make sure that you unzip or extract the folder using the latest version of:

- WinRAR/7-Zip for Windows
- Zipeg/iZip/UnRarX for Mac
- 7-Zip/PeaZip for Linux

The code bundle for the book is also hosted on GitHub at `https://github.com/PacktPublishing/Enterprise-Augmented-Reality-Projects`. In case there's an update to the code, it will be updated on the existing GitHub repository.

We also have other code bundles from our rich catalog of books and videos available at `https://github.com/PacktPublishing/`. Check them out!

Download the color images

We also provide a PDF file that has color images of the screenshots/diagrams used in this book. You can download it here: `https://static.packt-cdn.com/downloads/9781789807400_ColorImages.pdf`.

Conventions used

There are a number of text conventions used throughout this book.

`CodeInText`: Indicates code words in text, database table names, folder names, filenames, file extensions, pathnames, dummy URLs, user input, and Twitter handles. Here is an example: "Remove the text from it, and change the button name to `Home_button`."

A block of code is set as follows:

```
h1 {
  text-align: center;
  color: #000000;
  font-style: bold;
}
```

Bold: Indicates a new term, an important word, or words that you see on screen. For example, words in menus or dialog boxes appear in the text like this. Here is an example: "Select the **ARCamera**, and in the **Inspector** window click on **Open Vuforia Engine Configuration**."

 Warnings or important notes appear like this.

 Tips and tricks appear like this.

Get in touch

Feedback from our readers is always welcome.

General feedback: If you have questions about any aspect of this book, mention the book title in the subject of your message and email us at customercare@packtpub.com.

Errata: Although we have taken every care to ensure the accuracy of our content, mistakes do happen. If you have found a mistake in this book, we would be grateful if you would report this to us. Please visit www.packtpub.com/support/errata, selecting your book, clicking on the Errata Submission Form link, and entering the details.

Piracy: If you come across any illegal copies of our works in any form on the internet, we would be grateful if you would provide us with the location address or website name. Please contact us at copyright@packt.com with a link to the material.

If you are interested in becoming an author: If there is a topic that you have expertise in and you are interested in either writing or contributing to a book, please visit authors.packtpub.com.

Reviews

Please leave a review. Once you have read and used this book, why not leave a review on the site that you purchased it from? Potential readers can then see and use your unbiased opinion to make purchase decisions, we at Packt can understand what you think about our products, and our authors can see your feedback on their book. Thank you!

For more information about Packt, please visit packt.com.

1
Introduction to AR and How It Fits the Enterprise

This book was written for enthusiasts of emerging and interactive technologies who are interested in building AR applications for any market field from the very beginning, and learning about the latest tools to develop them. No prior AR experience is required.

The idea of this book is to introduce you to different AR frameworks by completing a set of projects in different enterprise environments. Although specific programming skills are not mandatory, minimal knowledge is desirable so that you understand the code in each example. Some object-oriented programming skills would be helpful, but they are not required. This book has been written from scratch, so you'll be able to follow any coding necessities step by step.

In this chapter, we will learn what **Augmented Reality** (**AR**) is and we will present a brief tour of its history, types, and how it works. We will also introduce the **Software Development Kits** (**SDKs**) that we will work with in this book. Finally, we will look at examples of the use of AR and, in particular, its application inside the enterprise. The main objective of this chapter is to understand how AR is being used today, including markets, technologies, devices, and development tools with a variety of AR recognition modes, such as target images, cloud markers, GPS-based, object or face tracking, and spatial mapping. You will also learn about the main AR tools we are going to use in this book and a brief introduction to their main features.

By the end of this chapter, you will have a basic understanding of how AR works and what its different uses are so that you can follow the technical chapters ahead more easily.

In this chapter, we will cover the following topics:

- Understanding AR
- Working with AR
- Using AR in enterprises

Understanding AR

AR is the term that's used to describe the technology that allows users to visualize part of the real world through the camera of a technological device (smartphone, tablet, or AR glasses) with virtual graphical information that's been added by this device. The device adds this virtual information to existing physical information. By doing this, tangible physical elements combine with virtual elements, thus creating augmented reality in real-time. The following image shows how AR works:

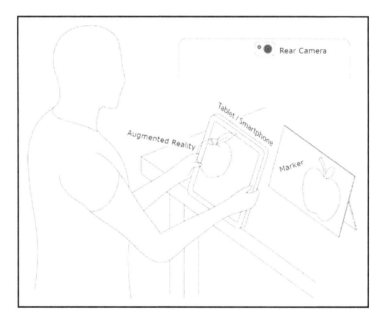

A user seeing a 3D apple in AR with a tablet

Now, we are going to look at the beginnings of AR and learn how AR can be divided according to its functionality.

Short history – the beginnings of a new reality

AR is not a new technology. The beginnings of AR begin with the machine that was invented by Morton Heilig, a philosopher, visionary, and filmmaker, when, in 1957, he began to build a prototype with an appearance similar to the arcade video game machines that were very popular in the 90s. The following image shows a schema of how the prototype worked:

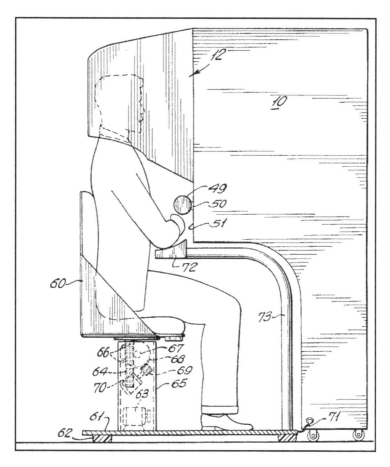

A schema on how the invention worked (This image is created by Morton Heilig)

Morton called his invention **Sensorama**, an experience that projected 3D images, added a surround sound, made the seat vibrate, and created wind that was thrown as air at the viewer. The closest similar experience we can feel today is seeing a movie in a 4D cinema, but these experiences were created more than 60 years ago.

In 1968, Harvard Electrical Engineering professor Ivan Sutherland created a device that would be the key to the future of the AR technology known as the **Human-Mounted Display** (**HMD**). Far from the AR glasses that we know of today, this HMD, called **the Sword of Damocles**, was a huge machine that hung from the ceiling of a laboratory and worked when the user was placed in the right place. In the following image, you can see what this invention looked like:

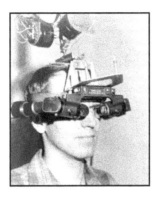

The Sword of Damocles (this image was created by OyundariZorigtbaatar)

In 1992, Boeing researcher Tom Caudell invented the term AR, and at the same time, AR technology was boosted from two other works. The first AR system, from L.B. Rosenberg, who works for the United States Air Force, is a device that gives advice to the user on how to perform certain tasks as they are presented, something like a virtual guide. This can be seen in the following image:

Virtual Fixtures AR system on the left and its view on the right (this image was created by AR Trends)

The other research in this area was led at Columbia University, where a team of scientists invented an HMD that interacted with a printer. The device, baptized as **Karma** (AR based on knowledge for maintenance assistance), projected a 3D image to tell the user how to recharge the printer, instead of going to the user manual.

The following diagram is a representation of the continuum of advanced computer interfaces, based on Milgram and Kishino (1994), where we can see the different subdivisions of the **MIXED REALITY (MR)** that go from the **REAL ENVIRONMENT** to the **VIRTUAL REALITY**. AR that's located nearer to the **REAL ENVIRONMENT** is divided between spatial AR and see-through AR. However, the appearance of mobile devices in the 21st century has allowed a different version of AR, where we can display it using the device screen and camera:

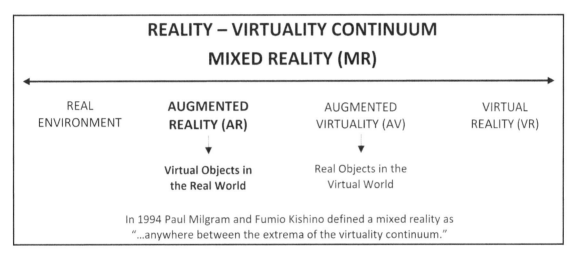

MIXED REALITY and its subdivisions

Now that we have introduced the beginnings of AR, let's learn how this technology can be classified depending on the trigger that's used to show virtual elements in the real world.

The magic behind AR

AR can be created in many ways; the main challenge is how to make the combination of the real and virtual worlds as seamless as possible. Based on what is used to trigger the virtual elements to appear in the real world, AR can be classified as follows:

- **GPS coordinates**: We use GPS coordinates, compasses, and accelerometers to locate the exact position of the user, including the cardinal point they are looking at. Depending on where the user is pointing to, they will see some virtual objects or others from the same position.
- **Black and white markers**: We use very simple images, similar to black and white QR codes, to project virtual objects on them. This was one of the first AR examples, although nowadays they are used less often as there are more realistic ways to create the AR experience.
- **Image markers**: We use the camera of the mobile device to locate predefined images (also called targets or markers) and then project virtual objects over them. This type of AR has substituted black and white markers.
- **Real-time markers**: The user creates and defines their own images with the mobile camera to project any virtual object in them.
- **Facial recognition**: Through the camera, we capture the movements of the face to execute certain actions in a request, for example, to give facial expressions to a virtual avatar.
- **SLAM**: Short for **Simultaneous Localization And Mapping**, this technology understands the physical world through feature points, thereby making it possible for AR applications to recognize 3D objects and scenes, as well as to instantly track the world, and overlay digital interactive augmentations.
- **Beacons**: eBeacons, RFID, and NFC are identification systems that use radio frequency or bluetooth, similar to GPS coordinates, to trigger the AR elements.

Now, you have a better grasp of what AR is and where it comes from. We have covered the basics of AR by looking at the first prototypes, and classified different types of AR according to the element that triggers the virtual images so that they appear on the screen. The next step is to see what is required to work with it.

Working with AR

AR projects need some basic elements to fulfill its function:

- Digital support, mainly tablet, mobile phone, or glasses. These will be the devices we will use to recognize what we are seeing and incorporate the information into AR.
- Sensors to perceive reality as a camera, GPS, 3D scanner, and so on. They are usually integrated into mobile devices.
- An algorithm or application to understand the reality that is being observed, interpreted, and displayed with the associated information.
- Digital content to enrich reality. This is all the information that you incorporate into AR.

The result is an interface in which reality is observed with additional information located in the space it needs to be in. The following subsections present different AR libraries and SDKs, as well as how they function.

ARToolKit – the first AR library

ARToolKit was the world's first open source software library and allows the creation of AR applications, in which virtual images overlap in the real world. It uses video tracking capabilities to calculate the position of the camera and the orientation relative to the position of the physical markers in real-time. Once the position of the real camera is established, the virtual camera is placed at the same point and a virtual layer of information, such as a 3D object, is superimposed on the real marker. ARToolKit was originally developed by Hirokazu Kato and the initial release was published in 1999 by the HIT Laboratory of the University of Washington. It is currently maintained as an open source project hosted at SourceForge with commercial licenses available at ARToolworks: `http://www.artoolkitx.org/`.

Introduction to the AR SDKs

Now, we will introduce the AR SDKs that we will use in this book. From the first appearance of ARToolKit, AR SDKs have very much evolved. Let's introduce and describe the different SDKs we are going to use in this book to create our own AR experiences:

- Vuforia
- EasyAR

- ARCore
- ARKit

Let's talk a little bit about each of them.

Vuforia

Initially developed by Qualcomm, and currently run by PTC, Vuforia is one of the oldest and most well-known AR SDKs, and it's one of the most stable and best-performing pieces of software in the market. Vuforia offers a wide variety of features, including 2D and 3D tracking, markerless AR, and fiducial markers called **Vumarks**. It provides multiple examples and extra features, such as virtual buttons, runtime image target creation, and background video texture manipulation.

EasyAR

An AR engine that allows us to create AR solutions in an easy way and offers multiple AR features, including technology that recognizes and tracks the position, rotation, and scale of a previously selected image in the real world, such as a book cover, a photograph, or a business card. It allows us to map a real place and keep track of the objects within it and contains technology to localize and track the position and orientation of real 3D objects instead of flat images and features, which allow us to take videos of the AR scene while we are playing it.

ARCore

The first version was launched in February 2018 and is Google's platform for creating AR applications for Android and iOS. It makes use of different capabilities, such as motion tracking, to estimate the position and orientation of the mobile device regarding the real world; the environmental location, to find and track horizontal surfaces such as the ground, tablets, or walls; and light estimation, to place 3D elements realistically into the real world. Targeted at Android 7.0 and above, not all devices in the market support this technology, although this number has increased greatly since the first SDK version.

ARKit

Apple launched the first version of ARKit in 2017, along with Xcode 9 and iOS 11, to bring AR to iOS devices. The framework, which is included in Xcode, lets users place virtual content in the real world. Months after its official release, it added new features such as 2D image detection and face detection. In 2018, with the iOS 12 release, ARKit 2 was launched with new features such as 3D object tracking, adding realistic textures to the scenes, and creating multiuser AR experiences. At the time of writing this book, the latest version is iOS 13, with ARKit 3 promising a huge improvement on the current state as it will add a new way of interacting with virtual elements, such as hiding virtual objects when a person is detected in front of them. It also allows users to interact with 3D objects via gestures and capture not only facial expressions but the body motions of a person.

Now that we are acquainted with the main AR tools we will use throughout this book, let's look at how we will apply this software to different enterprise fields.

Using AR in enterprise

AR can be a valuable asset and technology in multiple fields. In this section, we will learn how it is being used in sectors such as industry, marketing, retail, and tourism. In the first case, we will learn how industry 4.0 has put AR in the spotlight, since it's the natural interface for the human-machine interaction in areas such as production, maintenance, training, and more.

This section's main objective is to give you a better insight into how to apply AR in your own projects before you start to code. This way, you will be able to adapt the examples in this book to your own needs.

Let's start introducing the uses of AR in the industry field.

Using AR in industry 4.0

The use of this technology in the industrial sector is growing. Its application focuses, among other aspects, on being able to prepare for the breakdown of a machine and thus know what part has been damaged and how to proceed to repair it. This use of AR represents a significant cost saving as it favors rapid action before the breakdown in question. You can also use the AR to visualize a plant or product before carrying it out. This means that you can perfect what to build before turning it into something physical. The use of AR in industry favors the application of one of the enabling technologies of industry 4.0 that help us increase the competitiveness and productivity of a company.

Some examples are as follows:

- Smart assistance
- Virtual prototyping
- Logistics and warehouse management
- Digital Twins

Let's look at these examples in more detail.

Smart assistance

The use of AR with maintenance process management platforms provides direct support to operators during the operation of industrial machines, thus shortening the time and increasing accuracy in the performance of the task or repair. Some tasks you can have under this case are as follows:

- Follow guided instructions and workflows
- Assign activities in real-time
- Access checklists and list of assigned tasks
- Create a digital report of the interventions
- Automatically detect 3D objects
- View 3D manuals and work orders in real-time
- Have an expert remote collaborator through video calls
- Extract and display real-time data from machines

In this case, the use of AR technology improves business productivity by reducing costs and the possibility of errors.

Virtual prototyping

AR can be applied to visualize and configure 3D industrial plants and machinery in real-time. 3D models can be shown in the industrial environment where the validation is carried out, but also in exhibition spaces such as fairs and events. Through AR, you can visualize the hologram of the industrial machinery in the place where it will be installed to evaluate its dimensions, escape spaces, and safety margins. By doing this, you optimize the production processes. In addition, the packaging, shipping, or transport of heavy industrial machinery from one part of the world to another for presentation at fairs has a very high cost. With AR, you can see your product as if it were real in the center of your stand.

Logistics and warehouse management

Through 3D viewers or glasses connected to a warehouse management system, a warehouse operator receives information for the storage of merchandise directly on the device, which allows them to improve the times and quality of their work and, ultimately, the production yield.

Digital Twins

Thanks to AR technologies, you can create a virtual and dynamic replica of a real system, product, or service that, through the information that's obtained from sensors or automatisms, models its behavior. In this way, it allows intelligent monitoring and analysis, as well as the realization of simulations and experiments in the replica, without risks or costs, with the aim of improving the performance and effectiveness of the real system.

In this book, we are going to learn how to use AR for manufacturing by creating a prototype automation with an AR guide and training.

Using AR in other enterprise areas

The industry is not the only field where AR can be of value. The versatility of this technology makes it the perfect communication item between the users and the final product or process and adds a visual and interactive layer to engage them. Whether it's used to make a product more attractive or help users understand a process with added information, AR can be a great asset in many fields. Let's look at some other enterprise areas that we will later cover in this book where AR adds value.

AR for manufacturing

AR has many uses in this area, such as prototyping, production, and training. In these areas, AR can help speed up and reduce costs in prototyping by visualizing the designs over the real world and allowing designers, workers, and potential customers to walk around and through the model and manipulate its three dimensions.

AR for training

AR has become a valuable asset in education and training. It allows us to visualize concepts in three dimensions over an image or directly in the room so that we can access the information in a quicker and more dynamic way (just pointing with the camera instead of looking through a book or searching the internet for the information) or to create deeper personal projects (giving life to a painting, adding instructions or extra information over a handcrafted project, creating an animated presentation, and so on).

AR for marketing

Using AR, the user is in charge of their experience and can interact with it. Now, brands go beyond the *wow* effect and create functional experiences to promote and sell their products. Examples of this include augmented catalogs, which show the products in 3D over their flat images; virtual mirrors, where you can buy the glasses or complements you are trying on AR; packages that come to life to explain the elements inside the fabrication process; and so on.

AR for retail

Retail is one of the fields where AR offers a wider range of possibilities, from satisfying and engaging the consumer in order to reduce returned products, to linking products with social media or personalizing the shopping experience. Some examples of this include trying products before buying them so that users can visualize clothes, shoes, glasses, or even makeup over themselves before actually buying the products. By doing this, they can see how a product such as a piece of furniture, art, or even wall paint looks on their homes with AR.

Other examples include seeing extra information about a product, such as comments and reviews, before buying a product, receiving geopositioned information and discounts from the stores on it, and in supermarkets or big stores, orienting customers through sections to the product they want.

AR for automation

AR is the natural interface and connection to the **Internet of Things** (**IoT**) and Big Data. It allows workers to visualize and interact with the data coming from the machines and sensors of a factory in an easy and attractive way, either using mobile devices or AR headsets.

AR use in automation can go from the facial recognition of an employee to getting access to a concrete machine, to real-time on-site surveillance of the production process or remote access and control to the system through AR glasses.

AR for tourism

The thing that's attractive about AR is the visual content it displays over the real world. That makes this technology perfect for enhancing traveling experiences, from showing skyline information to making animals in a museum come to life or even translating signs and guides in real-time. Some of the most common uses of AR in tourism include serving as a live guide in the streets of a new city, where a user can go around the city while the AR app is showing them where the most interesting points to see are; showing attractions and **points of interest** (**POIs**) over a map when a user points at a map with the camera; giving all kinds of extra information on paintings, sculptures, or monuments so that when a user points at a painting it can show a video about the author, the place and time where it was painted, or even make it come to life in a 3D simulation. Apart from all these experiences, when AR is combined with other immersive technologies, such as virtual worlds or 360º videos, the experience goes one step ahead, allowing users to visit several places at the same time (for example, in a museum network, while visiting one of them, to be able to virtually visit the others).

In this section, we have looked at several examples of how we can use AR for very different fields, from visualizing a prototype before building it, to attracting customers or adding value to art pieces. Now, you have a better understanding of the possibilities AR offers in the world of enterprises and how to apply it according to the needs of each sector.

Summary

In this chapter, we have taken our first look at AR by learning what it is, where it comes from, and what type of software and elements we need in order to create it. We have learned about the names and main features of the SDKs we are going to use in this book and are now ready to start creating our own AR projects.

In the next chapter, we will introduce Untiy 3D, a 3D tool that can be used as the base for nearly any AR project since most AR SDKs are compatible with it. You will learn about how it works and create a simple example that will be the basis for the AR projects that follow.

Introduction to Unity for AR Development

2

This chapter will introduce you to Unity, a real-time 3D development platform that has become one of the main tools for multi-platform **Augmented Reality** (**AR**) development. Its versatility, extensive documentation, and active forums allow for a fast learning curve, and the already created scenes, examples, and varied resources of its Asset Store will help you create amazing AR experiences in a fast and simple way.

The main goal of this chapter is that you get comfortable around Unity before using it in AR projects. You will learn how to install and use Unity, how the user interface is distributed, and the names and purpose of the main components. Then, you will create a simple C# script to understand the power of scripting to be able to customize 3D scenes. By the end of this chapter, you will have basic knowledge under your belt so that you can explore Unity further by integrating and working with the AR **Software Development Kits** (**SDKs**) we are going to introduce in the following chapters.

Unity is one of the most powerful tools in AR development; it's multiplatform and most of the AR SDKs have specific packages that are compatible with Unity. In this book, Chapter 5, *AR for Marketing with EasyAR*, Chapter 6, *AR for Retail with Vuforia*, and Chapter 7, *AR for Automation with Vuforia and Epson Glasses*, will be developed with Unity and although their example projects are implemented in Android devices, they can also be built (except for the Epson glasses, which only run with Android OS) for iOS devices with nearly zero code changes. Furthermore, Chapter 3, *AR for Manufacturing with ARCore*, and Chapter 8, *AR for Tourism with ARKit*, can also be implemented within Unity.

Thus, the importance of this introductory chapter, where you will learn how to create a Unity 3D project and build it for a specific platform, serving as the basis for more complex projects.

In this chapter, we will cover the following topics:

- Introducing Unity
- Preparing your system for Unity
- Understanding the Unity interface
- Unity main components
- Scripting – first example in C#

Technical requirements

The technical requirements for this chapter are as follows:

Hardware (from `https://docs.unity3d.com/2019.1/Documentation/Manual/system-requirements.html`):

- CPU: SSE2 instruction set support
- GPU: Graphics card with DX10 (shader model 4.0) capabilities

Operating system:

- Windows: 7 SP1+, 8, 10, and 64-bit versions only
- macOS: 10.12+
- Linux: Fixed at Ubuntu 16.04, 18.04, and CentOS 7

Software for Android development:

- Java Development Kit (1.8.0 in this book)
- Unity 3D (2019.1.2f1 in this book)
- Android SDK (included in the Unity installation)
- Microsoft Visual Studio Community 2017 (included in the Unity installation)

The resources and the code files for this chapter can be found here: `https://github.com/PacktPublishing/Enterprise-Augmented-Reality-Projects/tree/master/Chapter02`.

 Although we will develop our Unity projects for Android devices, you can also build them for iOS. In this case, the requirements would be a macOS and Xcode 9.4 or higher.

Introducing Unity

When we think of tools that we can use to develop video games that have had a great impact in recent years, one name stands out above all others: Unity. Unity is a graphics engine that helps us in developing video games, interactive projects, visualizations, and 2D and 3D animations in real-time for different platforms. Unity offers a complete visual editor with scripting so that we can create applications with a professional finish.

For this purpose, Unity is composed of a package of tools that have been designed to facilitate the tasks of designing and programming the different aspects of a video game, including graphics, physics, animations, and artificial intelligence. Unity is a unique development system that focuses on assets and not on the code like other similar 3D modeling applications do. The content of the game is built from the editor and the game is programmed using the C# scripting language.

Unity also includes a land editor, which is where you can create a terrain (such as a blank sheet) using visual tools, paint, or textures, and also add other elements that have been imported from 3D applications, such as Blender, 3ds Max, and Maya.

Unity has had rapid growth in the market as has been adopted by companies and professionals due to certain characteristics. These characteristics make Unity stand out from other game engines:

- Unity is a multi-platform tool that allows us to publish 2D and 3D content for multiple platforms, such as Windows, OS X, GNU/Linux, Flash, Xbox One, PS4, Nintendo Switch, Android, and iOS, including web-based games over **Web Graphics Library** (**WebGL**) technology (a standard specification for rendering 3D graphics in any web browser).

- Unity possesses a fully functional free license for learning purposes and for independent developers, as well as different scalable pricing plans according to the business volume of the developer companies.

- Unity is one of the most popular engines for AR and **Virtual Reality** (**VR**) development, supporting the industry from an early stage. Around two-thirds of all AR and VR apps on the market have been built using Unity.

- Unity is an extensible environment, which can be increased by our own or third-party plugins, and grows in a scalable way with new elements and functionalities that it wasn't originally created to handle.

- Unity offers a portal that we can use to buy and sell all kinds of extensions and resources, both free and paid, called the Asset Store. This portal is not only useful for developers but also offers the business market the ability to create specific companies, whose business models are to create tools and content so that they can sell their own resources in this online store.

- Unity incorporates additional services, most of which are free, that allow us to generate profits in different business models of the video game world. Some of these services are, for example, Unity Ads, which allows you to add advertising; Unity Analytics, which provides information about the interaction of users; and Unity Networking, which provides infrastructure for the development of online games.

Now that we understand what Unity is and its many features, we can start preparing our system so that we can install the necessary software.

Preparing your system for Unity

In this book, we are going to use Unity to develop Android mobile applications. To create Android apps, we need to have the **Java Development Kit (JDK)** and Android **Software Development Kit (SDK)** installed.

 As we mentioned in the *Technical requirements* section, we can easily run the same projects for iOS, provided that we run Unity on a macOS computer with Xcode.

Since Unity directly provides the Android SDK installation, we will install the JDK first and then proceed to install Unity on our computer.

Installing Java Development Kit (JDK)

To install the JDK, follow these steps:

1. Go to Oracle's download page at `https://www.oracle.com/technetwork/java/javase/downloads/jdk8-downloads-2133151.html`:

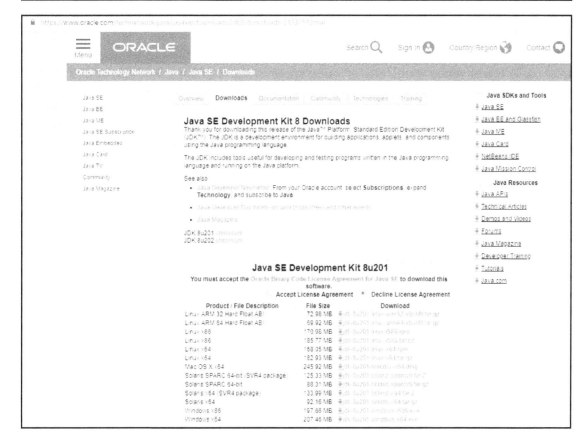

2. Ensure that you accept the **Oracle Binary Code License Agreement for Java SE**.

3. Select the latest **Java SE Development Kit** (in our case, this is the **Java SE Development Kit 8u201**).

4. Once downloaded, run the installation file and let it install JDK and JRE into their default folders.

 Starting with Unity 2019.2, the Unity installation allows you to install OpenJDK inside the **Android Build Support** options (see the *Installing Unity* section).

Now that you have installed the JDK, let's install Unity.

Installing Unity

We are going to install Unity using the Unity Hub, a tool that allows us to install and manage different versions of Unity on our computer. You can download the Unity Hub from `https://unity3d.com/get-unity/download`.

Follow these steps to install Unity:

1. Download and install the Unity Hub.
2. Run the Unity Hub. The first time you do this, it will notify you that the license is missing, as shown in the following screenshot. Click on **MANAGE LICENSE**:

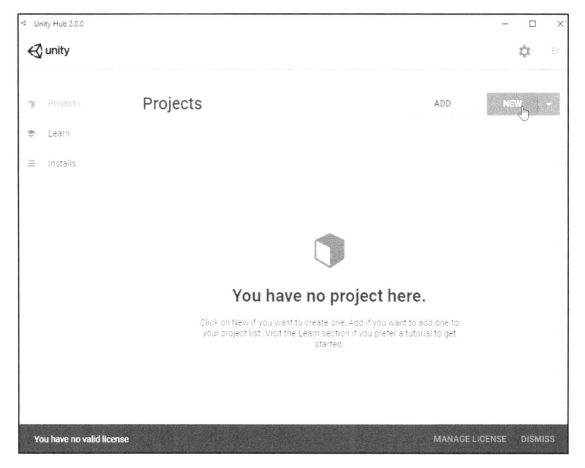

No valid license message

3. In the **License** window, another message will appear, asking you to log in in order to add a license. Click on **LOGIN**:

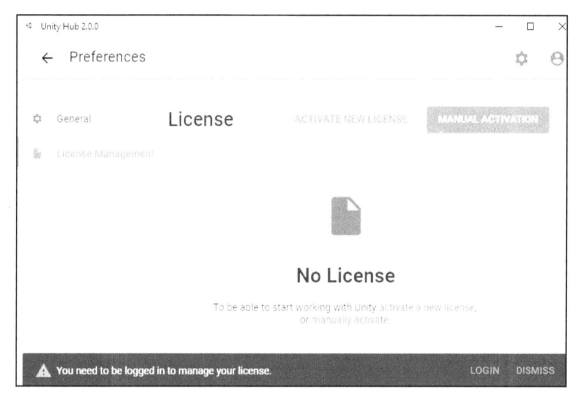

LOGIN message in the License window

4. A pop-up window will appear, asking for your **Email** and **Password**. If you don't have an account, you can create one by clicking on **create one**. You can also **Sign in with google** or **Sign in with facebook**:

Signing into Unity

5. Now, select one of the license options and click **DONE**. (You can use Unity for free with the **Personal** license if you meet the requirements. If you don't, you have to purchase **Unity Plus or Pro** on their web page (`https://store.unity.com`):

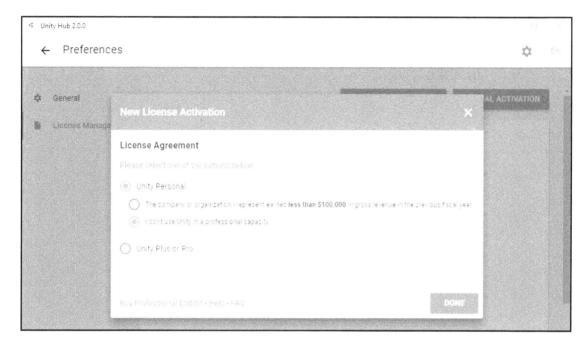

Selecting a license for the product

6. Now, go back, click on the **Installs** tab, and then on **ADD** to add a new Unity installation:

Adding a new Unity version

7. In the pop-up window that appears, select the **Unity Version** you want to install and the modules to add. In our case, we're using the **2019.1.2f1** version and we will install **Microsoft Visual Studio Community 2017** to code and **Android Build Support** and **Android SDK & NDK Tools** to develop in Android, as shown in the following screenshot:

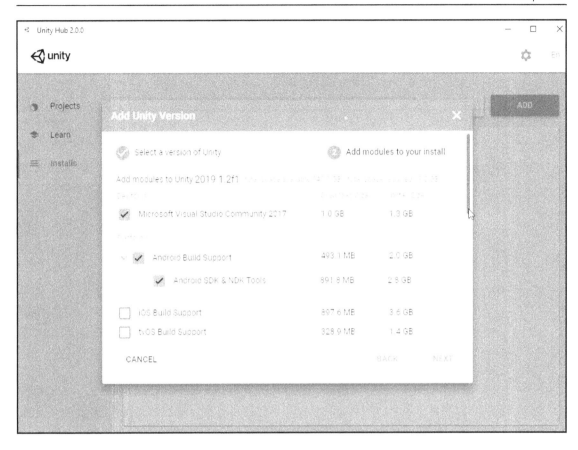

Choosing the Unity version and modules

 Unity Hub always shows the latest compilation of each version. If you want to install a specific version, such as the one we are using here, you can find it and install it through the Hub from the Unity Archive: `https://unity3d.com/es/get-unity/download/archive`.

 Starting with Unity 2019.2, a new option appears under **Android Build Support** so that you can directly install OpenJDK.

8. If you plan to develop with Vuforia, which is what we will do in `Chapter 6`, *AR for Retail with Vuforia*, and `Chapter 7`, *AR for Automation with Vuforia and Epson Glasses*, check the **Vuforia Augmented Reality Support** option shown in the following screenshot. Then, click **NEXT** and finish the installation:

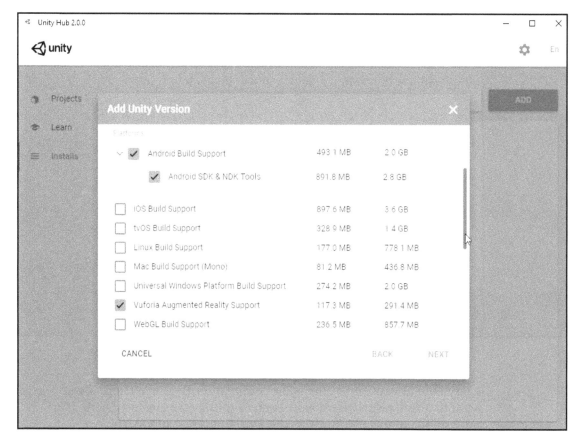

Selecting Vuforia Augmented Reality Support

 Most recent versions of Unity might not always support Vuforia. If you don't see Vuforia on the list, don't panic! It is because the latest version of Unity doesn't support it yet and an older version should be installed that supports Vuforia

9. When you've finished the installation, you will be sent back to the
   Installs window, where you will see the new version and the installed modules,
   as shown in the following screenshot:

Installs window with the new Unity version

10. If during the installation process you forgot to add a module or you want to add it at a later date, you only have to click on the three dots button in the top right corner and select **Add Modules**, as follows:

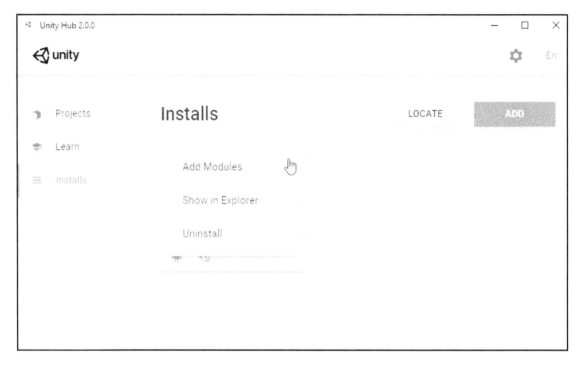

Adding a new module after finishing the installation

11. Now, click on the **Projects** tab. Here, we will create a new project by pressing on the **NEW** button, as follows:

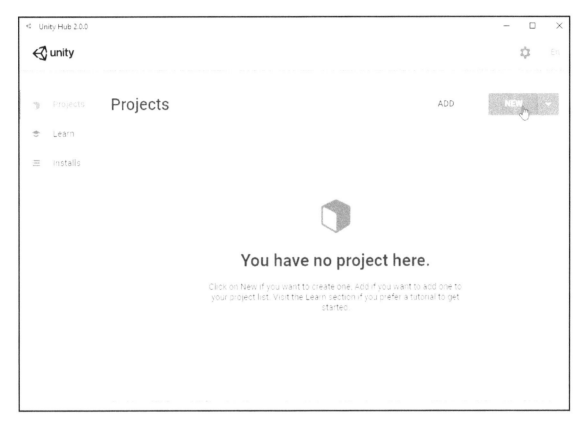

Creating a new project

12. We will create a **3D** project (already selected). In the **Settings** panel, give the project a **Name** and set a **Location**, as shown in the following screenshot. Then, click on **CREATE**:

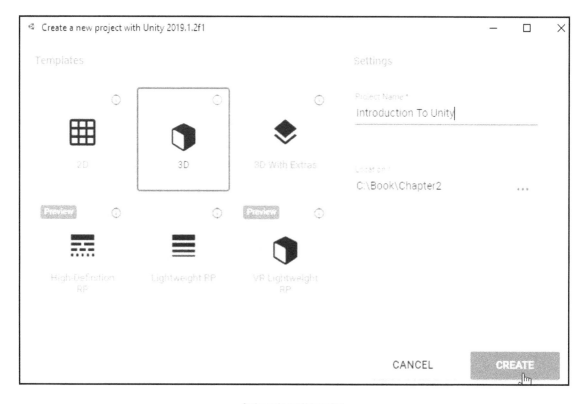

Setting up the new Unity project

13. Unity will now open the new project and you can start working with it. If you close the Unity window, you can reopen the project by selecting it from Unity Hub's **Projects** window, as shown in the following screenshot:

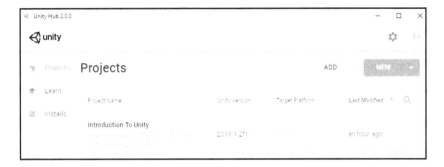

The new project appears in the Projects window

And that's it. Now, you have installed Unity on your computer and your first project is open so that you can start working with it. In the next section, we will provide a tour of the Unity interface in order to see the possibilities Unity offers and how to use each tool.

Understanding the Unity interface

The first time you open the Unity editor, you will see a layout with different bars and windows, similar to what can be seen in the following screenshot:

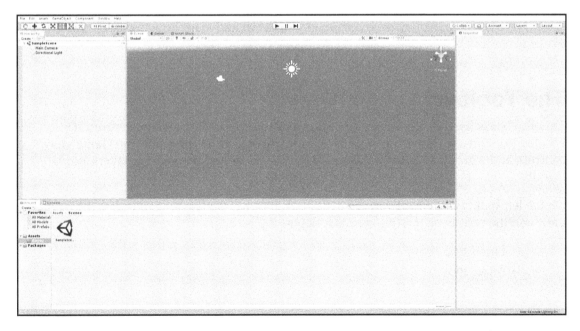

The initial Unity layout

At first glance, the Unity configuration slightly reminds us of 3D modeling tools, with the 3D scene in the middle, although it has more panels on the sides than modeling tools does. Although it can look a bit daunting to understand everything if you are not familiarized with 3D tools, the Unity interface is quite straightforward and has remained very much the same throughout the Unity versions. The main components that can be seen in the preceding screenshot are as follows (from top left to bottom right):

- **The Toolbar**: Here, we have the main buttons so that we can manipulate objects in the **Scene** view to test the scene.
- **The Hierarchy window**: The **Hierarchy** window shows the elements in the **Scene** view ordered hierarchically.
- **The Scene view, Game view, and Asset Store window**: These three tabs have different purposes. The **Scene** view shows all the elements in the 3D scene. The **Game** view shows, from the camera perspective, how the scene will look when built. The **Asset Store** window can be used to download packages and assets from the Unity Store so that we can include them in our project.
- **The Inspector window**: When an element is selected in the **Hierarchy** window or the **Scene** view, its features and components will appear in this window.
- **The Project window and Console window**: The former shows all the directories and files of the project that we can (or not) use in the scene, while the latter shows the log messages.

Now, we're going to explore each component in detail and learn how to change this layout to our needs and tastes.

The Toolbar

This Toolbar is fixed on the screen and allows us to access Unity's main features. It's divided into three sections: the tools to manipulate objects on the scene, the **Game** view controls, and a group of buttons to access Unity services and manage the layers and UI layout:

On the left-hand side, we can see the main tools that we can use to manipulate the **Scene** view and the objects on it. These are as follows:

- Hand tool
- Move tool

- Rotate tool
- Scale tool
- Rect tool
- Combined tool
- Center/Pivot button
- Local/Global button:

Buttons on the left of the toolbar

Let's take a look at these tools, one by one:

- **Hand tool**: This is the navigation tool for the scene. It has three uses:
  - **Move**: Left-click + Drag to move through the scene without altering any of its objects. A hand icon appears in the Toolbar and **Scene** view.
  - **Orbit**: *Alt* + Left-click + Drag to orbit in the scene. An eye icon appears in the Toolbar and **Scene** view.
  - **Zoom**: *Alt* + Right-click + Drag to zoom in and out of the scene. A magnifying glass icon appears in the Toolbar and **Scene** view.

You can use move at any time by pressing the wheel of the mouse and dragging. You can also access zoom in and out, using the mouse scroll wheel.

- **Move tool**: When this button is selected, you can move the objects on the scene into the three axes by dragging the corresponding arrow. You can also drag the small squares that appear on the intersection of the arrows to move the object into a plane (two axes) instead of a single axis:

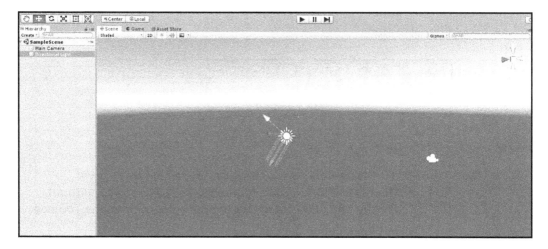

Moving a 3D element

- **Rotate tool**: When this button is selected, you can rotate the objects on the scene in the three axes by dragging the corresponding circle:

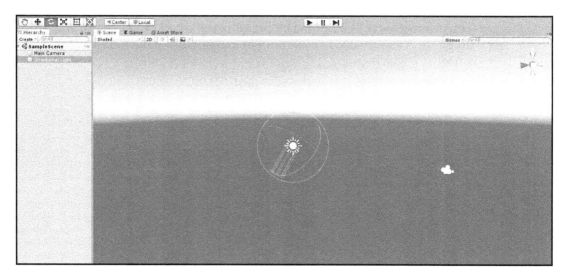

Rotating a 3D element

- **Scale tool**: When this button is selected, you can scale the objects on the scene in the three axes by dragging the corresponding arrow (ending on a small cube). You can also drag the central cube to scale the object uniformly on the three axes:

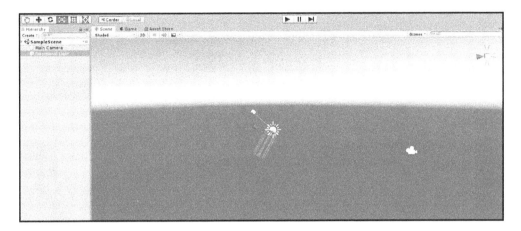

Scaling a 3D element

- **Rect tool**: The tools we have seen so far are thought to manipulate 3D models. The rect tool, however, is specifically used for the **User Interface** (**UI**) elements on the scene and it works in two dimensions. In the following screenshots, we are manipulating a button:
    - You can *move* a UI element by dragging it:

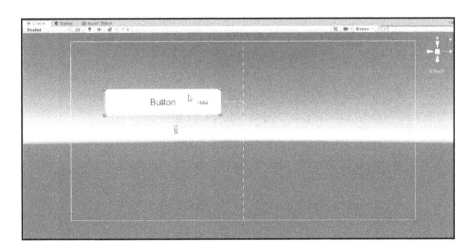

Moving a UI element

- To rotate an element, hover over the corner until the rotation icon appears. Then, click and drag:

Rotating a UI element

- You can scale the element by dragging it from the corners:

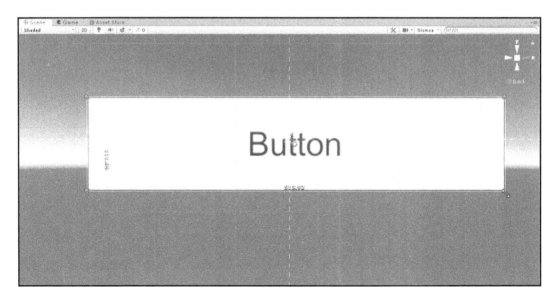

Scaling a UI element

- **Combined Move, Rotate, and Scale tool**: This button combines the Move, Rotate, and Scale options:

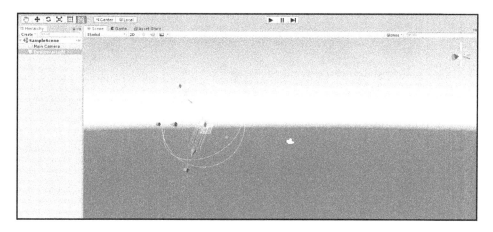

All the guides appearing together to manipulate the object

- **Center/Pivot button**: When **Center** is selected, the translation, rotation, and scale operations will be performed from the object's center point. In the following screenshot, the camera and directional light have been selected and the guide appears in the center point of the resulting group. In this case, the camera and light *will rotate around that central point*:

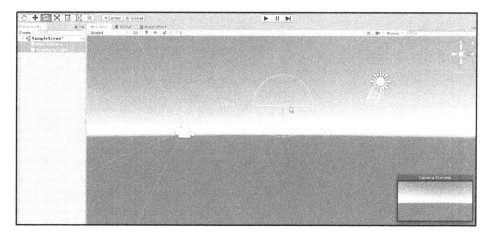

Center option active

When **Pivot** is selected, operations will be performed from each pivot point. In this case, the camera and light *will rotate around their respective pivot points*:

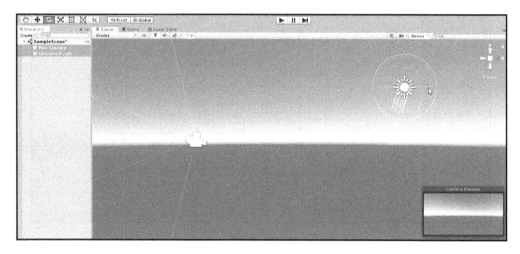

Pivot point option active

- **Local/Global button**: When **Local** is selected, the translation, rotation, and scale operations will be performed relative to the selected object's origin. In the following screenshot the light is rotated, and its coordinate system also appears rotated:

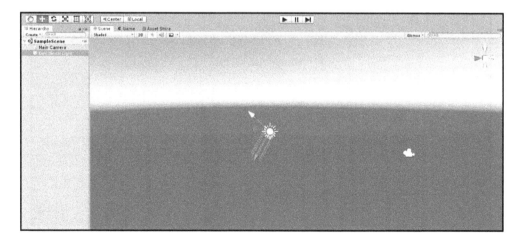

Local option selected

When **Global** is selected, the operations will be performed relative to the world's origin:

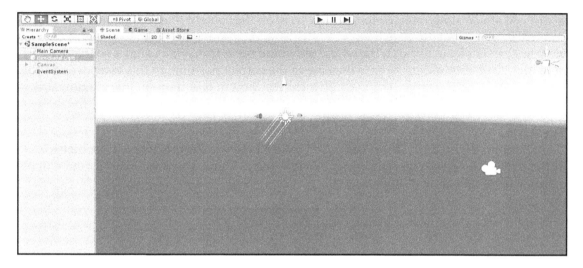

Global option selected

On the center of the Toolbar, we have the play, pause, and step buttons, which we can use to control the **Game** view:

Buttons on the center

On the right-hand side, we have some buttons that we can use to access Unity collaborate services, Unity cloud services (the cloud icon), our Unity **Account**, the **Layers** visibility menu, and the **Layout** menu. We will be using the **Layout** menu later in this section to create a custom layout for our projects:

Buttons on the right-hand side

Now that we have seen the functionality of the Toolbar, let's look at the **Scene** view.

The Scene view

The Scene view is the window where you will interact with the current scene and the 3D world you are creating on it. Here, you will have all the content that forms the scene and you will be able to manipulate them visually using the commands on the Toolbar. With this view, we can navigate through the whole scene and see it from all its angles so that we can place the 3D objects and make sure they are in the correct position. In this view, we can also manipulate the UI elements. The main element we want to talk about in this window is the Gizmo, which is located on the top right-hand side of the window.

The Gizmo: You can use the Gizmo to quickly change the view
(**Top**, **Bottom**, **Right**, **Left**, **Front**, **Back**) and switch between **Perspective** and **Isometric** (orthographic) modes. When changing the view, the *x*, *y*, and *z* arrows in the Gizmo will be pointing in the direction of each axis:

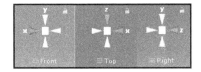

Gizmo with different arrows on the Front, Top, and Right views

The little icon on the left-hand side of the view name shows whether it's a **Perspective** or **Isometric** (orthographic) view, as shown in the following screenshot. You can switch between them by clicking on the little icon:

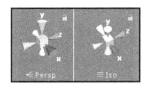

Perspective and Isometric (Orthographic) views allow us to adjust the objects in the scene

Now, let's look at the **Hierarchy** window and how it works.

The Hierarchy window

This window is a hierarchical view of the elements in the **Scene** view, which are represented by their names. On the top, we will always have the scene, and all the objects we add to the scene will hang from it. In the following screenshot, we have different elements, with some of them (**Cube**, **Canvas**) containing more elements.

The hierarchical view allows us to easily find the elements and the relationships between them (parenting) that affect the way they behave. For example, if we move the **Cube** element, its child object, **ChildOfCube**, will move along with it. However, if we only want to move the **ChildOfCube** element, we would select it in the **Hierarchy** window and move it, without affecting its parent **Cube**. In terms of the *local/global* positioning we explained in the previous section, the children's local position, rotation, and scale will be relative to those of the father:

The Cube object being selected in the Hierarchy window and Scene view

We will also use this window to quickly add new elements by right-clicking on it and selecting the one we want to add to the scene.

On the other hand, objects in the scene can be selected by clicking on them in the **Scene** view or in the **Hierarchy** window. The latter is very useful when an object has multiple children since we can ensure that we are selecting the correct element. In the **Scene** view, they could be overlapping.

A quick tip: double-clicking on the name of an object in the **Hierarchy** window makes the scene zoom into that object.

The **Scene** view and **Hierarchy** window are the two windows we can use to manipulate the elements in a scene, that is, the elements that we will build into our device. Now, we are going to learn how the **Inspector** window works when one of the elements in the scene is selected.

The Inspector window

This window displays the properties and components of the currently selected object. From here, you will be able to edit, delete, and add new components to the object. Since the different objects in the scene will have different properties, the **Inspector** window will change accordingly to show the corresponding information in each moment. This window can be seen in the following screenshot:

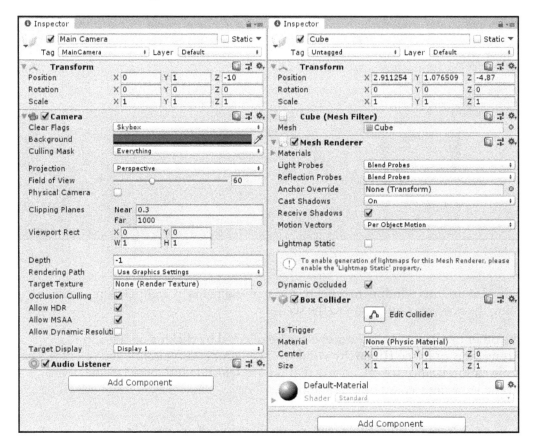

Two different Inspector windows for the Main Camera and a Cube

As shown in the preceding screenshot, every element in the scene will have a **Transform** component so that it can move, rotate, and scale that element in the scene. However, apart from this, the **Main Camera** and **Cube** elements of the image don't have more components in common. In the case of the camera, it has, as expected, a **Camera** component, while the **Cube** has a mesh, a renderer (to visualize the object), and a collider that marks the physical boundaries of such an object.

The components in the **Inspector** window can be maximized and minimized so that we can organize the view. This way, if we have many components in a GameObject, we only see the ones that we require at each moment. For that, we can use the small arrow next to each component, as shown in the following screenshot, where the same **Main Camera** has had its components collapsed:

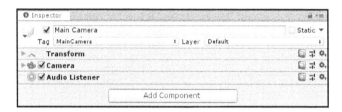

The Main Camera with its components collapsed

Now, let's look at how the **Project** window works.

The Project window

This window shows all the assets that are available for your project. When you import a new asset into your project, it will appear on this window and, from here, you will be able to drag it into your scenes. It's a hierarchical view with files organized in folders:

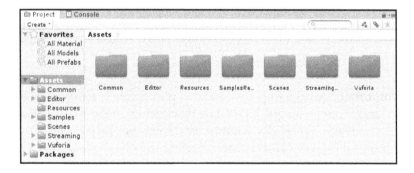

Project window displaying the main folders in the Assets folder

 Important! When building an application, not every asset that appears in the **Project** window will be built into it. Except for some special folders, which can be found here: `https://docs.unity3d.com/Manual/SpecialFolders.html`. **Assets** are only included in the final bundle if they are connected to the scene (directly appearing on it, called from scripts, and so on).

Now, we will take a look at the **Game** view, which, as we mentioned at the beginning of this section, is located in a tab next to the **Scene** view.

The Game view

This window shows how the scene has been rendered by the camera(s) in your world. You can use the play, pause, and step buttons from the Toolbar to play your scene and see how it will look when published:

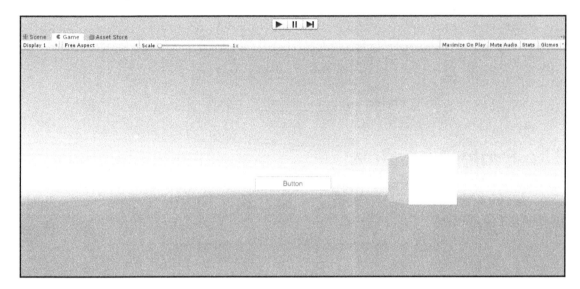

The Button and Cube objects from the Main Camera object's perspective

 Important! Any change you make in play mode is temporary and *will disappear* once you quit this mode by clicking on the play button again. This is useful when you want to try different approaches (for example, object rotation or color) before selecting the one that suits you, but make sure you don't lose important work because you forgot to switch play mode off!

The tab next to this window is the **Asset Store** window. Let's take a look.

The Asset Store window

This window connects to the Unity **Asset Store**, which is where developers and designers upload their assets. You can download and import any asset from the **Asset Store** for your project from this window:

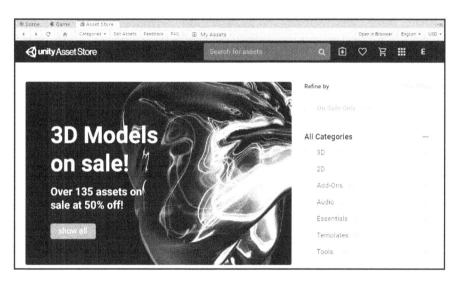

Asset Store window from within Unity

The Asset Store offers free and paid content, such as 2D and 3D models and scenes, audio files, templates, complete projects, and much more, all of which you can download and import directly into your projects. All of these assets make the process of creating a project easier and faster.

Last but not least, let's learn how the **Console** window works and what it is useful for.

The Console window

Here, you can find the log of your project. This window displays warnings, errors, and information logs about your project, as shown in the following screenshot. If you struggle while troubleshooting error codes, the Unity forums (`https://forum.unity.com/`) is a valuable tool so that you can search for similar cases and ask for help:

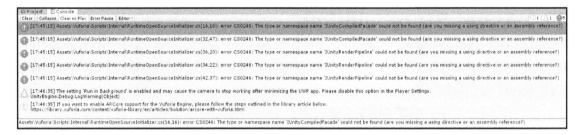

The Console window displaying different types of information, warning messages, and errors

The main elements of this window and their functions are as follows:

- The **Clear** button removes all messages except compilation errors. You will have to correct these errors before making any other changes to the current scene or playing it.
- You can use **Collapse** to join the same messages into an only message line.
- Use **Clear on Play** to delete all the messages the moment you hit the play button on the Toolbar.
- **Error Pause** allows you to pause the execution of the scene when an error occurs.
- Use the three buttons on the right-hand side to show/hide the different types of messages (information, warning, and error).

By now, you should have pretty good knowledge of how the Unity interface works. Before going any further, however, we are going to learn how to change the layout configuration. It's simple and useful to customize the various windows according to our needs and tastes.

Changing the layout

Now that we've looked at the main windows and know how they function, the first thing we are going to do is change the disposition of these windows on the screen so that they fit our project's needs. For this book, we are going to use a modified version of the **2 by 3** layout, which will allow us to see the AR scene and game at the same time. However, once you are comfortable using Unity, feel free to select the layout that suits you the most.

For the modified version, follow these steps:

1. First, select the **2 by 3** layout on the top right drop-down menu of the Toolbar, just above the **Inspector** window:

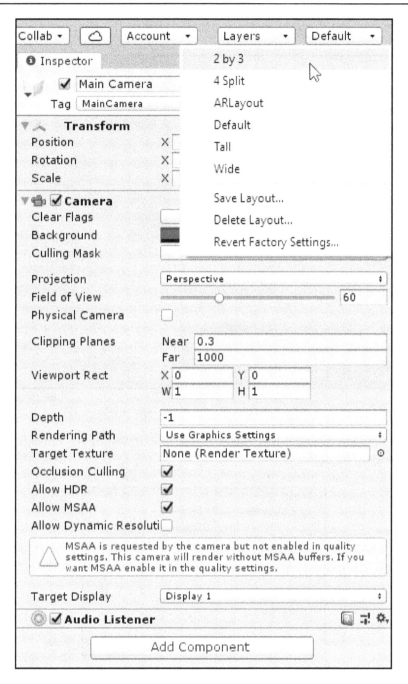

Selecting 2 by 3 on the Layout drop-down menu

2. Then, drag the **Project** window so that it's below the **Hierarchy** window:

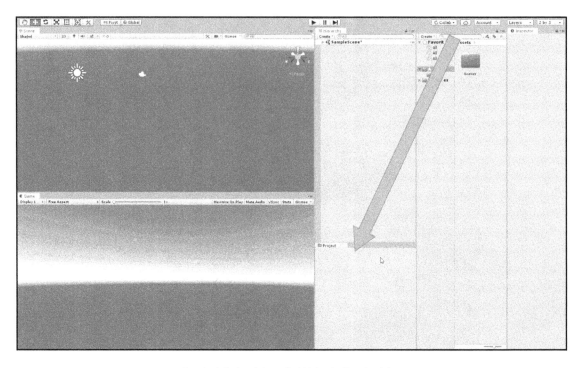

Dragging the Project window so that it's below the Hierarchy window

3. Select the list view on the **Project** window by dragging the bottom scrollbar all the way to the left:

Moving the horizontal scrollbar to the left

4. Create a new aspect ratio of the **Game** view called `1280 x 720` and insert the following values: **Width**: `1280`, **Height**: `720`:

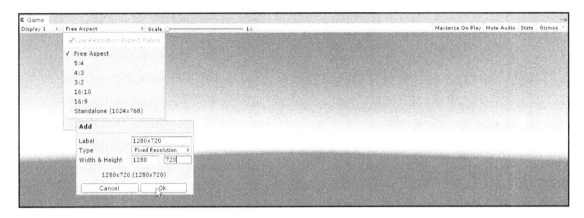

Creating a new Aspect Ratio

5. Open the **Console** window, press *Ctrl + Shift + C* or **Window|General|Console** and drag it so that it's a tab beside the **Game** view:

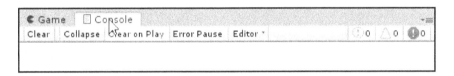

Dragging the Console window next to the Game view

6. Finally, to ensure this layout is available every time you open Unity, go to **Layouts**, select **Save Layout...**, and give it a name:

Saving the created layout

Now, we have our layout ready so that it can be used in our AR projects. By now, you should be acquainted with the different windows and tools Unity offers and how they work. In the next section, we will take a look at the main elements we can find in a Unity project.

Unity's main elements

An application built in Unity will be made up of a project. This project will contain all the necessary elements that we'll need in order to develop the application, such as models, scripts, plans, menus, and much more. When you start up Unity, you can open a project by pointing to its root folder.

Each project contains one or more documents, called **scenes**. The projects that are created in Unity are structured into scenes, where a scene can be any part of the project. When we talk about applications, a scene can be from the start menu to any level or area of it. A single scene will contain many elements, such as a user interface, 3D objects, scripts, and so on.

Some of the main elements you can find in a Unity project are as follows:

- Assets
- GameObjects
- Components
- Scripts
- Prefabs

First, we will look at **Assets**.

Assets

Unity refers to the files that will be used to create your project as an **asset**. They are the building blocks inside a Unity project and they can be in the form of image files, 3D models, sound files, code files, and so on. **Assets** from Unity, such as materials, textures, animations or scripts can be created in a *project* by either clicking on **Assets | Create** on the top menu bar or by right-clicking inside a folder on the **Project** window and selecting **Create**.

When we work with external assets, such as an image that's been downloaded from the internet or a 3D model we've designed, we can add them to the project by dragging them from an external folder (for example, from a folder on Windows Explorer) into one of the folders of the **Project** window or by right-clicking inside a folder of the **Project** window and selecting **Import New Asset...**.

Use one of these methods to add *two* images from your computer gallery to the project's
`Assets` folder (we will be using one now and the other later), as shown in the following
screenshot:

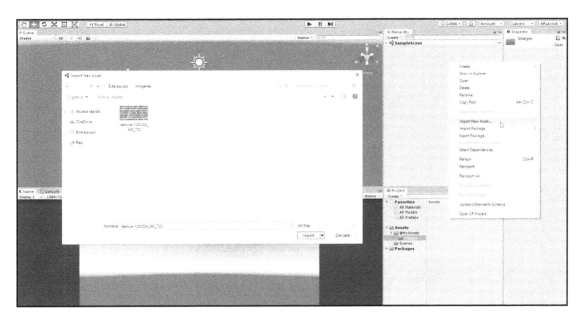

Adding an image to the project

Another way to import assets is to import a whole package containing several assets
through **Import-Package**. This option can be found in the **Assets** menu of the menu bar or
by right-clicking on the **Project** view.

To delete an asset from your project, right-click on it and press **Delete**. It's important to
notice that, once you delete an asset from the project, you can't recover it again.

Now, let's look at what GameObjects are.

GameObjects

When an asset is used in a scene, it becomes a GameObject. GameObjects can be added to
the scene by either clicking on **GameObject** on the top menu bar or by right-clicking in the
Scene view or **Hierarchy** window.

Use one of these methods to add a **3D Object|Cube** to the scene and move it so that it's in front of the **Main Camera** and is visible in the **Game** view:

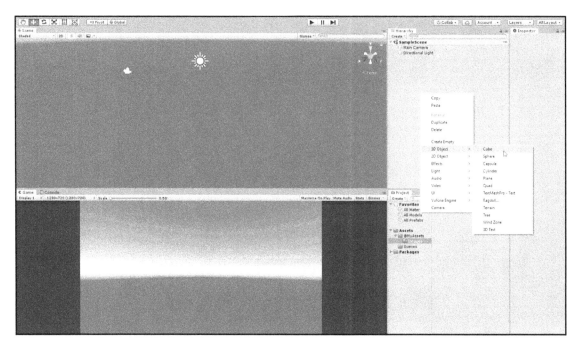

Creating a Cube in the Hierarchy window

Now, let's talk about components.

Components

Components come in different forms and they are in charge of adding functionality to GameObjects. They can be used to create behavior (for example, scripts), define the appearance of GameObject (for example, renderers), and influence other aspects of the function of an object in the project.

All GameObjects contain at least one component. We start with the **Transform** component. This component is in charge of telling the Unity engine the position, rotation, and scale of an object. Other common component elements include **Renderer** and **Collider**. We will be looking at their uses in the upcoming chapters in this book.

Components are added to a GameObject by selecting the object and then clicking on the **Component** menu of the menu bar or by hitting the **Add Component** button on the **Inspector** window.

Components can also be dragged from the **Project** window into the GameObject (for example, you can drag a script from the **Project** window onto a cube on the **Scene** view and the script will automatically appear in the **Inspector** window).

Drag one of the images you added to the **Project** window previously into the cube of the **Scene** view to convert it into a texture:

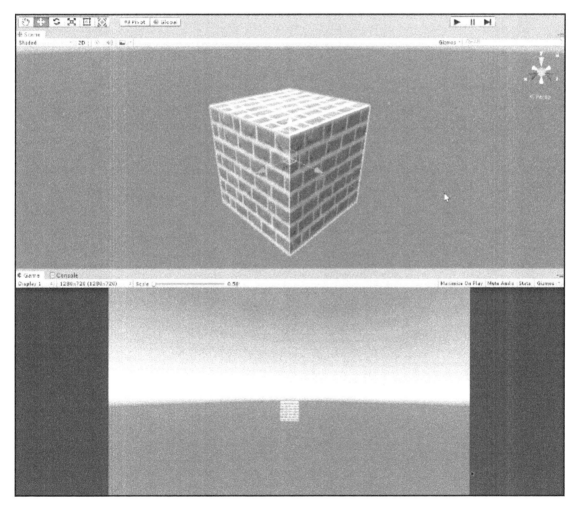

The cube in the scene with the image as a texture

Now that we know about the visible elements of a project, let's talk about the invisible ones: the scripts.

Prefabs

Prefabs are GameObjects with customized properties and components (for example, a light with a script added to it to make it blink) that you can store in your **Project** window so that you can reuse them in different scenes/moments. They can be created or copied at any time (including runtime) and, whenever you alter a property of the original prefab, unless otherwise defined, all its instances will be updated automatically.

Scripts

Scripts, which are actually a type of component, are an essential part of Unity since they define the behavior of the different elements in the project. You can manipulate (add/edit/delete) a script like any other component.

Right-click on the **Project** window and press **Create | C# Script** to create a new script and give it a name (for example, CubeHandler.cs):

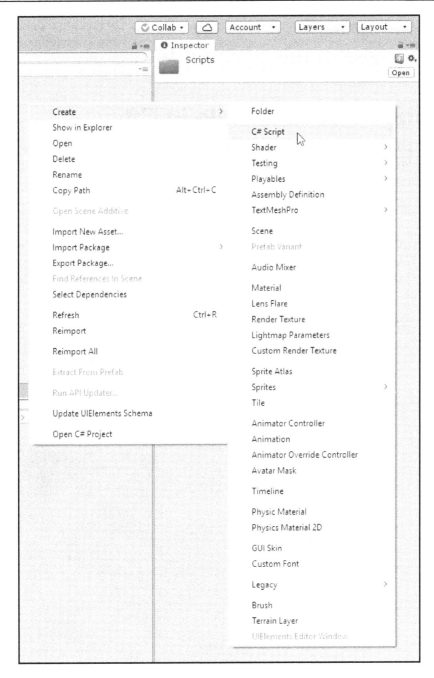

Creating a new script

In the **Inspector** window, you'll see that the newly created script has some default code in it. We'll talk about this code in the next section. Now that we have knowledge about the different elements of unity, let's learn to script in the following section.

Scripting – first example in C#

To see all the potential of scripts in Unity, we are going to take a look at the script we created in the previous section, `CubeHandler.cs`. As its name suggests, we are going to add some code to it to manipulate the cube in the scene.

Double-click on the name of the script in the **Project** window to open it in Visual Studio.

If you already had Visual Studio installed on your computer before you installed Unity, it's possible that Unity won't detect it automatically when double-clicking on the script. If so, you'll have to go to **Edit|Preferences** and go to **External Tools**. From there, select the path to the `.exe` file of Visual Studio:

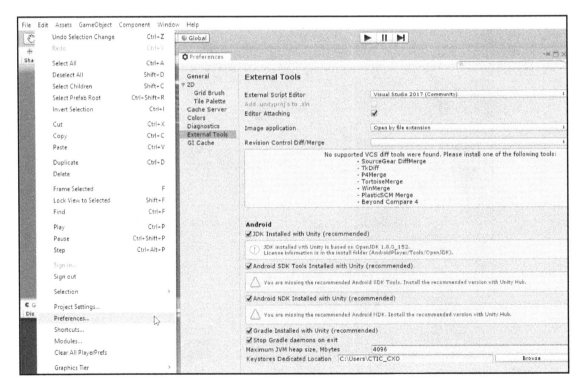

Preferences window with Visual Studio assigned as the External Script Editor

Upon opening the script, you will see the following auto-generated code:

```
using System.Collections;
using System.Collections.Generic;
using UnityEngine;

public class CubeHandler : MonoBehaviour
{
  // Start is called before the first frame update
  void Start()
  {

  }

  // Update is called once per frame
  void Update()
  {

  }
}
```

The first three lines are the calls to three references. The first two are commonly used collections, while the third one is the reference that we need so that we can work with the Unity engine.

Then, you have the class declaration. The name of the class must be the same as the `.cs` script. By default, the classes that are generated through Unity will inherit from `MonoBehaviour`, which allows us to use the following two methods:

- The `Start` method, which is called automatically as soon as the Unity scene is generated and before the first frame update. Therefore, this method is useful when it comes to initializing variables.
- The `Update` method is called once per frame, meaning that the code inside this method will be executed repeatedly.

Let's try to add some code to control the cube on the scene:

1. First, we are going to declare a variable called `speed`, just after the declaration of the class, and before the `Start` method:

   ```
   private float speed;
   ```

2. Then, we are going to initialize the value of `speed` in the `Start` method:

   ```
   void Start()
   {
   ```

```
        speed = 0.5f;
    }
```

3. Finally, we are going to use this variable in the `Update` method to tell the cube to rotate at a certain speed:

```
void Update()
{
    transform.Rotate(Vector3.up * speed);
}
```

This last line accesses the `transform` component of the current GameObject element, which is in charge of its position, rotation, and scale. We are telling the `transform` component that we want to rotate the object in the vertical axis (`Vector3.up`) with the speed we set previously.

4. By itself, the script won't do anything because it doesn't know which object's transform we are referring to. To tell the script which objects from the scene we want to manipulate, go back to the Unity editor and drag the script onto the cube. Make sure that it appears as one of its components in the **Inspector** window. This way, we are telling the script that it's the **Cube** we want to rotate. The full code should look as follows:

```
using System.Collections;
using System.Collections.Generic;
using UnityEngine;

public class CubeHandler : MonoBehaviour
{
    private float speed;
    public Texture2D texture;

    // Start is called before the first frame update
    void Start()
    {
        speed = 0.5f;
    }

    // Update is called once per frame
    void Update()
    {
        transform.Rotate(Vector3.up * speed);
    }
}
```

5. Now, if you press the play button on the Toolbar, the **Game** view will show the cube rotating:

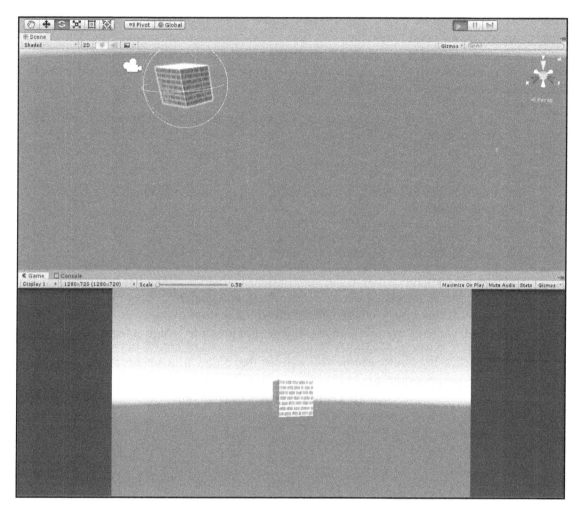

When playing the scene, the cube will start rotating

6. Press play again to stop the simulation. Try changing the value of the `speed` to see how it affects the rotation speed of the cube.

The `transform` component is a little special because it has its own name. To access any other component, we need to use the `GetComponent<ComponentName>()` function. As an example, we can use this if we want to change the texture of the cube (the image we dragged into it previously). The component that's in charge of materials and textures is the `Renderer`. Let's include this code in our script:

1. First, add the following line of code below the speed definition, which declares a variable of the `Texture2D` type:

```
public Texture2D texture;
```

2. Now, add the following two lines to the `Update` method, which is below the transformed line:

```
if (Input.GetKeyDown(KeyCode.A))
  GetComponent<Renderer>().material.mainTexture = texture;
```

Here, we are saying that, if the system detects that the *A* key has been pressed, the texture of the object's `Renderer` component will change to the new one. As you can see, in this case, we haven't initialized the texture in the `Start` method. Instead, we have made it `public` and we are going to assign it from within Unity.

3. Go back to the Unity editor. You will see that a new line has been added to the script component in the **Inspector** window. To assign the other image to it, you can either drag it from the **Project** window or click on the circle on the right and select it from the project:

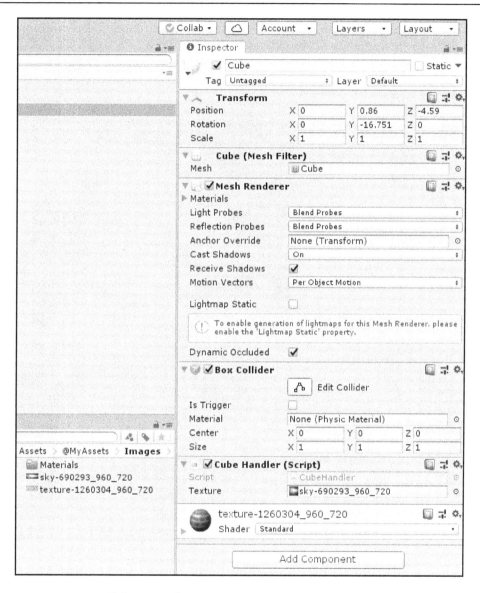

The last component of the cube is the script with the new line for selecting a Texture

4. Now, press play again. When the cube is rotating, press the *A* key. You will see how the texture of the cube changes:

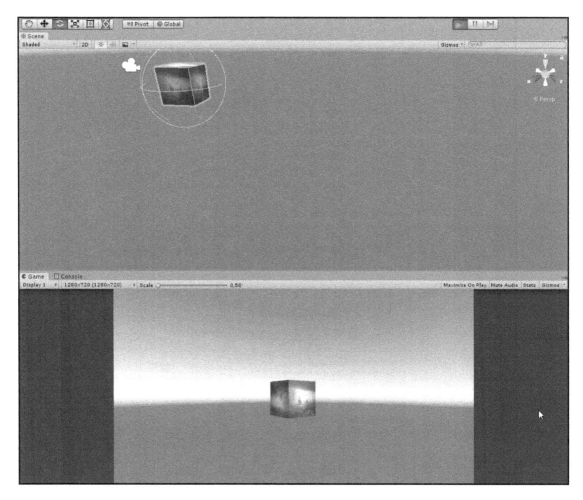

Pressing the A key on the keyboard to see the texture of the cube change

Now, you know about all of the logic behind a Unity project and have the basis to create more complex scripts. In the upcoming chapters, we will be using scripts for purposes such as showing elements in AR or interacting with the user through the user interface.

Summary

In this chapter, we learned how to install Unity and the necessary modules to make it work so that we can build mobile applications. We also introduced how the Unity interface is designed, its main windows, and how to customize their composition for our needs. We took a look at the main windows, their tools, and how to use them. Then, we learned about the main elements we can find in a Unity project and how to create/import them. Finally, we created our first script with a few lines of code to understand how easily we can control and alter objects on a scene.

In the next chapter and the ones that follow, we will work with all of the elements we learned about in this chapter in order to generate fully functional AR projects.

3
AR for Manufacturing with ARCore

In this chapter, we will create our first AR project using Google's ARCore tool. The main goal of this chapter is to introduce you to one of the latest and fastest-growing AR tools, ARCore. By the end of this chapter, you will have gained the necessary skills to create your own ARCore projects easily in Android Studio. At the same time, we present one of the uses of AR in manufacturing, that is, prototyping.

By the end of this chapter, you will have created a prototype viewer app where users will place 3D designs of industrial pieces, machines, and so on over flat surfaces, navigate around and through them, and manipulate them (move, rotate, and scale) with their fingers. With this knowledge, you will also be able to improve the current project and adapt it to your needs in this field.

In this chapter, we will cover the following topics:

- Using AR for manufacturing
- Exploring ARCore
- Creating a prototype AR viewer

Technical requirements

The technical requirements for this chapter are as follows:

- Android Studio (3.5.2 version for Windows in this book).
- Java Development Kit (1.8.0 in this book).
- Sceneform plugin (installed from inside Android Studio. 1.13.0 in this book).
- An ARCore supporting mobile device (see the list here: `https://developers.google.com/ar/discover/supported-devices`). The project has been tested on a Samsung Galaxy A5 (2017) and a Pocophone F1.

To install the Android Studio, the system requirements for Windows are as follows:

- 4 GB RAM minimum, 8 GB RAM recommended
- 2 GB of available disk space minimum, 4 GB recommended
- 1280x800 minimum screen resolution

For more details on other operating systems, you can find the official requirements at the end of this page: `https://developer.android.com/studio`.

The code files for this chapter can be found here: `https://github.com/PacktPublishing/Enterprise-Augmented-Reality-Projects/tree/master/Chapter03`.

Using AR for manufacturing

Industry 4.0, also known as the 4th industrial revolution, makes reference to the inclusion of digitalization and interconnectivity tools inside factories, covering production processes to maintenance and training. Although the term has been around for some years now, in the last couple of years, this industry 4.0 concept has taken on a new dimension thanks to the exponential growth (in quality and quantity) of technologies such as **Augmented Reality (AR)** and **Virtual Reality (VR)**, **Internet of Things (IoT)**, **Big Data Analytics (BDA)**, **Additive Manufacturing (AM)**, **Cyber-Physical Systems (CPS)**, and **Artificial Intelligence (AI)**.

The visual component of AR makes it the natural interface for users who can receive real-time information about processes, access remote systems for extra data, and control processes and machines, all with a mobile device or smart glasses.

AR in manufacturing has many uses in areas such as prototyping, production, and training. In this chapter, we will cover prototyping and, more specifically, where AR can help reduce costs in prototyping by visualizing a design in the real world. This allows designers, workers, and potential customers to manipulate a model in its three dimensions, scale it, interact with individual parts, and even walk through them together. ARCore is one of the examples of an AR tool that we can use for that.

Exploring ARCore

In preview since 2017, the first version of ARCore was launched in February 2018 and was Google's platform for creating augmented reality applications for Android and iOS. It makes use of different capabilities, such as motion tracking, to estimate the position and orientation of the mobile device regarding the real world along with environmental location, to find and track horizontal surfaces such as the ground, tablets, or walls, and light estimation, to place 3D elements realistically into the real world. A more detailed explanation of these features can be found at `https://developers.google.com/ar/discover/concepts`. Targeted at Android 7.0 and above, not all devices in the market support this technology, although the number has increased greatly since the first SDK version. You can consult the currently supported device list here: `https://developers.google.com/ar/discover/supported-devices`.

ARCore apps can be developed on different platforms such as Android Studio, Xcode for iOS, Unity3D, and Unreal Engine. When using Android Studio, developers can integrate Sceneform, a 3D engine that helps integrate 3D environments and models in an easier way than the OpenGL library. We will be using this plugin in our project to display 3D models.

 When developing an app using ARCore, make sure you disclose it in your app: `https://developers.google.com/ar/distribute/privacy-requirements`.

For this project, we will develop a prototype viewing app that will show three different engine models. The engine models that we will be using for this project have been taken from `https://sketchfab.com/3d-models/rocket-engines-6fba4dbbb9444e99ba68425bcb3a7f70`.

Now that we have seen the basics of ARCore, let's start developing the app.

Creating a prototype AR viewer

In this section, we are going to develop our AR viewer for prototyping. First, we are going to install all the required software tools—JDK and Android Studio—and then we'll create our Android application, learn how to enable and use ARCore in it, and how to use the Sceneform plugin to display the 3D elements.

Installing the Java Development Kit (JDK)

Android Studio requires that we install JDK. It's usually located in `C:\Program Files\Java\jdk_version`. If you don't have it installed, follow these steps:

1. Go to `www.oracle.com` and download the latest Java SE Development Kit.
2. Once downloaded, run the installation file and let it install the JDK and JRE in their default folders.

 If, during Android Studio's installation, it complains about not finding the JDK, you can solve this problem by going to **Start menu | Computer | System Properties | Advanced System Properties**, opening the **Advanced | Environment Variables** tab, and creating a `JAVA_HOME` system variable pointing to the JDK folder.

Installing Android Studio

Once the JDK is installed, we are going to do the same with Android Studio since it will be our main platform for developing our AR app:

1. Download Android Studio from Android's developer page: `https://developer.android.com/studio`.
2. Install the studio with the default values and when you're finished, run it:

Launching Android Studio when the installation finishes

3. The first time you open it after installation, the Android Studio setup wizard will launch to help you configure the last steps of the studio and download the Android SDK components:

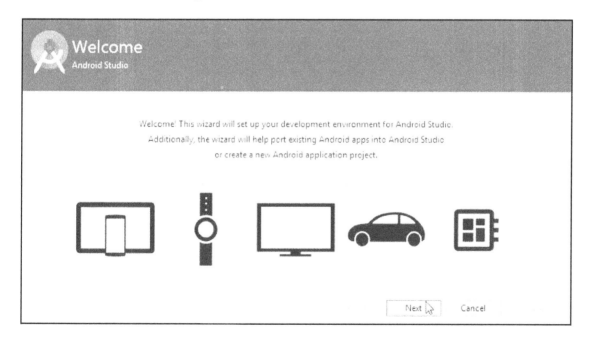

The setup wizard will appear the first time Android Studio is installed

4. Once finished, the **Welcome** window will be launched:

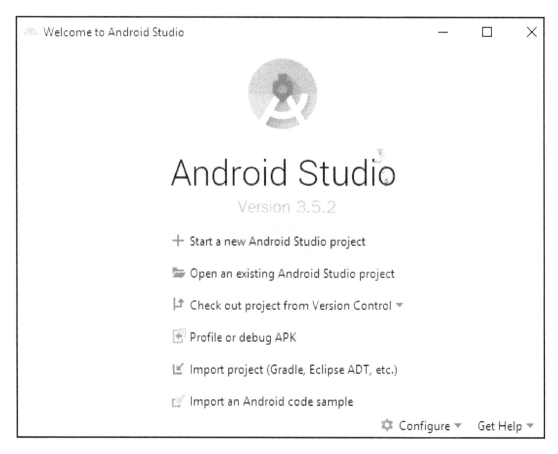

Android Studio Welcome window

Now that we have the software ready, we can start developing our app.

Creating the application

Now that we have the software installed, we are going to start creating our AR app. The first thing we have to do is launch a new Android Studio project and add the required libraries to it. Follow these steps to do so:

1. Click on **Start a new Android Studio project**.
2. Choose to create an **Empty Activity**:

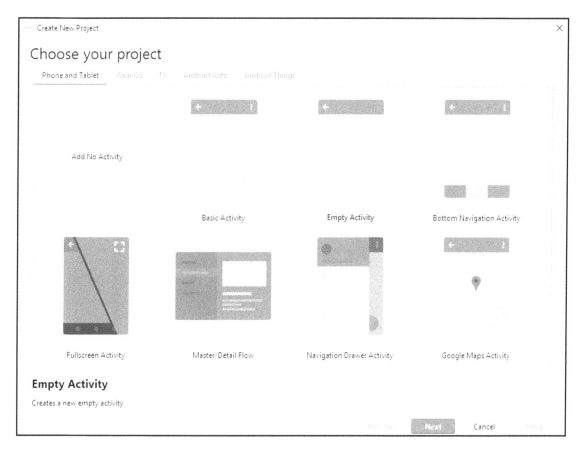

Choosing an activity type

3. Give the project a **Name**, **Package name**, and **Location**. Set the **Minimum API level** to at least **API 24: Android 7.0 (Nougat)** since it's the first that supports ARCore. Click on the **Finish** button to start the project:

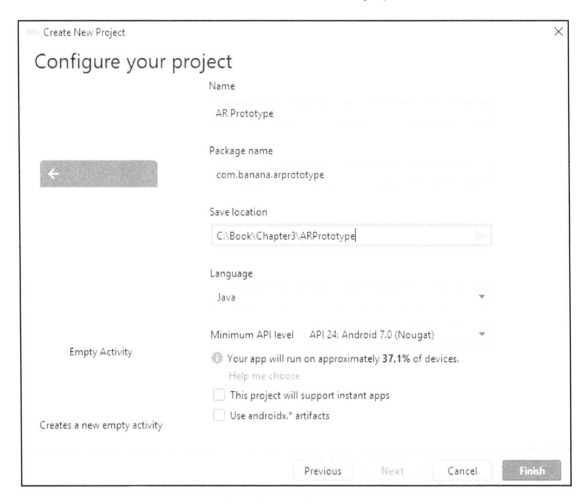

Configuration parameters for the new project

The next thing we need to do is enable ARCore in our project.

Enabling ARCore

In an AR project, ARCore can be set as **optional** or **required**. The former can work as a regular app on devices that don't support ARCore, while the latter will only appear in the Google Play Store to devices that support ARCore. Our app is a full AR application, so we will select the second option. To achieve this we have to modify some of the project files. Let's get started:

1. In the project window, unfold `app` and inside the `manifests` folder, open the `AndroidManifest.xml` file, as shown in the following screenshot. If you want to open the manifest externally you can find the file in `app/src/main` folder:

AndroidManifest.xml in the project

2. Add the following lines before the `<application>` tag:

```
<uses-permission android:name="android.permission.CAMERA" />
<uses-feature android:name="android.hardware.camera.ar" />
```

The first line is necessary in both cases (ARCore is **optional** and **required**) since it's the one giving permission to open the camera. The second line indicates the use of ARCore and is the one ensuring that only devices that support ARCore will have access to the app.

3. Now, add the following line inside `<application>`:

```
<application
    ...
    <meta-data android:name="com.google.ar.core"
android:value="required" />
</application>
```

This line sets ARCore as required and will make the Google Play Store download and install ARCore (if it's not already installed) when the app is installed.

4. Open your project's `build.gradle` file:

The project's build.gradle file in the Project window

5. Make sure it includes Google's Maven repository (it should be there; if not, add it):

```
allprojects {
    repositories {
        google()
```

6. Open your app's `build.gradle` file:

The app's build.gradle file in the Project window

7. Now, add the latest ARCore library as a dependency (1.13.0, in this book):

```
dependencies {
    ...
    implementation 'com.google.ar:core:1.13.0'
    ...
}
```

8. Synchronize Gradle in order for these changes to be effective by clicking on **Sync Now**, which can be found at the top right of the screen:

```
Gradle files have changed since last project sync. A project sync may be necessary for the IDE to work properly.                    Sync Now

1    apply plugin: 'com.android.application'
2
3    android {
4        compileSdkVersion 28
5        defaultConfig {
6            applicationId "com.banana.arprototype"
7            minSdkVersion 24
8            targetSdkVersion 28
9            versionCode 1
10           versionName "1.0"
11           testInstrumentationRunner "android.support.test.runner.AndroidJUnitRunner"
12       }
13       buildTypes {
14           release {
15               minifyEnabled false
16               proguardFiles getDefaultProguardFile('proguard-android-optimize.txt'), 'proguard-rules.pro'
17           }
18       }
19   }
20
21   dependencies {
22       implementation fileTree(dir: 'libs', include: ['*.jar'])
23       implementation 'com.android.support:appcompat-v7:28.0.0'
24       implementation 'com.android.support.constraint:constraint-layout:1.1.3'
25       implementation 'com.google.ar:core:1.13.0'
26       testImplementation 'junit:junit:4.12'
27       androidTestImplementation 'com.android.support.test:runner:1.0.2'
28       androidTestImplementation 'com.android.support.test.espresso:espresso-core:3.0.2'
29   }
```

Sync Now option to sync the project

 If you intend to create an app that works both with and without AR, the steps to follow to enable ARCore will differ from the ones shown here. Please refer to https://developers.google.com/ar/develop/java/enable-arcore to see what changes you have to make. Also, take into account that you will have to check whether the mobile running the app supports ARCore. You can do this by looking at your code.

Now that we have ARCore enabled, let's introduce Sceneform.

Adding Sceneform to the project

As we mentioned at the beginning of this chapter, Sceneform is an Android Studio plugin that will help us display 3D models in an easier and faster way than OpenGL.

Sceneform also provides ARFragment and other UX resources that will automatically handle the AR session after asking for the camera permission and checking if ARCore is installed and updated, without us having to include these verifications in our code.

 At the time of writing this book, the Sceneform Tools were still in Beta mode. If you encounter any problems when following these steps, please head to their GitHub page (`https://github.com/google-ar/sceneform-android-sdk`) for more information.

To import Sceneform into your project, follow these steps:

1. Open **File | Settings**.
2. In the **Plugins** tab, search for `Google Sceneform Tools (Beta)`. At the time of writing this book, the current version is **v1.13.0**:

Google Sceneform Tools plugin

3. Install it and press **Restart IDE** on the top right to activate the changes:

4. Once installed, open your app's `build.gradle` file and add the following compile options *inside* the `android` section. If we don't, when building our `ModelRenderable`, errors will appear. This is only necessary if `minSdkVersion` < `26` and we set the minimum to `24` (Android 7.0) when creating the project:

```
android {
    ...
    compileOptions {
        sourceCompatibility JavaVersion.VERSION_1_8
        targetCompatibility JavaVersion.VERSION_1_8
    }
}
```

5. In the same file, inside the `dependencies` brackets, we are going to add the following `implementation` line to include Sceneform in our project:

```
dependencies {
    ...
    implementation 'com.google.ar.sceneform.ux:sceneform-ux:1.13.0'
    ...
}
```

6. Your app's `build.gradle` file should now look similar to this:

```
app
    apply plugin: 'com.android.application'
    apply plugin: 'com.google.ar.sceneform.plugin'

    android {
        compileSdkVersion 28
        buildToolsVersion "29.0.2"
        defaultConfig {
            applicationId "com.banana.arprototype"
            minSdkVersion 24
            targetSdkVersion 28
            versionCode 1
            versionName "1.0"
            testInstrumentationRunner "androidx.test.runner.AndroidJUnitRunner"
        }
        buildTypes {
            release {
                minifyEnabled false
                proguardFiles getDefaultProguardFile('proguard-android-optimize.txt'), 'proguard-rules.pro'
            }
        }

        compileOptions {
            sourceCompatibility JavaVersion.VERSION_1_8
            targetCompatibility JavaVersion.VERSION_1_8
        }
    }

    dependencies {
        implementation fileTree(dir: 'libs', include: ['*.jar'])
        implementation 'androidx.appcompat:appcompat:1.0.2'
        implementation 'androidx.constraintlayout:constraintlayout:1.1.3'
        implementation 'com.google.ar:core:1.13.0'
        implementation 'com.google.ar.sceneform.ux:sceneform-ux:1.13.0'
        testImplementation 'junit:junit:4.12'
        androidTestImplementation 'androidx.test.ext:junit:1.1.0'
        androidTestImplementation 'androidx.test.espresso:espresso-core:3.1.1'
    }
```

The app's build.gradle file with the new lines added to it

7. Now, to use ARFragment in your app, open the `activity_main.xml` file in the `res/layout` folder and select **Text** mode at the bottom tabs of the view. By doing this, you can modify the elements in the text:

The activity_main.xml file's text view and visual preview

8. Remove the `TextView` block and add the following:

```xml
<fragment android:name="com.google.ar.sceneform.ux.ArFragment"
    android:id="@+id/ux_fragment"
    android:layout_width="match_parent"
    android:layout_height="match_parent" />
```

Sceneform is now ready to be used. Let's import our 3D model into the project.

Adding 3D models to the project

3D models, also called renderables, can be added in different ways:

- Created from basic shapes (sphere, cube, and so on) and materials and combined programmatically to generate more complex objects.
- Created from standard Android widgets via ViewRenderable. They are rendered as interactive flat cards in the scene.
- Imported from other programs as 3D assets. The supported formats include OBJ, FBX, and glTF (and glb). Animations are only supported in FBX.

We are going to use the first option and import a `.obj` file using Sceneform.

To import a model into our project, we have to create an external folder to contain the model (this folder won't be compiled into the final app) and then import the model into the project using Sceneform. Follow these steps to do so:

1. Create a `sampledata` folder in your project by right-clicking on the `app` folder of your project and selecting **New | Sample Data Directory**.

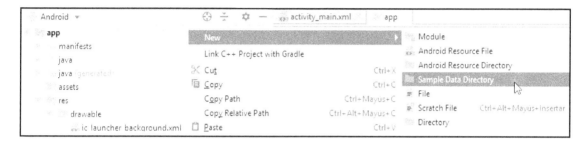

Adding a Sample Data Directory to the project

> If the `sampledata` folder doesn't appear automatically on your project, you can also create it manually from the file explorer, inside the `app` folder of your project. Call it `sampledata` and it will appear in Android Studio.

2. From the resources pack provided for this project, copy the `engine` folder into the `sampledata` folder:

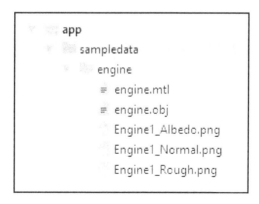

The newly added engine folder containing the model and its resources

Now, we will import the `.obj` file through Sceneform to include the 3D model as an asset.

3. Right-click the `engine.obj` file and select **Import Sceneform Asset**:

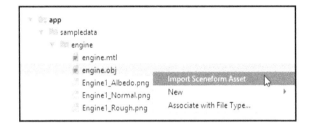

Selecting Import Sceneform Asset for our .obj file

4. Leave the default values as they are. This will create a Sceneform asset (`.sfa`) file inside `sampledata` and a Sceneform binary asset (`.sfb`) inside the `assets` folder:

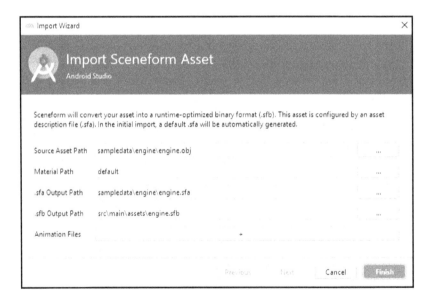

Default import values for the model

During the importing process, the following lines will automatically be added to the end of your app's `build.gradle` by Sceneform:

```
sceneform.asset('sampledata/engine/engine.obj',
        'default',
        'sampledata/engine/engine.sfa',
        'src/main/assets/engine')
```

5. Leave Gradle syncing. When it finishes, two windows will open: a text file with the model's description and its 3D preview:

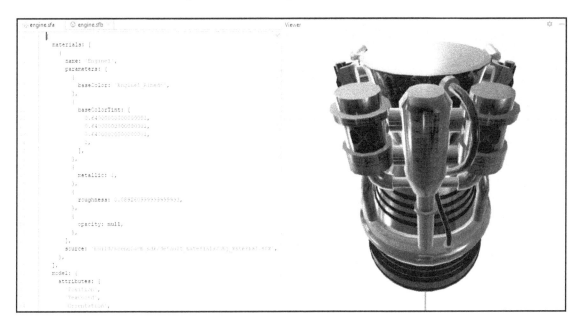

Our newly imported model's text view and preview

The final step will be to merge all the elements into the AR scene.

Forming the AR scene

Now that we have ARCore and Sceneform enabled and our 3D model included in the project, let's add the code that will make the model appear on the screen when a flat surface is detected and the user taps on the screen. Let's get started:

1. Open your `MainActivity.java` file from `app/java/com.banana.arprototype` and add the following imports:

```
import android.net.Uri;
import android.view.Gravity;
import android.view.MotionEvent;
import android.widget.Toast;
import com.google.ar.core.Anchor;
import com.google.ar.core.HitResult;
import com.google.ar.core.Plane;
import com.google.ar.sceneform.AnchorNode;
```

```
import com.google.ar.sceneform.rendering.ModelRenderable;
import com.google.ar.sceneform.ux.ArFragment;
import com.google.ar.sceneform.ux.TransformableNode;
```

2. Inside our class, create the following variables to control the AR scene and the 3D model:

```
private ArFragment arFragment;
private ModelRenderable modelRenderable;
```

3. Now, inside the OnCreate() method, add the ARFragment initialization:

```
protected void onCreate(Bundle savedInstanceState) {
    ...
    arFragment = (ArFragment)
getSupportFragmentManager().findFragmentById(R.id.ux_fragment);
```

4. Still inside the OnCreate() method, build the model in the scene using ModelRenderable, as shown in the following code:

```
ModelRenderable.builder()
        .setSource(this, Uri.parse("engine.sfb"))
        .build()
        .thenAccept(renderable -> modelRenderable = renderable)
        .exceptionally(
            throwable -> {
                Toast toast = Toast.makeText(this, "Unable to
                load the model", Toast.LENGTH_LONG);
                toast.setGravity(Gravity.CENTER, 0, 0);
                toast.show();
                return null;
            });
```

Here, we call the model from the assets folder using Uri.parse. It will launch an error message if it's unable to load it.

5. Finally, still in the OnCreate() method, we will place the model when the user taps the screen after a planar surface has been detected:

```
arFragment.setOnTapArPlaneListener(
    (HitResult hitResult, Plane plane, MotionEvent motionEvent) -> {
    if (modelRenderable == null)
    return;

    Anchor anchor = hitResult.createAnchor();
    AnchorNode anchorNode = new AnchorNode(anchor);
    anchorNode.setParent(arFragment.getArSceneView().getScene());
```

```
TransformableNode model = new
TransformableNode(arFragment.getTransformationSystem());
model.setParent(anchorNode);
model.setRenderable(modelRenderable);
model.select();
});
```

Here, when the user taps on a plane and the model renderable has been successfully loaded, an anchor is created to keep the model in place. Then, a new node for the model is created and attached to it.

6. Now, you can run the app either in an Android emulator or on an actual device. To run it in an emulator, the device must meet some requirements, and you will have to download ARCore from the Play Store manually on it (take a look at the *Prepare your device or emulator* section at `https://developers.google.com/ar/develop/java/quickstart`). Here, we will directly run the app in our device by clicking on the play icon and then selecting our connected device:

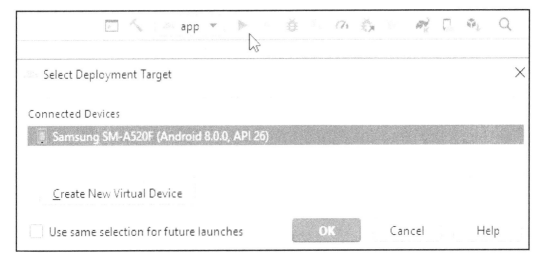

Running the app in a physical device

7. With this, the app will be installed on the mobile device. As we mentioned previously, the first time the app is run, it will check whether the latest ARCore version has been installed:

This application requires the latest version of ARCore.

CONTINUE

ARCore checking for the latest version of ARCore

8. You will have to install it through Google Play:

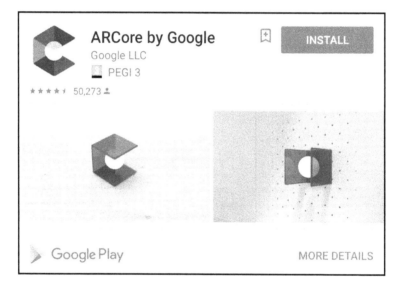

Installing the ARCore app

9. Once this initial step has been completed, you will be able to finish launching the app. Move the phone/tablet until a flat surface is detected:

The white dots form the plane surface where we can place the 3D objects

10. Tap on the screen to anchor your model:

The engine will appear standing in front of the camera

11. You can also resize, rotate, and move the model with your fingers while moving around it to see it from different angles. If you tap again, a new engine will appear:

Tapping multiple times causes multiple instances

Play around with the app and get comfortable with using it. You will see that, depending on the capacity of the device, the recognition of a flat surface will be faster/slower. You will also see that if you rotate the device (portrait/landscape), the model will disappear because the anchor is lost. Therefore, now that we have the basic setup, we are going to make some changes to improve the overall performance and give the user the option to add more models to the current scene.

Improving the basic app

Once we have the basic app ready, there are some things we can do to improve the overall working of the app:

- Make the screen orientation fixed. If we leave it in auto-rotation mode, rotating the screen will cause the phone to lose the anchor and the model will disappear from the screen.
- So far, we have seen that, for each screen tap, a new model appears. Since we are using the app for prototyping, the idea is that only one model is shown.
- We will also change the rotation and size of the model so that it's displayed better in the scene.

Let's change the code to add these features. For that, follow these steps:

1. Force the screen orientation so that it's in portrait mode by adding `AndroidManifest.xml` inside `<application>` and `<activity>`:

   ```
   <activity android:name=".MainActivity"
   android:screenOrientation="portrait">
   ```

   This way, the screen will always be in portrait mode and won't autorotate and lose the anchor, even if the user rotates the phone by mistake.

2. If you are using a tablet or prefer to see the scene in landscape mode, change this to the following:

   ```
   <activity android:name=".MainActivity"
   android:screenOrientation="landscape">
   ```

3. To display only one model for each tap on the screen, open `MainActivity.java` and create the following variables after the `ArFragment` and `ModelRenderable` variables:

```
private Anchor anchor;
private AnchorNode anchorNode;
private TransformableNode model;
```

4. Then, inside `setOnTapArPlaneListener()`, add the following lines after the `modelRenderable = null` check and before creating a new anchor, so that the previous one is released:

```
protected void onCreate(Bundle savedInstanceState) {
    ...
    arFragment.setOnTapArPlaneListener(
            (HitResult hitResult, Plane plane, MotionEvent
motionEvent) -> {
                if (modelRenderable == null)
                    return;

                //Remove previous anchor
                if (anchor != null)
                {
arFragment.getArSceneView().getScene().removeChild(anchorNode);
                    anchor.detach();
                    anchorNode.setParent(null);
                    anchorNode = null;
                }
```

This way, when the users tap on different places of the screen, the model will *move* from one place to the next one, instead of appearing duplicated in each one.

5. Now, remove the definition part of the `Anchor`, `AnchorNode`, and `TransformableNode` from the lines that follow, so that they make reference to the global variables:

```
anchor = hitResult.createAnchor();
anchorNode = new AnchorNode(anchor);
...
model = new
TransformableNode(arFragment.getTransformationSystem());
```

6. Finally, to rotate and scale the model, start by adding the following imports to the `MainActivity.java` file:

```
import com.google.ar.sceneform.math.Quaternion;
import com.google.ar.sceneform.math.Vector3;
```

7. Inside the `arFragment.setOnTapArPlaneListener()` method, add the following code before `setParent()`:

```
model.setLocalScale(new Vector3(0.55f, 0.55f, 0.55f));
model.setLocalRotation(Quaternion.eulerAngles(new
Vector3(-90,45,0)));
```

With this, the model will appear lying down on one side so that we can see the inside of it. This can be seen in the following image:

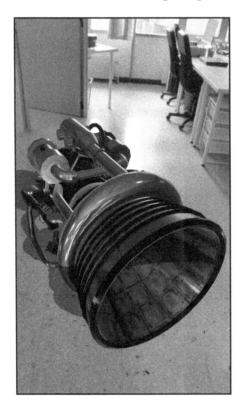

The engine in a rotated state

Now that we have improved on the basics, let's add two more prototypes and a simple UI so that we can switch between them. Follow these steps to do so:

1. From the `resources` folder of this project, copy the `engine2` and `engine3` folders into the `sampledata` folder.
2. Right-click on each of the `.obj` files and select **Import Sceneform Asset** to create the `.sfa` and `.sfb` files. Your `sampledata` folder should now look like this:

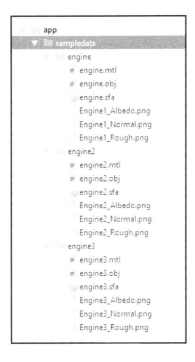

The sampledata folder with the new models

Your `assets` folder should have the three binary files for the models:

The assets folder with the three binary files

3. From the `resources` folder of this project, copy the three images corresponding to each of the engines into the `res|drawable` folder:

The res\drawable folder containing the new images

4. Open the `activity_main.xml` file located in **res|layout** in **Text** mode and add the following code:

```
<LinearLayout
    android:orientation="horizontal"
    android:paddingLeft="4dp"
    android:paddingTop="15dp"
    android:paddingRight="4dp"
    android:paddingBottom="1dp"
    android:layout_width="match_parent"
    android:layout_height="wrap_content"
    app:layout_constraintBottom_toBottomOf="@+id/ux_fragment">
```

Here, we're using `layout_constraintBottom_toBottomOf` to anchor it to the bottom of the screen.

5. If you are in landscape mode, you will probably want to locate the buttons on the right-hand side of the screen so that you have more space to play around. Make the following changes to the preceding code to do so:

```
<LinearLayout
    android:orientation="vertical"
    ...
    android:layout_width="wrap_content"
    android:layout_height="match_parent"
    app:layout_constraintRight_toRightOf="@+id/ux_fragment">
```

6. Now, add the three buttons:

```
<ImageButton
    android:id="@+id/engine1_button"
    android:layout_width="wrap_content"
 android:layout_height="wrap_content"
 android:layout_margin="10dp"
    android:src="@drawable/engine1"
    android:background="#7cc53a"
    android:layout_weight="1.0"/>

<ImageButton
    android:id="@+id/engine2_button"
    android:layout_width="wrap_content"
    android:layout_height="wrap_content"
    android:layout_margin="10dp"
    android:src="@drawable/engine2"
    android:background="#40000000"
    android:layout_weight="1.0" />

<ImageButton
    android:id="@+id/engine3_button"
    android:layout_width="wrap_content"
    android:layout_height="wrap_content"
    android:layout_margin="10dp"
    android:src="@drawable/engine3"
    android:background="#40000000"
    android:layout_weight="1.0" />
```

The first button has a green background (selected), while the other two have a semi-transparent background. Each of them has its corresponding image from `res`|`drawable`.

7. Finally, add the closing tag for `LinearLayout`:

```
</LinearLayout>
```

8. The preview should look similar to the following:

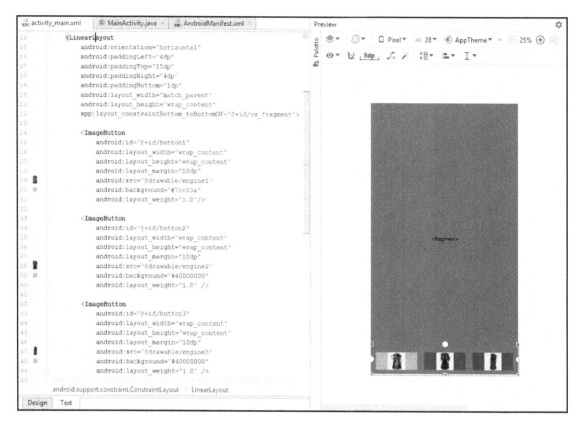

The activity_main.xml file's code on the left and the preview on the right in Portrait mode

9. By default, the **Preview** is in **Portrait** mode. To change it to **Landscape** click on the rotating phone icon and select **Landscape**:

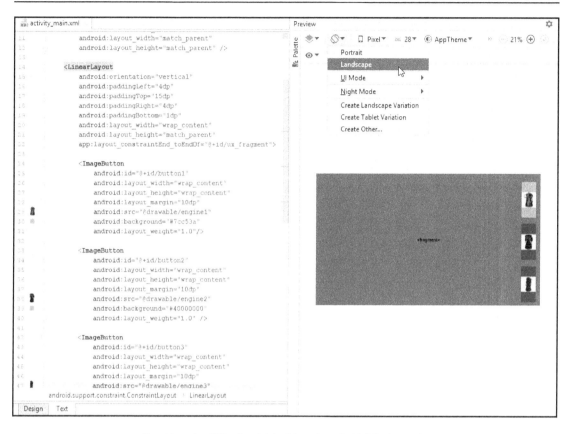

The activity_main.xml file's code on the left and the preview on the right in Landscape mode

10. Open the `MainActivity.java` file again and add the following libraries:

```
import android.widget.ImageButton;
import android.view.View;
```

11. Add three new `modelRenderables` below the preceding code:

```
private ModelRenderable modelRenderable2;
private ModelRenderable modelRenderable3;
private ModelRenderable currentRenderable;
```

We will use `currentRenderable` to find out which renderable is active every moment.

12. Now, add three new image buttons at the end of the variables:

```
private ImageButton button1;
private ImageButton button2;
private ImageButton button3;
```

13. Copy `ModelRenderable.builder()` and paste it *twice* to build the two new models.

14. Change their `Uri.parse` calls to `engine2.sfb` and `engine3.sfb`, respectively.

15. In the `.thenAccept` call, change the name of the `renderables` to the corresponding ones. The resulting code should look like this:

```
ModelRenderable.builder()
        .setSource(this, Uri.parse("engine2.sfb"))
        .build()
        .thenAccept(renderable -> modelRenderable2 = renderable)
        .exceptionally(
                throwable -> {
                    Toast toast = Toast.makeText(this, "Unable to
load andy renderable", Toast.LENGTH_LONG);
                    toast.setGravity(Gravity.CENTER, 0, 0);
                    toast.show();
                    return null;
                });

ModelRenderable.builder()
        .setSource(this, Uri.parse("engine3.sfb"))
        .build()
        .thenAccept(renderable -> modelRenderable3 = renderable)
        .exceptionally(
                throwable -> {
                    Toast toast = Toast.makeText(this, "Unable to
load andy renderable", Toast.LENGTH_LONG);
                    toast.setGravity(Gravity.CENTER, 0, 0);
                    toast.show();
                    return null;
                });
```

16. In the first `ModelRenderable.builder()`, modify the `.thenAccept` call:

```
.thenAccept(renderable -> currentRenderable = modelRenderable =
renderable)
```

Here, we're assigning `currentRenderable` to the first `renderable`. This way, the initial model that appears on the screen will be the first engine (remember that we have the first button highlighted as the selected one).

17. Finally, in the `setOnTapArListener()` method, change `modelRenderable` to `currentRenderable`:

```
if (currentRenderable == null)
    return;
...
model.setRenderable(currentRenderable);
```

18. To add the button's activities, we are going to make our `MainActivity` implement `OnClickListener`:

```
public class MainActivity extends AppCompatActivity implements
View.OnClickListener
```

19. This way, we can simplify our buttons initialization like so, at the bottom of the `onCreate()` method:

```
button1 = findViewById(R.id.engine1_button);
button2 = findViewById(R.id.engine2_button);
button3 = findViewById(R.id.engine3_button);

button1.setOnClickListener(this);
button2.setOnClickListener(this);
button3.setOnClickListener(this);
```

The first three lines initialize our buttons and the next three make a call (the same call in all three cases) when the user clicks on them.

20. To receive these clicks, create the `onClick()` method:

```
@Override
public void onClick(View view)
{
    switch (view.getId()) {
        case R.id.engine1_button:
            currentRenderable = modelRenderable;
            button1.setBackgroundColor(0xFFA4FF50);
            button2.setBackgroundColor(0x40000000);
            button3.setBackgroundColor(0x40000000);
            break;
        case R.id.engine2_button:
            currentRenderable = modelRenderable2;
            button1.setBackgroundColor(0x40000000);
            button2.setBackgroundColor(0xFFA4FF50);
            button3.setBackgroundColor(0x40000000);
            break;
        case R.id.engine3_button:
```

```
                        currentRenderable = modelRenderable3;
                        button1.setBackgroundColor(0x40000000);
                        button2.setBackgroundColor(0x40000000);
                        button3.setBackgroundColor(0xFFA4FF50);
                        break;
            }
        model.setRenderable(currentRenderable);
    }
```

This method will assign a different `modelRenderable` to the `currentRenderable` and highlight its corresponding button, depending on which button has been pressed, after the `onCreate()`. The last line swaps the current visible model to the newly selected one.

21. Run the app and try the three different engines. Just select one of the engines and place it on the floor or a desk. The following image shows the yellow engine on the floor:

Engine 2 is in view in the scene

22. To change the engine, just press another button and the current model will change. You can also find another spot and click on it to make it appear:

Engine 3 appearing on the surface

In this section, you have learned how to create a simple interface to change the models that appear in AR. With this, you now have the basic skills to go further and build more complex apps so that you can show and manipulate your own prototypes.

Summary

In this chapter, we have made an introduction to AR using Google's ARCore to create a prototype viewer app. We learned how to integrate the capabilities of ARCore and the Sceneform library to make the task of generating an AR scene easier and we have included our own external 3D models. We also created a basic UI that allows us to switch between different models.

Now, you have the skills to create your own application with ARCore. You can improve the current project by adding your own prototype, or prototype pieces, make the model break down into smaller pieces when the user presses a button, or change the color of the model with another button. This chapter has given you the basis to explore the possibilities of AR that's displayed on flat surfaces.

You also have a better knowledge of how AR can be useful in the manufacturing field and you can explore the further possibilities it offers beyond the example that's been provided here.

In the chapters that follow, we will explore other AR tools and technologies. Some of them will be related to ARCore, such as WebAR, while others will be completely different, such as Augmented Class!, EasyAR, and Vuforia.

Further reading

If you want to go further with the project we completed in this chapter, we recommend that you explore the following options:

- AR images: Instead of placing objects on surfaces, you can attach them to physical images (pictures, planes, and so on). You can find a starting point on how this works at `https://developers.google.com/ar/develop/java/augmented-images/`.
- Explore the available samples using Sceneform, you will only have to download and open them with Android Studio: `https://developers.google.com/ar/develop/java/sceneform/samples`.
- In `Chapter 2`, *Introduction to Unity for AR Development*, we introduced Unity 3D. ARCore can be used inside the Unity platform, which also makes the process of adding 3D models easier. It also accepts a greater number of extensions. You can find more information about how to get started here: `https://developers.google.com/ar/develop/unity/quickstart-android`.

4
AR for Training with WebAR and Augmented Class!

In this chapter, we will explore two different tools that work on Android devices that can be applied to the training field. The first one will be based on WebAR, specifically, the Google Web Component `<model-viewer>`, which will let us visualize 3D models in a real environment through a web page using ARCore. We will be able to select a model from a series of them on the web page, place it in the real world, and manipulate it (move, rotate, and scale it).

The second one will be Augmented Class!, an educational-oriented authoring tool that will let us create AR training projects to show different elements (images, audio files, videos, and 3D models, among others) over images or real-life pictures, add interactivity to our projects, and exchange them between users.

The main goal of this chapter is to introduce you to two AR tools in a slightly different context than the rest of the chapters have. The main idea of this chapter is for you to discover other forms of AR that are different than the rest of the SDKs that we have covered or will be covering, and their value for such a transversal field as training. By the end of this chapter, you will be able to create your own AR viewer through the web with ARCore, but you will have also discovered the possibilities of interactivity to enrich the user experience in AR applications using the Augmented Class! tool.

At the time of writing this book, both tools are under constant development and improvement, with new functionalities and integrations being added. Currently, they only work on Android devices, but it is expected they will soon work on iOS.

In this chapter, we will cover the following topics:

- Using AR for training
- Exploring WebAR with Google Component `<model-viewer>`
- Exploring Augmented Class!

Technical requirements

The technical requirements for this chapter are as follows.

For the `<model-viewer>` project, you will need the following:

- An ARCore-supporting Android device (see the list here: `https://developers.google.com/ar/discover/supported-devices`). The project has been tested on a Pocophone F1.

For the Augmented Class! project, you will need the following:

- An Android device with Android 5.0 or above

The resources and the code files for this chapter can be found here: `https://github.com/PacktPublishing/Enterprise-Augmented-Reality-Projects/tree/master/Chapter04`.

Using AR for training

AR has been present in the educational field for more than 20 years, especially inside the university scope, although its growth has been much slower and less noticed than in more commercial fields such as marketing or tourism.

With the evolution of the supporting hardware (phones, tablets, and digital whiteboards, for example), AR has become a valuable asset in education and training. It allows students to visualize concepts in three dimensions over an image or directly in the room so that they can access information in a quicker and more dynamic way (just pointing with the camera instead of searching on a book or the internet for the information) or to create deeper personal projects (giving life to a painting, adding instructions or extra information over a handcrafted project, creating an animated presentation, and more).

One important consideration to make is that AR in education/training is transversal to all ages and subjects: a child can use it in the classroom to learn forms and colors, while a company can use it to train workers on its occupational risk prevention plan—it just depends on the tool and the target of the AR content.

In this chapter, we will learn how to use two different and easy tools that will help us create two different educational projects in little time. For that, we will be using the following 3D models:

- `https://sketchfab.com/3d-models/gearbox-planetary-2bee7992d266456aaef1f1394b0ebb98`
- `https://sketchfab.com/3d-models/warm-gearbox-e7fedd86a90b4c46a53fe88882e66aa3`
- `https://sketchfab.com/3d-models/gearbox-conical-60f023924ee0456daa758eb590b6064b`

Let's get started with WebAR by learning about what the Google Web Component `<model-viewer>` is and how it works.

Exploring WebAR with Google Web Component <model-viewer>

Before smartphones hit the market, AR was exclusively developed on computers. Later on, web applications appeared, first written in Flash and then in HTML5, but always requiring the webcam from a computer. Since the appearance of the ARCore (Google) and ARKit (Apple) toolkits, AR is also arriving on smartphones through the web.

WebXR Device API is one of the current standards that's working to provide the specifications for accessing both VR and AR from the web, including the use of devices' sensors or **head-mounted displays** (**HMDs**). This standard specification is being written by the **World Wide Web Consortium** (**W3C**) and it's currently under development. At the time of writing, the integration of AR in this WebXR specification is still unstable and thus it's not presented in this chapter. It is expected that this functionality will be further developed during the following months. For more information on the standard and its progress, you can check their website (`https://www.w3.org/TR/webxr`) and GitHub (`https://github.com/immersive-web/webxr/`).

In this section, for the development of a WebAR application, we will be using Google's `<model-viewer>` Web Component, which allows us to easily embed 3D models into a web page and visualize them in AR using a smartphone or tablet.

 A Web Component is a custom HTML element that is based on existing web standards and works across modern browsers.

Google's `<model-viewer>` Component was first launched in February 2019 to allow users to display 3D models in web pages. In May 2019, they announced AR compatibility through the `ar` attribute. It's based on the ARCore functionality Scene Viewer and at the moment it only works on Android devices that support this technology. We will see that its use is quite straightforward and works on any browser. In `Chapter 3`, *AR for Manufacturing with ARCore*, we learned how to implement a whole AR mobile project. In this case, we will only have to use its web feature using the mentioned `<model-viewer>` Component. We will see which type of models we can use, how to create a web page to contain the component, and how to actually add the component and make it work on a mobile device.

Now that we have looked at the tool we are going to use, in the next section, we will cover the 3D models that are accepted by this component (at the time of writing).

Working with 3D models

Because we are displaying our models in the browser, the supported format is **GL Transmission Format (glTF)** 2.0/glb, a format that's designed to minimize the size and runtime processing, making it the best option for web transmission. Nowadays, many 3D designing programs such as Blender, 3ds Max, and Maya, as well as some 3D model platforms, such as Sketchfab, provide exporters to this format.

 You can find more information on the functionality of glTF and its possibilities at `https://www.khronos.org/gltf/` and `https://github.com/KhronosGroup/glTF/blob/master/README.md`.

The 3D models' textures can be in `.jpg` or `.png` format, the tool supports animations, and, because models are going to be displayed via a web browser, they should not be very heavy on keeping the AR experience fluid.

More information on these requirements can be found at `https://developers.google.com/ar/develop/java/scene-viewer`.

For this project, we are going to use three static models called `gearbox_conical.glb`, `gearbox_planetary.glb`, and `gearbox_worm.glb`. These models provide good detail for a more realistic AR experience, and we are going to use them in the project in the next section with Augmented Class!.

Now that we have understood the basics of how the `<model-viewer>` Component works, let's start creating a web page.

Creating a simple web page

The first thing we are going to do is create the web page where the 3D models will be displayed and ready to be launched in AR. For this, we are also going to use Glitch, an online tool that will help us create this project.

First, we are going to learn how to prepare a Glitch project before actually coding the style sheet and HTML page.

Coding with Glitch

Glitch is a simple tool for creating web apps with a strong collaboration component. It allows us to remix existing apps or clone projects from services such as GitHub or GitLab. In our case, since we'll only want to create a simple demo web page, we will use Glitch to store both the HTML page and the 3D models. To create a new Glitch project, follow these steps:

1. First of all, go to `https://glitch.com` and click on the **Sign-in** button. It will automatically create an account.

2. In the top-right corner of the page, click on **New Project** to start a new project. Then, click on the first option, **hello-webpage**:

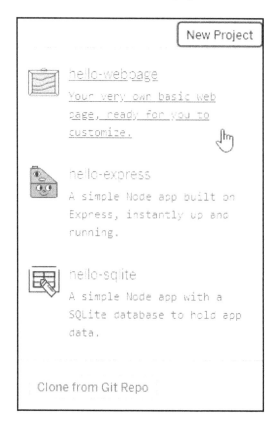

Selecting our project template

3. You will be directed to a board that will look similar to this:

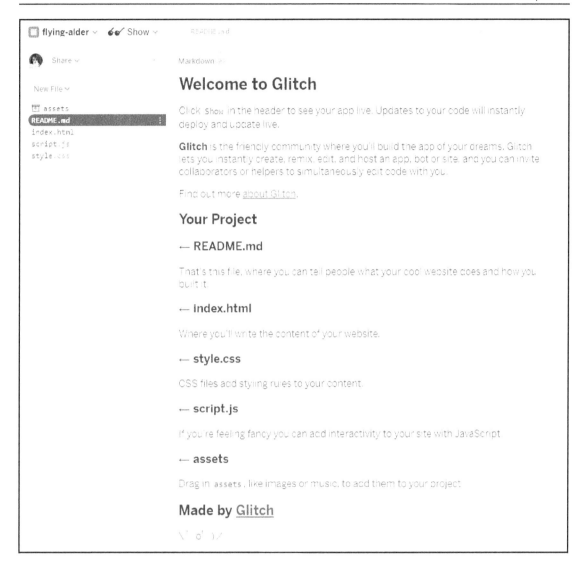

The Gitch board

Take a look at the **README** file as it explains the main functionality of the page.

4. The next step will be to change the name of the project that Glitch has provided us. Click on the name in the top-left corner of the page and provide a name and description:

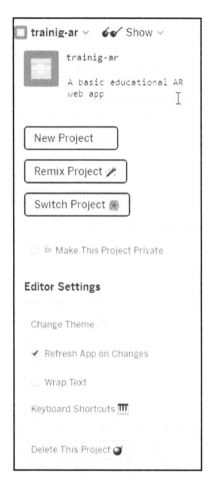

Changing the default name of the project

5. Now, from the dropdown button '**Show**', select '**Next to The Code**':

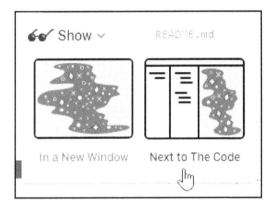

Selecting how to see the final web page

6. This will divide our window to show us the result of the code we are writing:

The window shows the code on the left and the result on the right

7. Let's upload our models. Click on assets on the left-hand bar and drag and drop the three models of this project, that is, `gearbox_planetary.glb`, `gearbox_worm.glb`, and `gearbox_conical.glb`, onto the square:

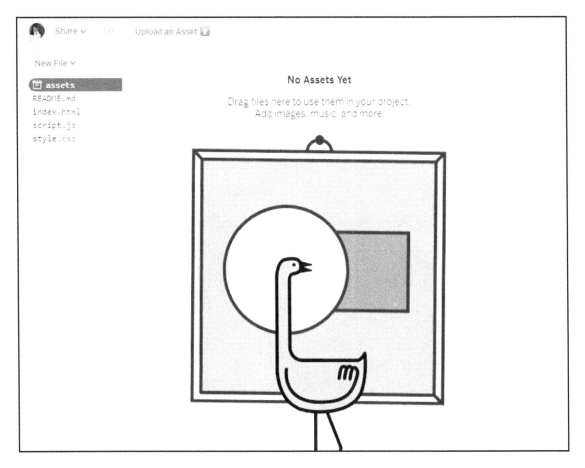

The assets window

8. Once the models have been uploaded, they will appear on the dashboard:

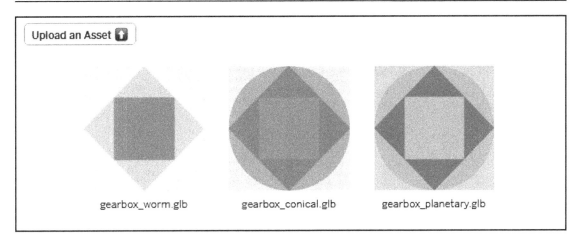

Assets listed in the assets window

9. Selecting each model will allow you to **Copy** the link to the asset or `Delete` it:

Link to the assets and a button to delete it

Glitch saves every key we press, so there is no need for us to manually save the code.

With our basic elements ready, let's write the web page code, starting with the style sheet and then the HTML page.

Coding the style sheet

In the style sheet, we are going to decide on the appearance of our web page. Since our main goal is to show the AR, we will keep it simple for now. The Glitch `style.css` file will already have some code in it. Let's modify this file and adapt it to our needs. Follow these steps to do so:

1. We are going to leave the body brackets as they are:

   ```
   body {
      font-family: "Benton Sans", "Helvetica Neue", helvetica, arial,
   sans-serif;
      margin: 2em;
   }
   ```

   Here, we specify the font we are going to use for the web page and the margins of the body element.

2. Next, we're going to modify the `h1` title element:

   ```
   h1 {
     text-align: center;
     color: #000000;
     font-style: bold;
   }
   ```

   Now, the title will be centered, black, and in bold.

3. Let's add some class elements:

   ```
   .box{
     max-width: 600px;
     margin: 4em auto;
     border-radius: 8px;
     box-shadow: 3px 3px 10px rgba(0, 0, 0, 0.7);
     text-align: center;
     overflow: hidden;
   }
   ```

   This class will encapsulate the 3D models when they are displayed over the web page (not in AR). They will appear inside a box, with rounded borders and a soft shadow on it. The text we will add will be centered inside the box and the `overflow: hidden` parameter will prevent the content from overflowing from the box.

4. Now, we'll add another class for the CC BY message of the models, which is required for these types of models:

```
.cc{
    display: flex;
    justify-content: flex-start;
    margin: 0.5em;
    font-style: italic;
}
```

Here, we are locating the content on the left-hand side and with italic text.

5. We'll also change the appearance of the cc class' images:

```
.cc img{
  height: 1em;
  opacity: 0.6;
}
```

With these two lines, we are selecting the height of the images inside this class and making them a little bit transparent.

6. Finally, we are going to modify the <model-viewer> Component's style:

```
model-viewer {
    width: 100%;
    height: 580px;
}
```

With this, we will make the model viewer take the width of the container box and set its height.

Now that the style sheet is ready, we can create our page.

Coding the index.html page

Now open the index.html and, at the beginning of the document, change the title of the web page from Hello! to AR Training Web App. You can leave the rest of the code between the <head> </head> tags as it is. Now, remove everything between the <body> </body> tags (if you want, you can leave the last two lines with the Glitch button).

Now, let's add the title and the three boxes for the models inside the `<body>` tags:

1. Add the title between `<h1>` tags so that it uses our `.css` file's style:

   ```
   <h1>Select a gearbox to display in AR</h1>
   ```

2. Now, after the title, add the first box with the title on top and the CC BY message at the bottom:

   ```
   <div class="box">
      <h2>Planetary Gearbox</h2>
      <div class="cc">
        <a href="https://creativecommons.org/licenses/by/2.0/"
   target="_blank">
           <img
   src="https://mirrors.creativecommons.org/presskit/icons/cc.svg">
           <img
   src="https://mirrors.creativecommons.org/presskit/icons/by.svg">
        </a>
          
        <a
   href="https://sketchfab.com/3d-models/gearbox-planetary-2bee7992d26
   6456aaef1f1394b0ebb98" target="_blank">T-FLEX CAD ST (Free)</a>
      </div>
   </div>
   ```

   The main component is the `box` class. Inside it, we have the title in `<h2>` format and the `cc` class with a link to the license, the two images from `creativecommons` to identify the CC BY license type, and the author of the model with a link to the Sketchfab page where it comes from.

3. Do the same for the other two models:

   ```
   <div class="box">
        <h2>Worm Gearbox</h2>
        <div class="cc">
          <a href="https://creativecommons.org/licenses/by/2.0/"
   target="_blank">
             <img
   src="https://mirrors.creativecommons.org/presskit/icons/cc.svg">
             <img
   src="https://mirrors.creativecommons.org/presskit/icons/by.svg">
          </a>
             
          <a
   href="https://sketchfab.com/3d-models/warm-gearbox-e7fedd86a90b4c46
   a53fe88882e66aa3" target="_blank">T-FLEX CAD ST (Free)</a>
   ```

```
      </div>
    </div>
    <div class="box">
      <h2>Conical Gearbox</h2>
      <div class="cc">
        <a href="https://creativecommons.org/licenses/by/2.0/"
target="_blank">
          <img
src="https://mirrors.creativecommons.org/presskit/icons/cc.svg">
          <img
src="https://mirrors.creativecommons.org/presskit/icons/by.svg">
        </a>
           
        <a
href="https://sketchfab.com/3d-models/gearbox-conical-60f023924ee04
56daa758eb590b6064b" target="_blank">T-FLEX CAD ST (Free)</a>
      </div>
    </div>
```

At the moment, your project should look like this:

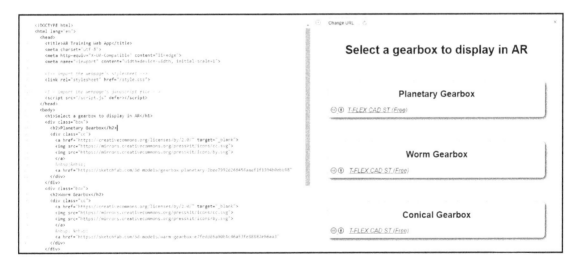

The web page with the three boxes

Now, we have to include the 3D models with the `<model-viewer>` Component.

Adding the <model-viewer> Component to our page

Adding the <model-viewer> Component is quite straightforward. Follow these steps to do so:

1. First of all, we have to add the following two lines at the end of the <body> element:

```
<script type="module"
src="https://unpkg.com/@google/model-viewer/dist/model-viewer.js"></script>
<script nomodule
src="https://unpkg.com/@google/model-viewer/dist/model-viewer-legacy.js"></script>
```

   With these lines, we are adding the module to our page and making it work in new and old browsers.

 If you want to work with a specific version of the module, add the version number on the URL after model-viewer, like this: /model-viewer@0.3.1/.

2. Then, we can call it inside the box class, after the h2 title and before the cc class, making reference to the models' URLs (put your own model's URL in the src attribute):

```
<model-viewer
src="https://cdn.glitch.com/6f8eb042-0e74-4182-9d39-4f877746edb1%2F
gerabox_planetary.glb?v=1566506940560" alt="Planetary Gearbox"
background-color="#42697b" auto-rotate camera-controls ar></model-viewer>
```

   The code interface can be seen in the following screenshot:

```
<body>
  <h1>Select a gearbox to display in AR</h1>
  <div class="box">
    <h2>Planetary Gearbox</h2>
    <model-viewer
      src="https://cdn.glitch.com/6f8eb042-0e74-4182-9d39-4f877746edb1%2Fgerabox_planetary.glb?v=1566506940560"
      alt="Planetary Gearbox"
      background-color="#42697b"
      auto-rotate
      camera-controls
      ar
    ></model-viewer>
    <div class="cc">
      <a href="https://creativecommons.org/licenses/by/2.0/" target="_blank">
        <img
          src="https://mirrors.creativecommons.org/presskit/icons/cc.svg"
        />
        <img
          src="https://mirrors.creativecommons.org/presskit/icons/by.svg"
        />
      </a>
        
      <a
        href="https://sketchfab.com/3d-models/gearbox-planetary-2bee7992d266456aaef1f1394b0ebb98"
        target="_blank"
        >T-FLEX CAD ST (Free)</a
      >
    </div>
  </div>
</body>
```

Final code for the <model-viewer>

As you can see, the <model-viewer> tag supports several attributes:

- The src, background-color, and alt attributes define the source URL, the color of the background, and the description, respectively.
- The auto-rotate attribute will have the model rotating by default on the web page (flat view, not in AR).
- With camera-controls, we can rotate/scale the model while it's in a flat view.
- The really important attribute for us here is ar; without it, the option of seeing the model in AR will not be available.

3. Do the same with the other two models:

```
...
<model-viewer
src="https://cdn.glitch.com/6f8eb042-0e74-4182-9d39-4f877746edb1%2F
gearbox_worm.glb?v=1566506941410" alt="Worm Gearbox" background-
color="#42697b" auto-rotate camera-controls ar></model-viewer>

...

<model-viewer
```

```
src="https://cdn.glitch.com/6f8eb042-0e74-4182-9d39-4f877746edb1%2F
gearbox_conical.glb?v=1566506963689" alt="Conical Gearbox"
background-color="#42697b" auto-rotate camera-controls ar></model-
viewer>
```

4. With this, you should see the three models loaded and rotating on the web page:

The web page with the 3D models in the display

We have finished coding. Now, let's take our mobile phone or tablet and see the models in AR.

Visualizing the 3D models in AR

To see the models in AR, you need to open the web page with an ARCore-supporting device. Once you have one, the steps to visualize the model are as follows:

1. Get the URL to your final page by clicking on the **Share** button in the top-left corner of the Glitch web page and selecting **Live App**.

2. Now, copy the URL and paste it into your mobile device. You should see the 3D models loading (it might take a little more time than it would on a computer since they are detailed models):

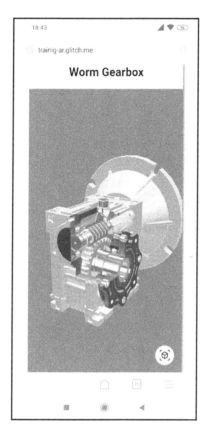

The web page displayed on the mobile phone

3. In the bottom-right corner of each model, you will see a little box that doesn't appear in the computer's browser. Click on it.

4. The first time you do this, a message will appear, asking if the page can open **Google Play Services for AR**, and if you don't have it installed, it will ask you to install it:

Google Play Services for AR in the Google Play Store

5. Now, you will see the 3D model in fullscreen, along with a button at the bottom to **View in your space** (AR). Click on it to launch the camera and point it at a flat surface:

The model displayed fullscreen with the button to see it in AR below

6. Once the model has been fixed to a surface, we can move around it. By touching the screen, you can move, rotate, and scale it:

The model in AR over the real floor

7. Now, you can play with the size and position of the model to view it from different angles and to move inside it.

 Important! 3D models must be accessed through an HTTPS connection. Otherwise, when clicking on the little box in the bottom-right corner, the **View in your space** button won't appear for the model. Keep this in mind if you use your own server in a future application instead of Glitch.

And that's it. Now, you know how to display models in AR using the Web Component `<model-viewer>` and ARCore.

As we mentioned previously, the Component is quite new and constantly changing. To see the latest features and accepted properties, you can take a look at `https://googlewebcomponents.github.io/model-viewer/` and `https://github.com/GoogleWebComponents/model-viewer`.

In the next section, we will create another training project using the same 3D models but with the Augmented Class! tool instead. We will use an image marker and add interaction to our final project.

Exploring Augmented Class!

Augmented Class! is an educational authoring tool born from the motivation of a group of developers and teachers/professors and provides a complete solution that allows all the members of the educational community (teachers, students, and parents) to create and share interactive AR projects without technical knowledge and without the usual constraints of these kinds of tools, such as limited content and functionalities.

Currently, in its 3.0.30 version, it's freely available in the Google Play Store and in private beta versions for PC. The application uses image markers, which are known as targets in other tools. This means it displays the virtual content over a real image, such as a picture, book cover, and so on, instead of over a flat surface like ARCore does. Augmented Class! allows a wide variety of content (images, audio files, videos, 3D models, and text), also we can add interaction (touching the screen, playing with the distance from the camera to the marker, and playing with the distance between two markers) and share our projects between users. It's free in this version and it is expected they will launch more free and pro functionalities in the upcoming months. For more information, visit `www.augmentedclass.com`.

In this chapter, we will use the Android app to create a simple project to display a 3D model of a gearbox. Then, we will add user interaction to display further information. Finally, we will create another marker and create an interaction between them. For that, we will prepare our material (images and 3D models) on the mobile device, create a simple project, add some user interaction to it, and create an interaction between two different markers.

To do this, we'll need to prepare all the material for our mobile device.

Preparing the material

Before we start the project, we have to prepare the material in our mobile device so that we can access it quickly:

1. The first thing we need to do is register on their web page (`http://creativitic.es/augmentedclass/beta/`) and download the Android app at `https://play.google.com/store/apps/details?id=com.AugmentedClass.AClasshl=es_419`. The app allows us demo access without us having to log in, but it has more restrictions for projects than it does with registered access.

2. Now, on your phone or tablet, create a folder called `AClass` in the `root` folder and copy the model file, `gearbox_worm.glb`, and the markers, `gearbox_worm.jpg` and `component_desc.jpg`, into it. Creating a folder isn't required, but it will make using and searching for content from the app easier.

Now, we are ready to start the app.

Creating a simple project

We are going to start by creating a simple project to see how AR can be used in a training project using image-based markers. Let's get started:

1. Open the app, give the required permissions, and on the login page, enter the username and password you should have received from the email address you provided previously:

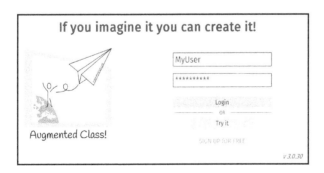

Augmented Class! app login window

2. The first time you open the app, you will be asked to complete a simple tutorial, where you have to follow some basic steps to create a very simple project with some given resources:

Initial tutorial

3. Once you have completed the tutorial, from the main menu, press **Go to Inventor**.

4. In the inventor window, click on the created **New Project** to select it and delete it by pressing the delete icon:

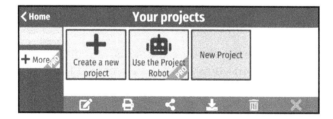

Inventor window with the project created and the tutorial deleted

5. Now, click on **Create a new project** to enter the blackboard window.
6. Before anything else, give the project a name so that you can identify it later.
7. Here, we can select our type of marker. They are as follows:

  - **Simple Marker**: Shows the AR content over the selected image
  - **Camera Interaction**: Shows some AR content when the camera is far from the marker and another different AR content when the camera is close to the marker
  - **Marker Interaction**: Shows an AR content in each marker when they are separated and other content in each one when they are close

Choose **Simple Marker**:

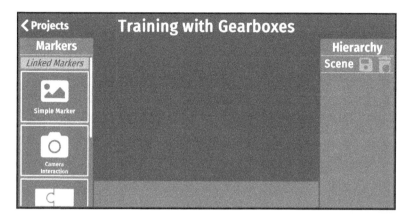

Giving the project a name from the top bar

8. The first thing we need to do is select a marker. We could select a previous one, take a picture of an image from our camera, or upload a marker. Drag the square **Load MARKER** over the white square in the middle and select the gearbox_worm.jpg image from your mobile device:

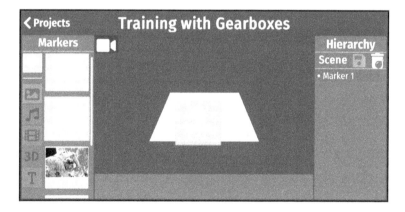

Dragging the Load MARKER square from the left scrollview to the middle

9. Now, we can add our 3D model to the marker. Click on the **3D** button on the left and drag **Load model** to the marker in the middle of the screen:

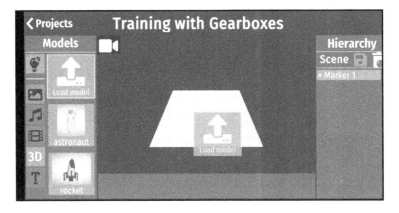

Dragging the Load model square to the marker in the middle

10. Navigate to the `AClass` folder we created earlier and select `gearbox_worm.glb`. As you can see, many file types are accepted:

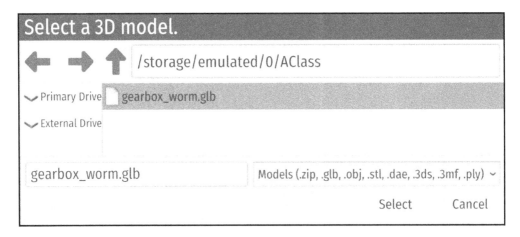

Selecting our 3D model

11. Wait until the model has loaded. You will see that the model is selected by default and that new buttons are being displayed on the top bar. Select the hand icon to manipulate the model. Using the move/rotate/scale buttons, manipulate the gearbox until it looks as follows:

3D model rotated and scaled down

The multi-gesture option allows you to manipulate the model with fewer buttons.

12. Now, press on the **Scene** save icon under the **Hierarchy** panel. Our current marker will be saved and a thumbnail will appear on the bottom bar:

The current marker appears as a thumbnail in the bottom bar

13. Click on the **Projects** button in the top-left corner to quit the blackboard. Then, from the top-left corner, click on the **Home** button to go to the main menu. There, press **Go to Viewer**. Here, we can see our project on the grid:

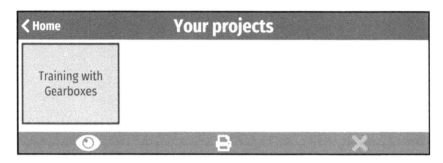

The viewer window with our project

14. Since we only have one project and it's already selected, press the eye icon to load the AR. Then, point with the camera to the marker to see the 3D model appear over the image. Move and rotate the image and get closer to/further away from it to see the model from all angles:

The gearbox appearing over the image marker

 Both the inventor and the viewer windows have a printer button so that you can print a PDF with the markers in case you don't have them at hand.

That's it. We have the basic project ready. Now, let's add some interaction to it.

Adding user interaction

Let's add some interactivity to our project by letting the user touch the screen so that they can view more AR information when hovering over the marker. Follow these steps to do so:

1. Go back to the **Inventor** window and select our project. Press the pencil icon to edit it:

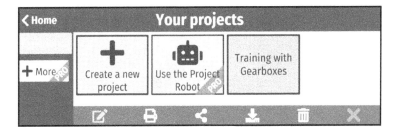

Editing a project

2. Press the thumbnail and then the pencil icon to edit the marker's scene:

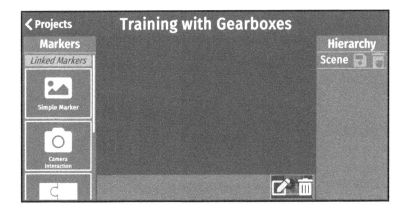

Selecting and editing the scene

3. Let's add some information. On the left-hand bar, press the texts button and drag one of the fonts over the marker:

Dragging a text element over the marker

4. Enter the text `Worm gear` and, with the manipulation buttons, move it until it's next to the gold-colored gear (the worm gear) of our 3D model:

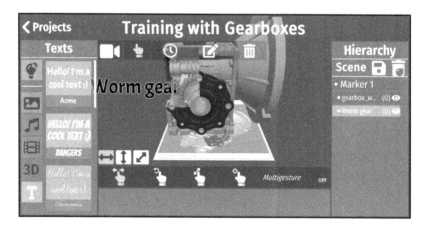

Locating the text next to the object it makes reference to

5. To make it easier to place, you can change the camera perspective by pressing the camera icon and then on the camera with the eye:

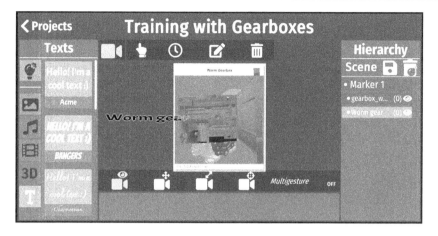

Switching the camera view to top view

6. Now, with the text selected, press the clock icon to add the interaction and select the hand icon. This way, the text will appear when the user touches the screen once the model is visible:

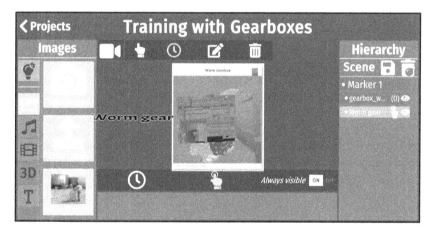

Selecting the interaction of the text

You can select the different elements on the scene by pressing them or on their names in the **Hierarchy** panel.

7. Save the scene and go back to the viewer window to launch the AR. Now, when the model appears over the image, press it. The text will appear:

The text appearing when touching the element on the screen

In this section, we've learned how to add basic interaction to our marker. In the next section, we will create a marker interaction instead.

Creating interaction between markers

Now, we will create a marker interaction. We will have two markers: the model, as in the previous sections, and some simple text, `Component Description`.

For this example, we will keep it simple, and when we focus on the model's marker with the camera, it will show the 3D model. However, when we put both markers together, the description text will appear.

Because we are going to reuse our 3D model's marker, we will create another project. Inside a project, single markers can't be repeated as the viewer won't know which content it should display over the marker. Thus, we will start a new project and create the necessary interaction. Let's get started:

1. In the project window, create a new project, and in the blackboard window, call it `Interactive Gearbox`. For this project, select two marker interactions:

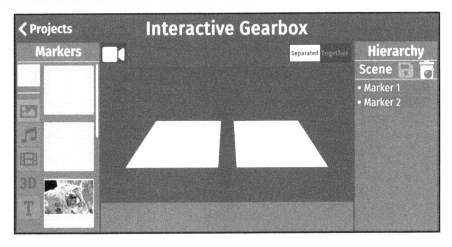

The new project with two markers

As you can see, a new button will appear in the top-right corner: **Separated/Together**. This button will switch between the two modes (when the markers are separated and together), allowing us to place different content over the markers in each case.

2. Now, from the list of markers, make `gearbox_worm` the first marker:

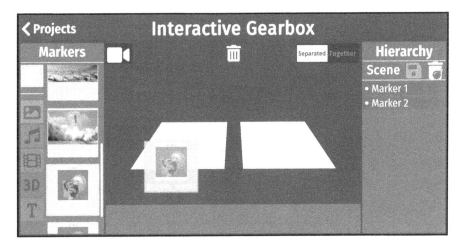

Dragging the previously uploaded gearbox_womr1 image onto the first marker

3. Now, drag the **Load MARKER** square onto the second one to load the `component_desc.png` picture on it:

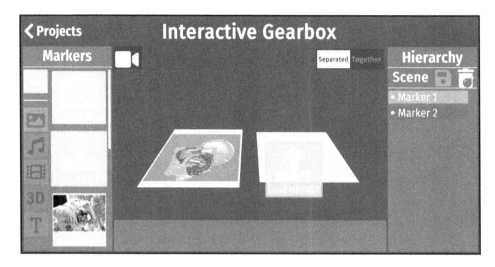

Dragging the Load MARKER square to load an image from the mobile device

4. Press the **3D** button and drag and drop the `gearbox_worm` model from the scrollview's end over the first marker. This will be our content for when markers are separated:

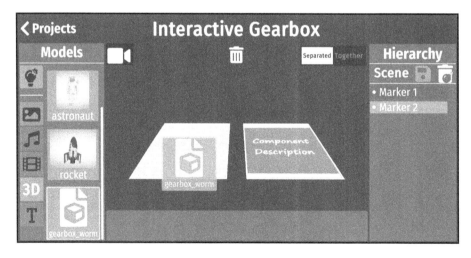

Dragging the previously uploaded model

5. Now, click on the **Together** button to change to the content that's going to appear when we put them close to each other. You will see that the previous content will disappear from the scene:

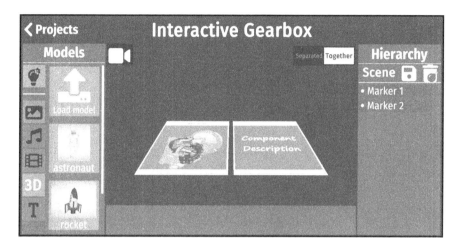

The scene changed to the Together mode

6. Repeat *step 4* to place the model over the first marker.

7. Select the text button and drag and drop one of the fonts over the first marker in two separate instances to create two different sets of text. Select and place them like so:

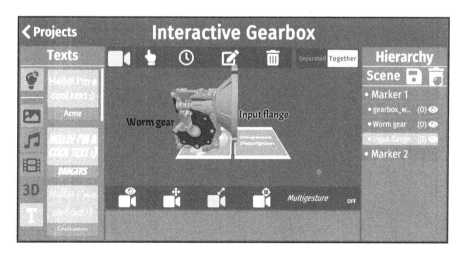

The scene with the model and the information text

8. You can make use of the camera's buttons to reduce the scene and see it from the top in order to place the text properly:

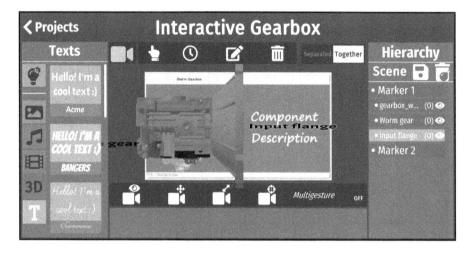

The same scene from above after changing the camera view

9. That's it. Now, press the save button and go back to the viewer window to launch the AR. Select the current project in the grid and press the eye icon:

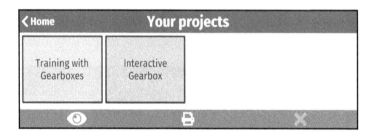

Selecting the current project to display in AR

10. Now, you will see that, when they are separated, the gearbox shows the 3D model:

When the markers are separated, only the model appears

11. Now, when they're put together, we're shown the 3D model and the text we added earlier:

When the markers have joined the model and the information is displayed

Beyond this example, this kind of interaction is very useful for complex explanations such as chemical reactions (we have different components that behave in one way when they are separated and in another way when they are together), for word-forming, for commands (we can have markers such as **Component Description**, **Assembly**, or **Basic Maintenance** and, depending on which one we put close to the model, different information will appear), and more.

Sharing the project

All the projects that are created on a device are stored locally. However, you may want to share one or more with your students or colleagues. For that, follow these steps:

1. Go to the projects window.
2. Select the project and press the share icon:

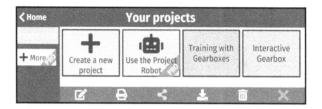

Sharing the selected project

3. For multiple selection, long-press on a project until the checkboxes appear and select as many as you want:

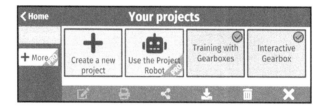

Sharing multiple projects

4. A window will open so that you can share your project file via email, social networks, and so on:

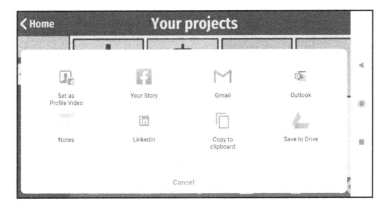

Selecting how to share the project(s)

To import another person's project (or a project you created in another device), follow these steps:

1. Download the projects file from your email or drive, or where you had shared it (remember the folder you downloaded it from):
   - Go to the projects window.
   - Click on the download icon (the only active one when a project is not selected):

Selecting to import a project file

2. Browse to the folder where you downloaded the file and select it:

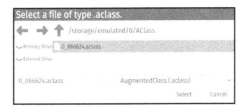

Choosing the project file

The project(s) will be imported automatically.

Once the new projects have been imported into your projects window, you can edit and delete them like any other project you have created.

What's next?

So far, you've learned how to create a simple marker and two marker interactions, and added interaction for touchscreens. To do so, we've used a 3D model and some text, but you can try enriching the current projects with video files or audio explanations.

On the other hand, Augmented Class! offers more options, including interaction with the camera (content changes when the camera is far from the marker and when it's close to it), delayed showing of the content (elements appear after a time and they can disappear again or not), and content editing (video and audio loop, text color and style, and so on). Once you've tried out all of these options and you're familiar with them, design and create a fully interactive project using every possible interaction.

Summary

In this chapter, you have learned about two different tools for training projects. The first one is based on ARCore's web feature, which allows us, without having to code much, to add AR visualization to any 3D model that's displayed on a web page. The second tool, Augmented Class!, has allowed us to easily create interactive educational projects that can serve different purposes, such as learning the basics of a piece, training a maintenance engineer, and so on.

Now, you have a better understanding of the versatility of AR, how it can be used on mobile devices and through web apps, and how interaction can help create a deeper and more valuable experience. With the skills you've acquired in this chapter, you can try to migrate your projects into other areas and needs, as well as exploring both tools even further so that you can improve the current projects.

In the next chapter, we will start using the Unity 3D environment and some other AR tools that can be integrated into it. Here, you will learn how to use the EasyAR tool's image recognition process to create an AR catalog.

AR for Marketing with EasyAR

5

This chapter will introduce you to EasyAR, an easy and intuitive AR SDK with multiple functionalities that can be used alone or, like in this chapter, integrated into Unity 3D. You will learn what image-based AR is and how it works with EasyAR by using your own images as markers. You will also learn how to import a custom 3D model into Unity to display it using AR over an image marker. Finally, you will create an augmented catalog where your furniture will come to life.

This chapter has two main goals: to learn EasyAR and its features and to understand the possibilities of AR as a marketing tool. Nowadays, EasyAR is, along with Vuforia, one of the most versatile AR SDKs that can be used for many purposes. By the end of this chapter, you will have the basic skills to continue improving the current project or create new and improved ones by exploring the rest of the functionalities EasyAR has to offer. As you will see, AR is a very powerful marketing tool for different purposes, such as impacting the user, presenting the product in a more visual and appealing way, and offering discounts and prizes that are integrated into the AR experience. The idea of this chapter is that, by the end of it, you will understand the basic use of AR in this field so that you can explore its possibilities afterward.

 Important! In this chapter, we will be using Unity 3D, so if you haven't done it already, we recommend that you read `Chapter 2`, *Introduction to Unity for AR Development*, first to familiarize yourself with its layout, nomenclature, and features.

In this chapter, we will be covering the following topics:

- Using AR for marketing
- Understanding EasyAR
- Building image-based AR
- Working with custom 3D models
- Creating an AR catalog

Technical requirements

The technical requirements for this chapter are as follows:

- A Unity 3D-supporting computer (see the latest requirements here: `https://unity3d.com/es/unity/system-requirements`). This chapter's example project has been developed on a Windows 10 x 64 computer.
- Unity 3D (2019.1.2f1 in this book).
- Microsoft Visual Studio Community 2017 (included in the Unity installation).
- EasyAR SDK (3.0.1 in this book).
- A mobile device with Android 4.2 and above, or iOS 8.0 and above (EasyAR requirements: `https://www.easyar.com/doc/EasyAR%20SDK/Getting%20Started/3.0/Platform-Requirements.html`). The project has been tested on a Samsung Galaxy A5 (2017) and a Pocophone F1.

The resources and code files for this chapter can be found here: `https://github.com/PacktPublishing/Enterprise-Augmented-Reality-Projects/tree/master/Chapter05`.

 The project in this chapter has been tested using a Windows 10 PC, and a Samsung Galaxy A5 (2017) and Pocophone F1 Android devices. For iOS development, you will also need to develop using an Apple computer because Unity will build an Xcode project.

Using AR for marketing

Marketing is one of the first fields where AR landed when it first began. The visual impact of this technology makes it very attractive to potential customers, and it can be used from generating a *wow effect* to explaining the qualities of the products.

When it began, AR was mainly used to impact users. A new technology, close to the concept of holography, that let us see ourselves and others surrounded by virtual elements and characters, was a good enticement. Big brands started using it in commercial centers where people could see themselves on a big screen next to virtual animals, dinosaurs, or famous characters. With mobile devices being widespread, AR marketing techniques have changed: the user is now in charge of the experience and can interact with it. Brands could now go beyond the *wow* effect and create functional experiences to promote and sell their products. Examples of this include augmented catalogs that show the products in 3D over their flat images, virtual mirrors where you can buy the glasses that you are trying on in AR, packages that come to life to explain the elements inside the fabrication process, and so on.

The main idea behind AR's marketing success is that it has to be meaningful and engaging to make sure that users will want to download the app and use it and, after the experience, they will remember your brand, will return to you, or will have purchased from you.

In this chapter, we are going to use AR to create a furniture catalog where chairs will come to life from its pages. We will also give users the possibility to change these chairs' colors.

When focusing on using mobile devices to view the catalog's pages, we want our potential customers to see the product from all its angles so that they can get a better idea of what they are buying and feel more attached to the product. The possibility of customizing certain aspects of the product, such as its color, in real-time can help spark an interest in it.

For our project, we will be using the real catalog pages and 3D models from the company Euro Seating (`https://www.euroseating.com/en/`), a seating manufacturer that's present in more than 100 countries all over the world. Using their high-quality 3D models and real catalog will help us visualize this project as a real-life AR application that can be used in any other marketing context.

The models and images that will be used in this chapter have been released by the company for their use in the context of this book.

Before we start working on this project, let's have a quick look at what EasyAR is and how to integrate it into Unity.

Understanding EasyAR

EasyAR is a multiplatform augmented reality SDK for Android, iOS, UWP, Windows, Mac, and Unity editor. An AR engine allows us to create AR solutions in an easy way and offers multiple AR features, including the following:

- **Planar image tracking**: A technology that recognizes and tracks the position, rotation, and scale of a previously selected image in the real world, such as a book cover, photograph, or a business card.
- **Surface tracking (SLAM)**: A technology to detect surfaces and keep track of the objects within it.
- **3D object tracking**: A technology to localize and track the position and orientation of real 3D objects instead of flat images.
- **Screen recording**: A feature that allows us to take videos of the AR scene while we are playing it.

Some of the main features of EasyAR are as follows:

- It has an intuitive target management interface so that targets can be generated at runtime without us having to upload or download anything from their website, such as other tools.
- It supports both local and cloud recognition.
- It supports multitracking (simultaneous multiple target tracking) of different targets and the same targets.
- It supports 3D tracking to detect and track 3D objects with rich textures in real environments.

EasyAR has a web-based platform through which users can register their projects and obtain the licenses that they need in order to test and release their applications. EasyAR SDK is available in two different kinds of editions:

- EasyAR SDK Basic is free for commercial use without any kind of limitations or watermarks. It offers AR capacities based on image targets, it can load and recognize up to 1,000 offline targets, and it supports multi-target tracking, surface recognition, transparent and streaming video playback, and QR recognition. We need to make it known that the app has been developed with EasyAR.
- EasyAR SDK Pro includes all the features of the Basic edition, plus 3D object tracking, multi-type target detection, and screen recording. The Pro edition costs $499.00 per license key, but offers a free trial version with limited uses (up to 100 per day). A feature comparison, pricing, and payment details are listed on the EasyAR SDK product page https://www.easyar.com/view/sdk.html.

For our project, the functionalities from the basic license will be enough. Let's get started with EasyAR.

 Before we start using EasyAR SDK, we need to integrate it into Unity (take a look at Chapter 2, *Introduction to Unity for AR Development*, *Preparing your system for Unity* section to learn how to install and use Unity for the first time).

In order to download and import EasyAR SDK into Unity, follow these steps:

1. Create an account by navigating to EasyAR's web page at `https://www.easyar.com/view/signUp.html`. You will need to accept the developer agreement to create one.

2. After creating your account, you will receive a confirmation email so that you can activate it and log in.

3. Once you're logged in, go to the EasyAR download page (`https://www.easyar.com/view/download.html`) and, in the right-hand column, in the Unity Packages section, select **EasyARSense_3.0.1-final_Basic_Unity.zip** to download it. This package contains the engine and the basic examples for the different uses of the tool. Unzip it to obtain the `.unitypackage` file.

4. Now, we can create the Unity project. Open the Unity Hub and, from the top bar, click on **NEW**:

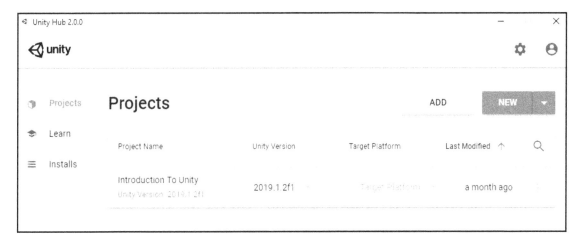

Opening Unity Hub to create a new project

5. Give the project a **Name** and a **Location** and click on **CREATE**:

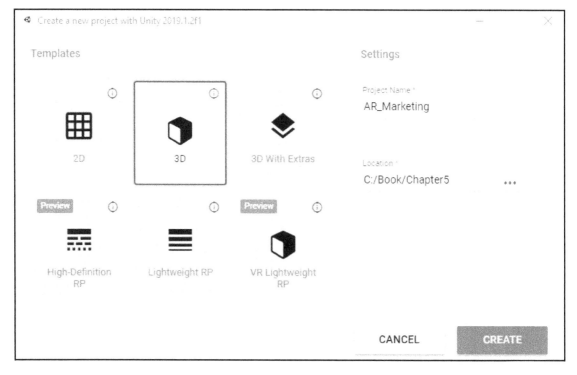

Giving the project a name and location

6. Once the project has been created, import the EasyAR package into Unity. To do so, once you've unzipped the compressed file, you can either double-click on the resultant .unitypackage file (the quickest way) or, from inside Unity, you can click on **Assets | Import Package | Custom Package...** and select the .unitypackage file.

7. A new window will appear with all the files inside the EasyAR package. Click on **Import:**

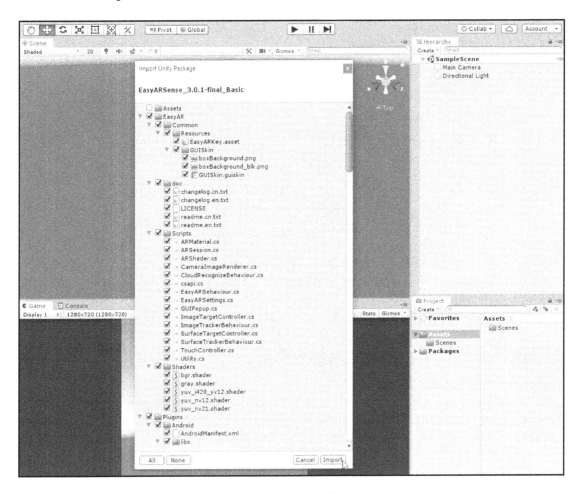

Importing EasyAR SDK into Unity

8. As you will see, four new folders will appear on your **Project** window: **EasyAR** and **Plugins**, which include the main resources and code to build EasyAR for different platforms, and **Samples** and **StreamingAssets**, which contain the sample resources and code:

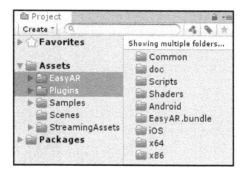

Four new folders have been added to the project

At this point, we have a new clean project with the EasyAR engine and samples included. In the next section, we will learn how to use it to build an app that detects a real image and displays a virtual cube on it.

Building image-based AR

You can build AR using different techniques; the most common one is image-based AR, which consists of tracking a previously selected image (target) and superposing the virtual content to it while taking into account the image's position, rotation, and size. This kind of tracking requires the use of different algorithms that differentiate images one from another through characteristic points of the design, and position the image in three dimensions on the camera feed. Don't worry—EasyAR will do this work for you. All you will need to do is decide which images will act as the targets and what virtual content will go on top of them.

To create this project, we will use EasyAR's **ImageTarget** sample project as a reference since it already has all the components we need for our app. But before we start with the AR elements, we will set up our project folders:

1. The first thing we are going to do is create our personal `Assets` folder, `@MyAssets`, to differentiate it from the rest of the assets we've imported into Unity. Here, we will add all the external resources, such as marker images and 3D models. For that, right-click on the **Project** window and select **Create|Folder**. Name it `@MyAssets`:

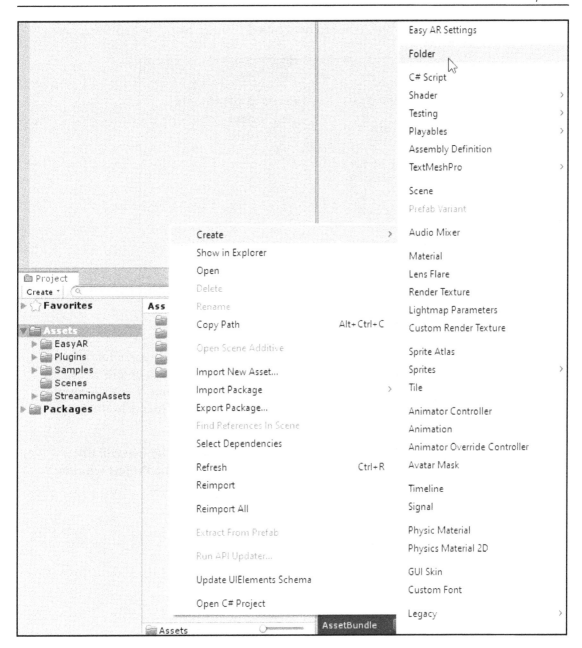

Create a new folder under the main Assets folder and call it @MyAssets

2. Inside this, create three other folders called `Images`, `Models`, and `Scripts`:

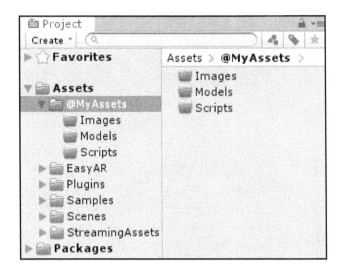

@MyAssets folder with the three folders inside it

Note: This project currently has six folders under the `Assets` folder. As you can see, projects tend to increase in size quickly and before we realize it, our resources are lost in the chaos of folders and files. Taking a couple of minutes to create a basic structure for our project folders is always good practice.

3. Now, we can create our AR scene. As we mentioned earlier, we will use EasyAR's sample scene as a reference. To do that, from the **Project** window, double-click on the **HelloAR_ImageTarget** scene located at **Assets | Samples | Scenes** to open it:

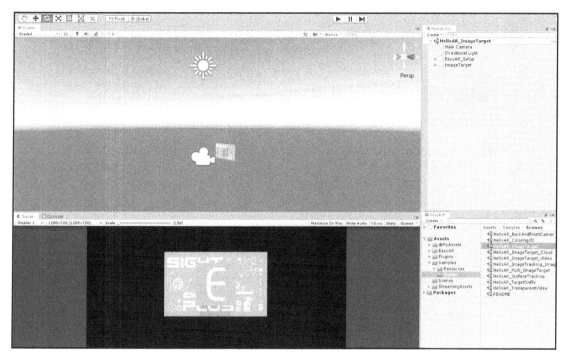

The HelloAR_ImageTarget sample scene

Here, we have all the elements we need to replicate our own AR project.

4. Now, click on **File|Save As...** and save the scene inside the **Assets|Scenes** folder with the name `ARScene`:

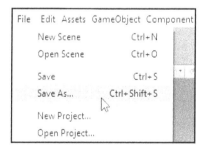

Saving the scene with another name

By doing this, we've created a duplicate of the sample scene. If anything happens to our scene, we can always go back to the original one.

Now that we have the initial scene, we can take a look at each component and customize them for our needs.

Understanding our AR scene

An AR scene has two main components that are common to any image-based AR SDK:

- **The ARCamera**: The camera object that will receive the feed from the camera device and process those frames in search of the selected image (target).
- **The ImageTarget**: The representation of the real image where we will put the virtual elements. When the camera finds this **ImageTarget** in the real world, it shows the virtual elements attached to it.

In EasyAR, we have three main elements (apart from the **Directional Light**):

- The **Main Camera**, which is the element that will render the image coming from our mobile device.
- **EasyAR_Setup**, which is in charge of the main operations of the app, such as initializing and handling the EasyAR engine, attaching the physical camera device to the **Main Camera** element of the scene, or implementing the image target detection and tracking through the **ImageTracker**:

The EasyAR_Setup element and its elements

- **ImageTarget**, which is the representation of the image we want to recognize. It contains the virtual elements that will appear and disappear when the image is detected/lost in the real world. In this case, the **ImageTarget** already comes with two children: a **Quad**, which represents the image we will track, and a **Cube**, which we will use to initially test the scene. The values of the image to recognize appear in the **Inspector** window in the **Image Target Controller**, as shown in the following screenshot:

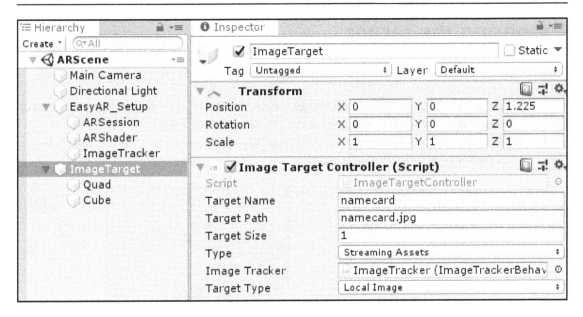

ImageTarget with its children on the left and the component values on the right

The parameters in the **Image Target Controller** are as follows:

- **Target Name**: The target's name. This doesn't have to be the image's name.
- **Target Path**: This is the full path to the image we want to use as a target. It's directly related to the **Type** option.
- **Target Size**: Size of the target. We will usually leave it at 1.
- **Type**: Whether the image of the target will be stored inside the assets of the project (specifically, the `StreamingAssets` folder, which we already have in our **Project** window) or if the **Target Path** is absolute.
- **Image Tracker**: This is the **ImageTracker** that will search for this **ImageTarget** in the camera feed.
- **Target Type**: Here, we will be using the first option, **Local Image**, since our image will be included locally inside the project.

Now that we have seen the main elements of the scene, the next thing we need to do is create our own target.

Preparing the target

Let's create our target. We'll start by adding the necessary images and resources to our project. Follow these steps to do so:

1. Drag the `Target_Maia.jpg` image located in the `Images` folder from the project resources provided to the `StreamingAssets` folder, and the `Target_Maia_texture.jpg` image to our `@MyAssets/Images` folder, as shown in the following screenshot:

Target_Maia.jpg and Target_Maia_texture.jpg images in their respective folders

The first image will be our target. We will use the second image, which is smaller than the first one, to guide us on the target's size in the editor.

 We can't reuse the image from the `StreamingAssets` folder because the files in this folder are not processed by the Unity editor, so they can't be used inside the scene directly like regular files.

2. In the **Hierarchy** window, select the **ImageTarget** and change the **Name** and **Path** values in the **Inspector** window, as shown in the following screenshot:

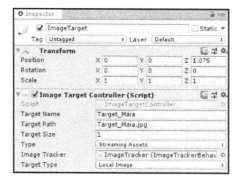

Image Target Behaviour parameters

With these parameters, we are telling **ImageTracker** to find the target called `Target_Maia.jpg` inside the streaming assets of the project.

 Note: You can use the folders inside the `StreamingAssets` folder to organize your targets. In that case, you will have to add the folder to the **Target Path** property (for example, `MyFolder/Target_Maia.jpg`).

3. The **ImageTarget** doesn't have an image associated with it, meaning that we can't actually see it in the editor. To visualize how our target will look, and especially to see how the virtual content will look over the real image (size, position), we will use the **Quad** element we already have as a child of the **ImageTarget**. By the end of the project, when we no longer need it, we will delete this **Quad** element. Drag the `@MyAssets/Images/Target_Maia_texture` image from the **Project** window to the **Quad** to make it its texture:

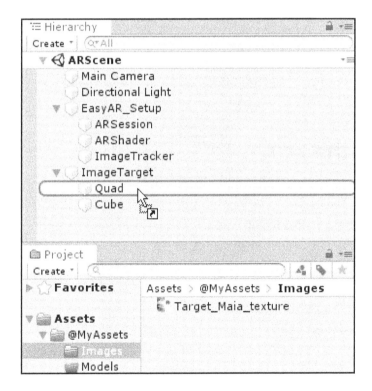

Target_Maia_texture being dragged to the Quad

4. Now, we have to adjust the aspect ratio of the **Quad** so that it matches our image's aspect ratio. We'll do that by setting the **Y** scale to 0.7, as shown in the following screenshot:

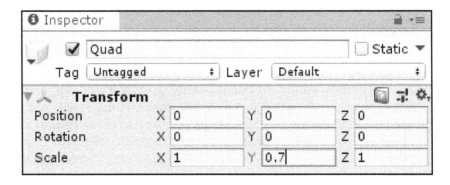

The Quad's Transform component and its values

Our scene is ready. We have the **Main Camera**, the **EasyAR_Setup**, our **ImageTarget** has the path to the image we want to recognize in it, and the **Quad** and a **Cube** are children so that they will appear when the marker is recognized. The next thing we need to do is get the EasyAR key to test the scene.

Obtaining the key

To test the current scene, we need to add the key to the EasyAR GameObject. This key is generated by EasyAR to license the app:

1. Go to the EasyAR develop center (`https://www.easyar.com/view/ developCenter.html#license`), log in if you aren't already, and click on **Add SDK License Key**.
2. There, select **EasyAR SDK Basic** and provide the following details:
   - **App Name:** `AR Catalogue`
   - **Bundle ID (iOS):** `com.banana.arcatalogue` (you only need to fill this in if you are going to build your app on iOS)
   - **Package Name (Android):** `com.banana.arcatalogue` (you only need to fill this in if you are going to build your app on Android)

These names correspond to the app name and bundles (*com.companyname.productname*) in Unity.

If you want to change these names in the future, you will have to make sure to change them in the key generation panel and copy/paste the resulting key into Unity again.

3. Select the created key in the panel and copy the **SDK License Key** (valid for EasyAR SDK 3.x) into the **Easy AR Key** element located in **Assets│EasyAR│Common│Resources**:

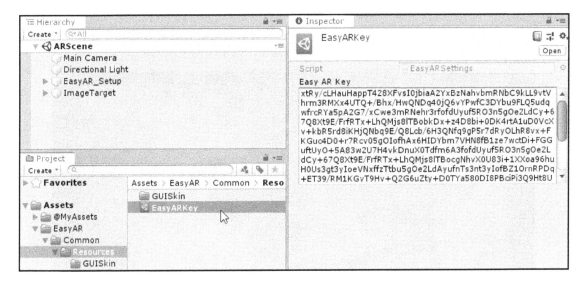

EasyARKey settings script

Once we have the key, we are ready to test the scene.

Testing the scene

Now, let's test the scene: press *Ctrl + S* to save everything again, make sure you have a webcam connected to your computer and hit the play button at the top of the Toolbar. The system should launch the webcam automatically. If you point at the marker (either printed or displayed in the screen), you should see the quad in the background and the cube popping from it in the **Game** view:

> To view the scene in full-screen mode, you can press **Maximize on Play** in the top right of the **Game** view before pressing play.

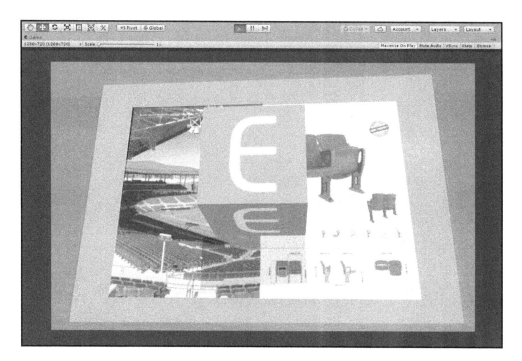

The Game window maximized, showing the cube appearing in AR over the target

Hit the play button again to stop the simulation.

> **Important!** Remember that to hit the play button to stop the simulation or any changes that are made in the scene afterward while you're still in simulation mode won't be saved.

Troubleshooting

If you can't see the AR scene correctly, you can go to the **Console** tab (it's in the bottom bar or the tab next to the **Game** view) and look at the information there.

If everything worked correctly, it should show only information messages, namely the successful initialization of EasyAR, its version, and so on. However, if there is an error message of **404 Not Found**, this means that the target has not been set up properly. Please review all the steps, especially the **Path** parameter in the **ImageTarget** to make sure it's pointing to the correct file. In the following screenshot, the target name is `Target_Maia2.jpg` instead of `Target_Maia.jpg`:

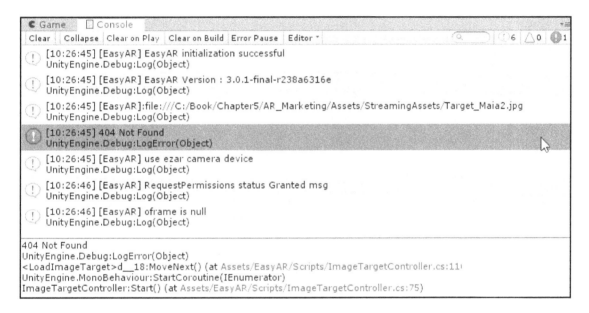

The console showing common information messages and an error

In any case, you can try to troubleshoot the errors either in the Unity forums (`https://forum.unity.com/`) or in the EasyAR forums (`https://forum-test.easyar.com/`).

 This step of testing the scene is not necessary, although it's highly recommended. Building an app into a device takes time, so it's advisable to test it first and make sure it works as you want it to.

Now, let's build the app.

Building the app

To build a new Android app, there are some steps you will always have to follow:

1. The first thing you need to do is select the platform. For that, click on **File**|**Build Settings**.
2. Click on **Add Open Scenes** to add our current scene to the (empty) list of scenes that will be built in the app.
3. Under **Platform**, select **Android** and click on **Switch Platform**. Wait until Unity recompiles the resources for the selected platform:

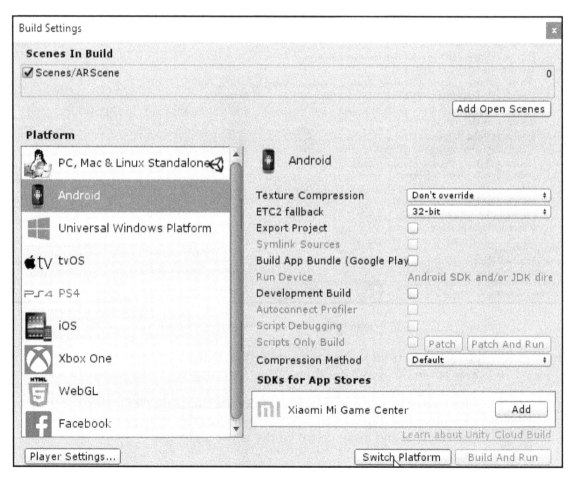

The Build Settings window with the current scene added and the Android platform selected

4. Then, click on **Player Settings...** to configure the app settings. In the pop-up window, we are going to change a few things for the time being:

- **Company Name**: Banana
- **Product Name**: AR Catalogue

These names are the same ones we used in the generation of the EasyAR key code.

The following image shows the **Project Settings** window with the newly added **Company Name** and **Product Name** fields:

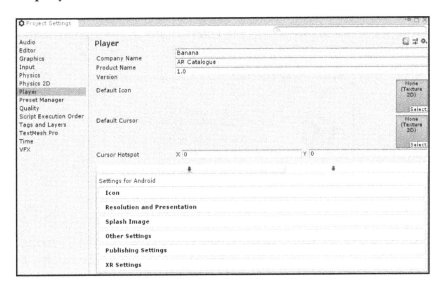

Filling in the company and product names in Project Settings

5. Then, on **Other Settings|Identification**, set the following:

- **Package name**: com.banana.arcatalogue (make sure it matches the name from the EasyAR key generation, otherwise the app will launch an error on its initialization saying the package name doesn't match the key)
- **Version**: 1.0
- **Minimum API Level**: Android 5.0 'Lollipop' (API level 21)
- **Target API Level**: Automatic (highest installed):

According to EasyAR's documentation, the SDK is compatible with Android 4.2 and above, but for performance reasons, and in order to have a fluid AR experience on users' devices, we recommend setting the minimum API level to 5.0.

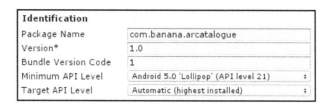

Identification section inside the Other Settings tab

6. In case you have Android SDK installed outside Unity, before opening the **Player Settings**, Unity will most likely tell you it found an Android SDK and whether you want to use it. If that's the case, click **Yes**:

Using the installed SDK if we already have it installed

7. Close the **Player Settings** window, connect your mobile device to the computer with a USB cable, and make sure your device has USB debugging activated in order to deploy the app directly into it from Unity. To activate this option, the general steps are as follows:

- Enable **Developer Mode** by going to **Settings | About Device**.
- Then, tap seven times on the build number until a notification appears stating that the **Developer Options** are available.
- Go to the **Developer Options** and activate **USB Debugging** to allow the computer to install and start the app on it.

Important! As we mentioned earlier, these steps are general. If you have any doubts, please try to find the specific case for your device as the names of the options may vary from one manufacturer to another.

- Now, click on **Build And Run** in the **Build Settings** window, call your APK `arcatalogue.apk`, and hit **Save**. Unity will immediately start the compilation by looking for the Android SDK (if it doesn't detect it, it will ask you to select the folder where it's installed) and searching for a suitable device (if the device isn't plugged in correctly or **USB Debugging** isn't activated, it will tell you it can't find the device). Then, it will start the building process until it copies the APK into the device and launches it.

- Once the app has launched, point the camera to the target in order to see the cube:

Screenshot of the cube over the target on a mobile device

If for any reason, you don't want/can't build the APK into the mobile device, you can use **Build** instead of **Build And Run** to create the APK without installing it.

When the compilation process finishes, you will have to manually copy the resulting APK into your device and install it.

Note: This process is for Android devices only. To compile the app on an iOS device, you have to build and run the Unity project from an Apple computer and, when the building process finishes, it will automatically launch Xcode where the building will end up (you will have to assign your Apple ID in order to play the app on an iOS device, just like you need to with any other iOS app developed in Xcode).

In this section, you have learned how to use EasyAR to detect an image and display a virtual cube on it. Now, we will substitute the test cube for an external 3D model we will import into our project.

Working with custom 3D models

In the previous section, we learned how to create a simple AR app with EasyAR to display a cube. In this section, we are going to import our own 3D model into Unity to visualize over the target and play with its materials and textures.

For this project, we are going to work with `fbx`, an exported format that allows us to include materials, textures, and animations. To see a list of all the exported and native 3D formats Unity accepts, please visit `https://docs.unity3d.com/Manual/3D-formats.html`.

Before including the models in our project, we will make a few changes to our scene to improve it:

1. Select **Directional Light** in the **Hierarchy** window. Then, in the **Inspector** window, set the **Shadow Type** to **No Shadows**. Shadows are quite resource-consuming and, in this case, the AR experience will benefit from not having shadows:

Directional Light properties in the Inspector window

2. Now, select **ImageTarget** and change its **Transform** values so it rotates on the x axis. This way, in the scene, the objects will appear to be popping up from the ground:

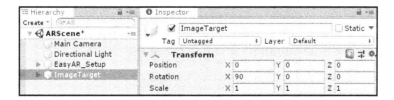

ImageTarget Transform values

3. Finally, select **Main Camera** and rotate and move it so that it's pointing at the target:

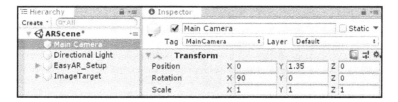

Main Camera Transform values

Now, it's time to include the 3D models. Let's get started:

1. Delete the **Cube** from inside **ImageTarget** in the **Hierarchy** window by right-clicking on it and selecting **Delete**, or just by selecting it and pressing *Delete* on your keyboard:

Deleting the Cube model

2. Drag the `Models/Maia` folder from the code resources provided into the **Project** window on `@MyAssets/Models`. This will import the `.fbx` mesh object and its texture files inside the `textures` folder, as shown in the following screenshot.

3. Drag the `maia.fbx` file inside **ImageTarget**. Remember to make sure it's inside **ImageTarget** so that it appears/disappears when the target does. Move, rotate, and scale the model until it looks good over the target:

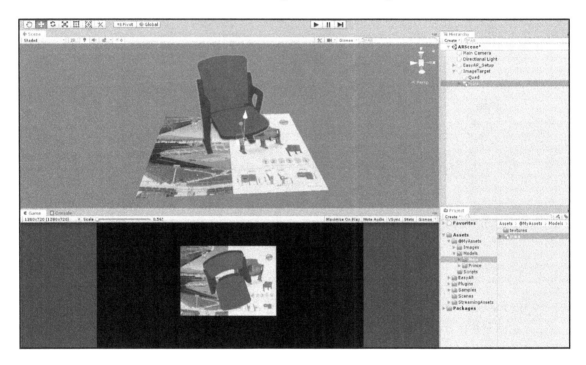

The maia model inside the target

4. Now, hit the play button at the top of the Toolbar to test the current scene. The moment the target is detected, the seat will appear:

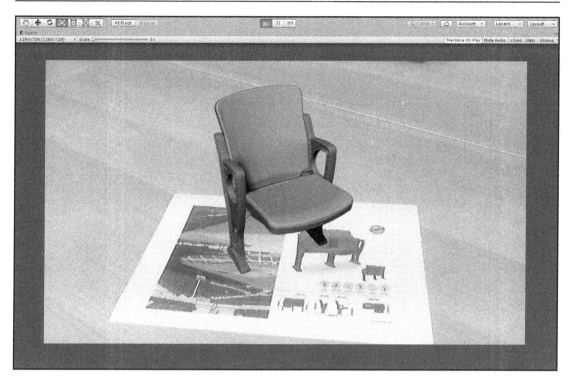

The seat appears when the target is detected

5. Hit the play button once more to stop the simulation and then save the scene (*Ctrl + S*). Connect the mobile device to your computer and press *Ctrl + B*, or go to **File | Build Settings | Build And Run**, to build the app into your device.

Now that we have our basic AR scene, in the next section, we will create our AR catalog by adding another chair and creating the UI to allow users to interact with our furniture.

Creating an AR catalog

Now that we have created the basic scene, we will create a small AR catalog:

- We will use two **ImageTargets** to show two different chairs.
- We will allow users to change the color of the chairs while they are looking at them.

Modifying the AR scene

In this section, we are going to modify the current AR scene by adding a new **ImageTarget**. To do this, we will follow the same steps that we followed in the previous section:

1. From the resources of the project, drag the `Target_Prince.jpg` image into the `Assets/StreamingAssets` folder.

2. Then, drag the `Target_Prince_texture.jpg` image into the `Assets/@MyAssets/Images` folder:

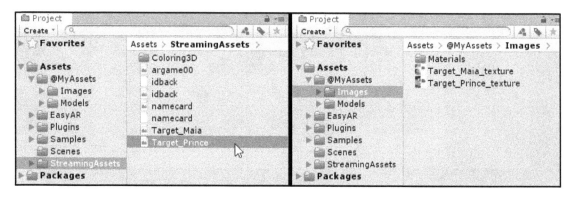

Target_Prince and Target_Prince_texture in their respective folders

3. Then, drag the `Prince` folder, which contains the model, into `Assets/@MyAssets/Models`:

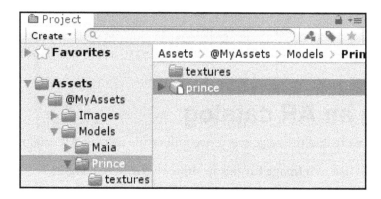

The prince model

4. Right-click the **ImageTarget** and select **Duplicate** so that we can use it as template for the new **ImageTarget**:

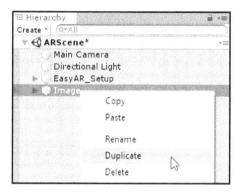

Duplicating the ImageTarget

5. Rename the first **ImageTarget** to `ImageTargetMaia` and the current one to `ImageTargetPrince` so that you can distinguish between them. Move them on the scene so that they don't overlap.

6. Copy the following **Target Name** and **Path** parameters into the **Image Target Controller** of our **ImageTargetPrince** in the **Inspector** window:

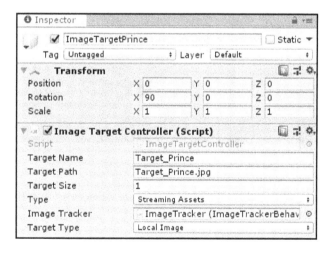

Image Target Controller parameters

7. Drag the `Target_Prince_texture.jpg` image from
the `Assets/@MyAssets/Images` folder onto the **Project** window to the **Quad**
of **ImageTargetPrince** in the **Hierarchy** window in order to apply it as a texture.

8. Remove the **maia** model from **ImageTargetPrince** (right-click and **Delete**) and
drag the **prince** model there instead.

9. Move, rotate, and scale the **prince** model until it's in the middle of the marker
and looks good.

The following screenshot shows our scene with the two **ImageTargets** and their respective
seats:

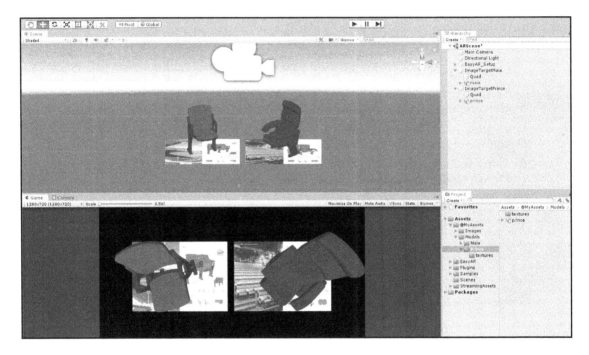

The scene with the two targets and models

10. Before testing our scene, let's hide the **Quad** objects so that they don't appear in
AR and we only see the chairs. For that, select both **Quad** GameObjects
(*Ctrl* + left click for multiple selection) and uncheck their **Mesh Renderer**
components:

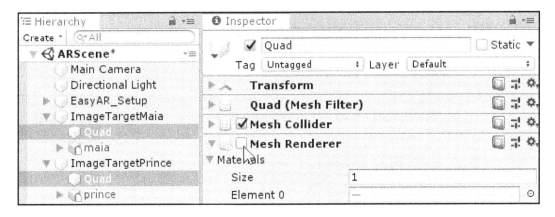

Hiding the Quad GameObjects

11. Now, hit play to test that everything is set up correctly. Point with the camera to one of the targets and then to the other to see the chairs.

12. Hit play again to stop the simulation and continue making changes.

13. At the moment, **ImageTracker** of the **EasyAR_Setup** GameObject has been set to detect only one marker at a time. Let's increase this value to 2 so that our users can see both chairs together:

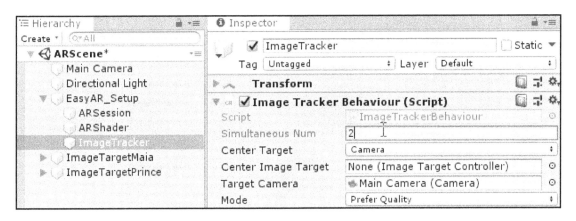

Changing the number of simultaneous targets

Now, test this out—you should see both chairs appear at the same time.

The next thing we need to do is create the script that will let the user change the textures of the seats.

Creating the controller script

In this section, we are going to create a script that will control the scene and allow our users to change the textures of the seats. Let's get started:

1. In **@MyAssets | Scripts**, create a new C# script by right-clicking and selecting **Create | New C# Script**. Call it `MainController` and double-click on it to open it in Visual Studio:

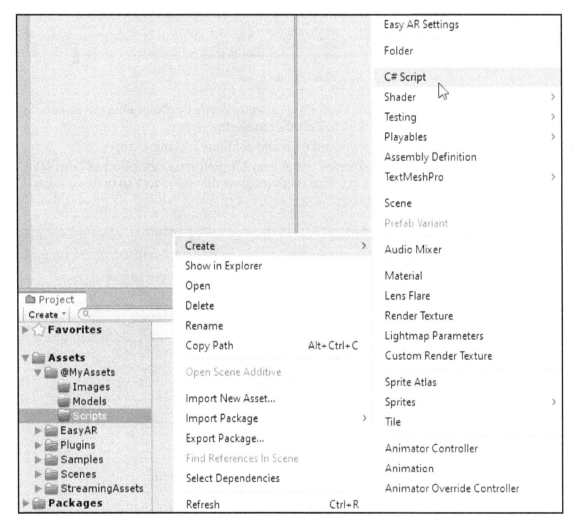

Creating a new C# Script in the @MyAssets/Scripts folder

2. If you installed Unity by following the steps in `Chapter 2`, *Introduction to Unity for AR Development*, you will already have Visual Studio installed and configured, and it will open the script with the default code, as shown in the following screenshot:

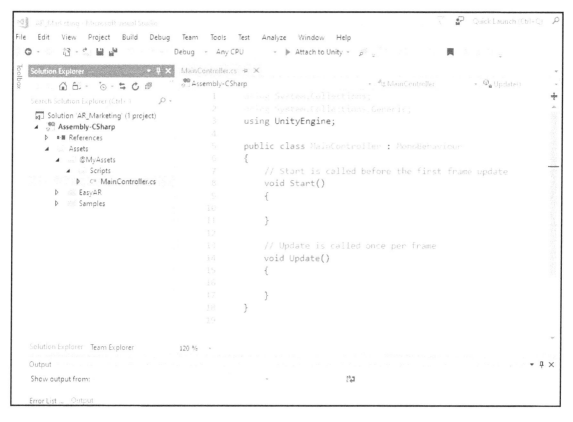

MainController script in Visual Studio

3. If you installed Visual Studio prior to Unity or used another program such as MonoDevelop, you can configure Unity to open scripts with it by clicking on **Edit | Preferences | External Tools | External Script Editor**, as shown in the following screenshot:

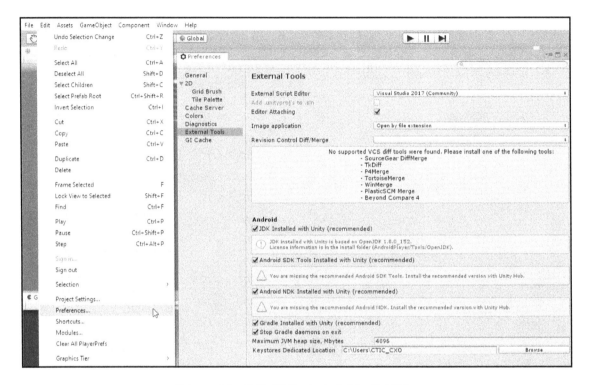

Preferences window with Visual Studio assigned as the External Script Editor

4. In the script, start by adding the following lines after the class declaration:

```
public class MainController : MonoBehaviour
{
    public Material[] materials;
 public Texture2D[] textures;
...
```

Here, we are declaring the `materials` array, which is where we will store the materials of both chairs. We will use it to change those materials' texture properties. The `textures` array will contain the actual images (red and blue) that we will apply to those materials. Both variables are public because we will initialize them from the Unity editor.

5. Inside the `Start()` method, add the following loop:

```
foreach (Material material in materials)
{
    material.mainTexture = textures[0];
}
```

With this loop, we are assigning each material inside the `materials` array to the first image of the `textures` array.

6. After the `Update()` method, we are going to create a new method:

```
public void ChangeColor()
{
    foreach (Material material in materials)
    {
        if (material.mainTexture == textures[0])
            material.mainTexture = textures[1];
        else
            material.mainTexture = textures[0];
    }
}
```

This method changes the texture (red or blue) of the materials of the chairs. It checks which texture is selected and assigns the other one to both chairs.

7. Now, go back to the Unity editor and drag the script to the **EasyAR_Setup** GameObject so that the script will affect the current scene.

Remember that a script will only be executed if it's attached to one GameObject (or more) of the scene. Otherwise, it will only exist in the **Projects** window but not in the actual scene.

Since this script doesn't make direct reference to the element it's attached to, it could go on any element that is active in the scene all the time (so it's always available). We have put it in **EasyAR_Setup** because it's a root element that fulfills this rule.

8. Unfold the two variables of the script, that is, **Materials** and **Textures**, and, in **Materials**, set **Size** to 2 and select **tela** and **Material #5**. These are the materials that correspond to the fabric in each model:

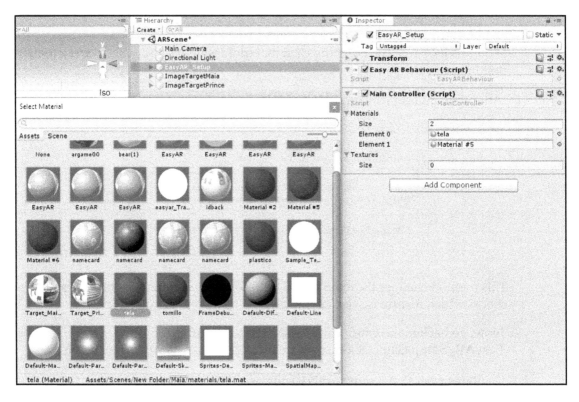

Assigning the materials to the variables

9. In **Textures**, set **Size** to 2 and select the red and the blue elements, that is, **Acapulco 3011** and **Acapulco PANTONE 2935 C**:

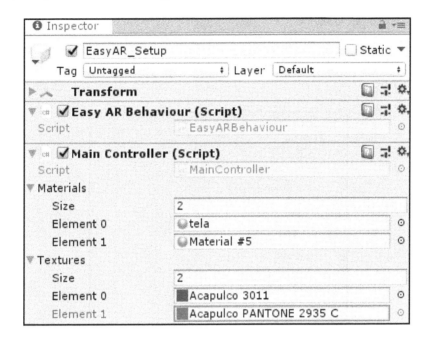

Assigning the textures to the variables

The **Controller** script is ready. Now, we have to create the user interface and the button that will trigger the color change through the ChangeColor() method we have just created.

Creating the interface

Let's create a simple interface to allow our users to change the features of the AR objects they are seeing. Let's get started:

1. First, right-click on the **Hierarchy** window and select **UI** | **Canvas**. The **Canvas** element is the main element on the Unity interface and contains all the other elements:

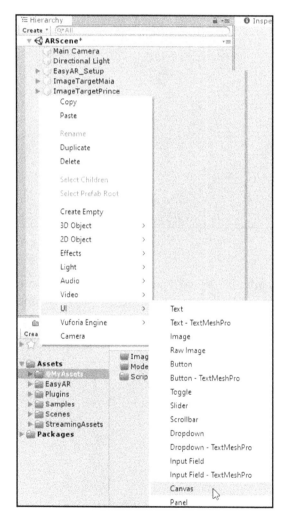

Creating a Canvas element on the scene

2. By default, the **Canvas** is located in the (0,0) point, facing back, overlaying the whole 3D scene, and with the current screen size. Double-click on its name in the **Hierarchy** window so that the scene focuses on it.

3. In the **Inspector** window, include the following values for **Canvas Scaler**:

   - **UI Scale Mode**: **Scale With Screen Size**. With this parameter, we are telling the canvas to adapt itself to the different screen sizes (useful when compiling for different mobile devices).
   - For **Reference Resolution**, we will use 1280 x 720.
   - **Screen Match Mode** allows us to adapt the UI elements to the width and/or height of the screen. A value of 0.5 tells it to adapt to both:

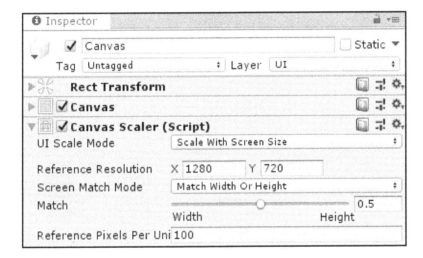

Canvas Scaler values on the Inspector window

To manipulate the UI elements (move, scale, and so on), select their specific tool in the toolbar:

4. We are going to use an icon for our color button. For that, import the `circle_icon.png` image into `Assets/@MyAssets/Images`. Select it in the **Project** window. Then, in the **Inspector** window, modify its **Texture Type** so that it's **Sprite (2D and UI)** in order to use it in the UI. Then press **Apply** to save this change:

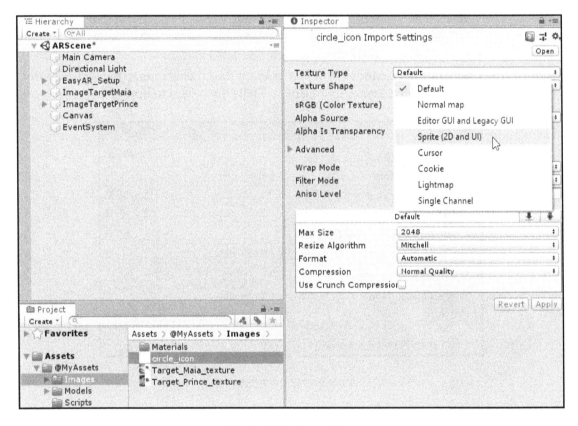

Converting circle_icon into a sprite image

5. Now, right-click on **Canvas** in the **Hierarchy** window and select **UI/Button**:

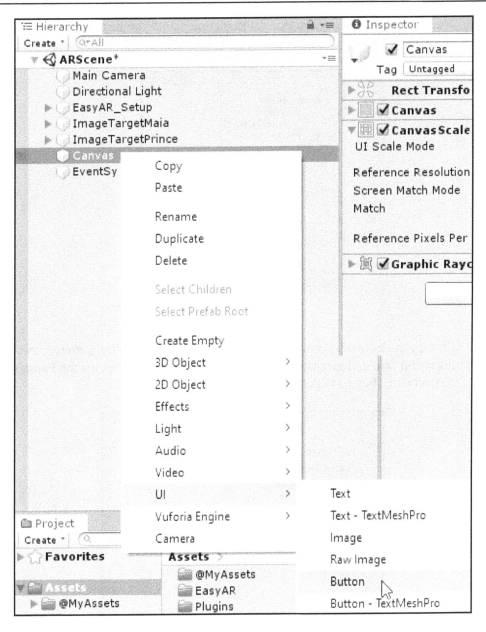

Creating a button inside the canvas element

6. We don't need the text component that comes with the **Button**, so right-click on it and **Delete** it:

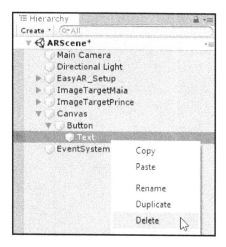

Deleting the text component of the button

7. Change the button's name to `Color_button` and assign the icon we previously imported into its **Image** component to **Source Image**. Click on the **Preserve Aspect** checkbox to make sure it's always round:

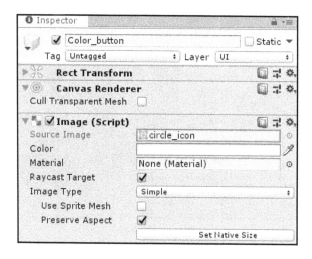

The Color_button image component in the Inspector window

8. Now, let's place the button in the top-right corner of the screen. For the **Rect Transform** component, click on the square and select the top-right option to move the button's anchors:

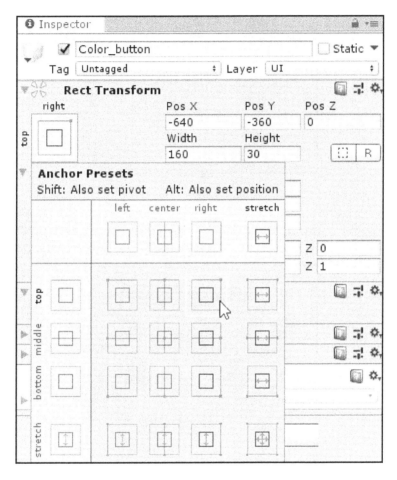

Selecting the top-right anchor for the button

9. Then, change the **PosX**, **PosY**, **Width**, and **Height** values to adjust the button's position and scale, as follows:

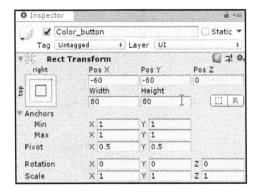

The button's new Rect Transform values

10. Now, with the button selected, under the **Button** component on the **Inspector** window, go to the `On Click ()` method and press the + symbol to create a new action:

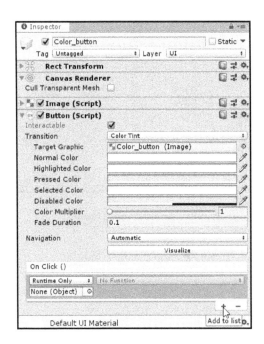

Creating a new action in the On Click() method

11. Drag the **EasyAR_Setup** element from the **Hierarchy** window to the **None (Object)** box and, from the drop-down menu on the right, select **MainController | ChangeColor**. With this, we are telling the UI that whenever the **Color_button** is pressed, the `ChangeColor()` method from the `MainController` class that's attached to the **EasyAR_Setup** GameObject will be executed:

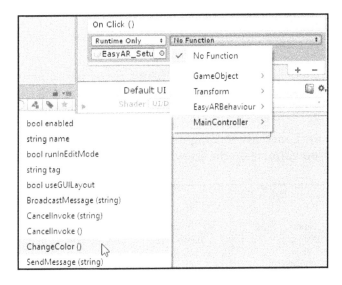

Selecting the ChangeColor() method for the Color_button

12. Play the scene to test it. You will see that when you click on **Color_button**, the texture of the chairs changes. However, there is still a small detail: the button is not intuitive because it doesn't change its own color. To solve this, we are going to add a few lines to our code in Visual Studio.

13. Go back to Visual Studio and in the `MainController` script import the `UnityEngine UI` library at the beginning of the file:

    ```
    using UnityEngine.UI;
    ```

14. Add the following variables *before* the `Start()` method:

    ```
    public Image color_button;
    private Color32 red = new Color32(159, 40, 40, 255);
    private Color32 blue = new Color32(40, 74, 159, 255);
    ```

    We'll use the first one to assign the button in Unity editor (that's why it's `public`) and the two colors as reference.

15. Add the following line inside the `Start()` method, after the loop segment, to initialize the button to `red`:

```
color_button.color = red;
```

16. Add the following lines *inside* the `ChangeColor()` method:

```
if (color_button.color == red)
  color_button.color = blue;
else
  color_button.color = red;
```

Here, we are telling the button to evaluate the current color and, if it's `red`, to change it to `blue` and vice versa. This way, the button will change its color at the same time as the textures of the seats do.

17. Finally, in the Unity editor, drag the **Color_button** GameObject to the **Color_button** variable on the `EasyAR_Setup` GameObject to assign it:

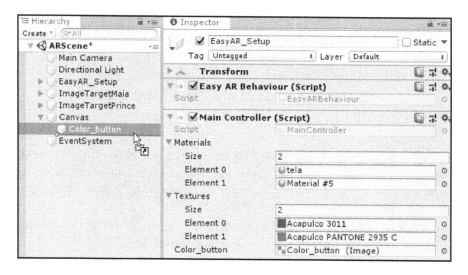

The Color_button GameObject dragged to the last variable of the Main Controller

18. Save and test the scene in the editor to see how the button changes color initially and whenever it's pressed.

19. Now, **Build And Run** the app in your mobile device and enjoy seeing how the seats come to life in AR:

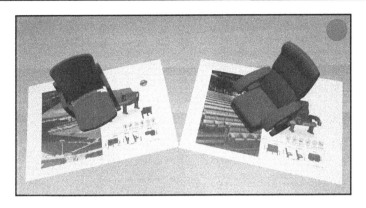

Mobile phone screenshot with both seats in red

You can move the camera around the seats, get close to them, or move the targets to see them in detail. You can press the color button to switch their texture color. Now that the app is complete, you can even delete the Quad planes from the scene since they are no longer needed. With this, your project is ready.

Summary

In this chapter, you learned how to create an AR catalog using the EasyAR SDK. You learned how to import the SDK into Unity and create a scene showing a cube on an **ImageTarget**. Then, you learned how to import models from outside Unity and modify some of their features, such as materials and textures. Then, you merged the models into the initial scene to make a seat come to life from its catalog. Finally, you added a script and UI elements to control the color of the models.

By the end of this chapter, you have acquired the basic skills to continue developing with EasyAR and try out some of its other features. For that, we recommend opening the rest of the sample scenes located at **Assets** I **Samples** I **Scenes** and try them out to understand how they work. You have also acquired an understanding of how AR can be used to create a catalog, magazine, or similar product for marketing. You can now improve this project in order to, for example, link the products with e-commerce, offering the consumer the full experience and attracting them to buy your products. You can now use basic tools to create your own AR experiences in marketing.

In the next chapter, you will learn how to use another SDK, Vuforia, to place the same seat models in a real environment, instead of using **ImageTargets**. You will learn how to use Vuforia's Ground Plane features to place and manipulate 3D models on flat surfaces, such as tables or on the ground, to create an interactive retail experience.

6
AR for Retail with Vuforia

In this chapter, you will work with Vuforia, one of the most well-known AR SDKs that offers a wide variety of options (working with and without image targets, web and local recognition, and more), as well as examples that can be directly downloaded and tested. It has also the advantage of being integrated into the Unity editor, making it easier to develop with it.

This chapter's first main goal is to introduce you to the Vuforia SDK and how it works. Among its many features, you will learn how to use spatial recognition and augmentation to place 3D objects in the real world without the need for previously printed image targets. You will learn how to use Vuforia fusion with and without ARCore and you will acquire the skills to use Vuforia's elements in Unity. This chapter's second goal is to present you with an attractive use of AR in retail to show potential customers products such as furniture, paintings, decorations, and more in their own spaces. With these kinds of applications, they can decide on which elements they want to buy and how they will look in their own homes, making them more involved in the buying process.

In this chapter, we will cover the following topics:

- Using AR for retail
- Exploring Vuforia
- AR on the go – using Ground Plane
- Creating an AR furniture viewer

Technical requirements

The technical requirements for this chapter are as follows:

- A Unity 3D-supporting computer (see the latest requirements here: `https://unity3d.com/unity/system-requirements`). This chapter's example project has been developed on a Windows 10 x 64 computer.
- Unity 3D (2019.1.2f1 in this book).
- Microsoft Visual Studio Community 2017 (included in Unity installation).
- The latest version of Vuforia that's included with Unity 3D (8.3.8 in this book).
- A mobile device supporting Vuforia Fusion (see `https://library.vuforia.com/content/vuforia-library/en/articles/Solution/ground-plane-supported-devices.html`).

The resources and the code files for this chapter can be found here: `https://github.com/PacktPublishing/Enterprise-Augmented-Reality-Projects/tree/master/Chapter06`.

Using AR for retail

Retail is one of the fields where AR offers a wider range of possibilities, from satisfying and engaging the consumer in order to reduce returned products, to linking products with social media or personalizing the shopping experience. Some examples of this are as follows:

- Trying products before buying them. This is where users visualize clothes, shoes, glasses, or even makeup before actually buying the products.
- Seeing how a product such as a piece of furniture, a piece of art, or even wall paint looks in their homes with AR.
- At the store, seeing extra information about a product, such as comments and reviews, before buying it.
- In a commercial center, receiving geopositioned information and discounts from the stores in it.
- In supermarkets or big stores, orienting customers through sections to the product they want.

This field also allows us to display AR on various hardware, including customers' mobile devices, tactile screens, and virtual fitting rooms. Therefore, in the past few years, AR solutions in retail have multiplied, especially since ARKit (from Apple) and ARCore (from Google) appeared on the market. These two pieces of software allow us to easily recognize the environment using the camera and sensors of the mobile devices and place virtual elements over flat surfaces such as the ground or tables.

In this chapter, we will take advantage of Vuforia Fusion, Vuforia SDK's ground detection features, which can also be combined with ARCore, to place virtual objects in our surroundings without any kind of printed target, creating an AR furniture viewer that customers can use to see how the furniture fits in their homes.

For our project, we will be using the real catalog pages and 3D models from the company Euro Seating at `https://www.euroseating.com/en/`, a seating manufacturer present in more than 100 countries all over the world. Using their high-quality 3D models and real catalog will help us visualize this project as a real-life AR application that can be used in any other marketing context. The models and images that are used in this chapter have been handed over by the company for their use in the context of this book.

We will start by exploring Vuforia and how to integrate it into our Unity project.

Exploring Vuforia

Initially developed by Qualcomm, and currently run by PTC, Vuforia is one of the oldest and most well-known AR SDKs. It's one of the most stable and best-performing pieces of software on the market and, along with ARKit and ARCore, one of the favorite choices for AR developers.

Vuforia offers a wide variety of features, including 2D images and 3D objects tracking, markerless AR where there is no need for a reference image to launch AR content (the one we will be using in this chapter) and barcode-like markers called Vumarks. It provides multiple examples and extra features, such as virtual buttons, runtime image target creation, and background video texture manipulation.

Like other AR software, Vuforia requires a license for it to be deployed on mobile devices. Vuforia offers a free development key generator, which will have to be switched to a deployment key when the app is in the production stage. You can consult its pricing options on their web page: `https://developer.vuforia.com/pricing`.

The Vuforia SDK can be downloaded for Android and iOS, and can also be used in the Unity 3D platform. Since the Unity 2017.2 version, it comes directly integrated into the Unity editor, just like any other main asset, and it has to be installed and activated inside it. Now, we'll incorporate Vuforia into a new project and set it up so that we can build it on an Android device. Let's get started:

1. When you first installed Unity on your computer (see `Chapter 2`, *Introduction to Unity for AR Development*), you should have selected the option of adding the Vuforia module. If you didn't install it or you are in doubt, open the Unity Hub, go to the **Installs** tab, and check the installed modules at the bottom of your Unity version:

Current Unity installation with Vuforia support

2. If Vuforia is not there, click on the top-right button and click on **Add Modules**. Select **Vuforia** and install it:

Adding new modules to the current Unity installation using Unity Hub

 Vuforia usually comes included with stable versions; if you are trying a beta version or a very recent version of Unity, it's possible that Vuforia might not appear among the options and you will have to install a previous version to use it.

3. Now, open the Unity Hub. On the **Projects** tab, click on **NEW**:

Creating a new project in the Unity Hub

4. Fill in the **Project Name** and **Location** fields and click on **CREATE**:

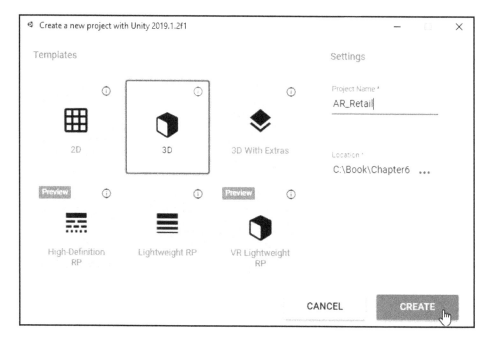

Creating a new 3D project

5. Click *Ctrl + N* or go to **File | New Scene**. Now, press *Ctrl + S* or go to **File | Save**. Name the file OnTheGo and save it in the Scenes folder:

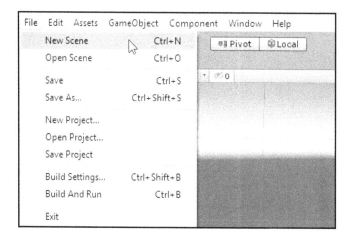

Creating a new scene for the current project

6. You can also delete the **SampleScene** that comes with the project from the **Project** window:

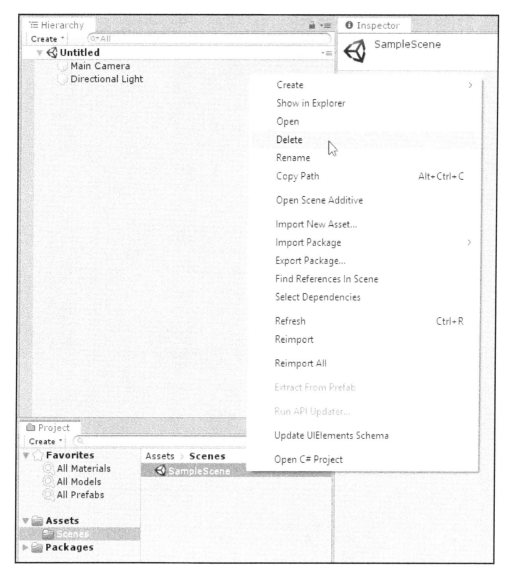

SampleScene is no longer needed

7. AR requires a special camera that retrieves the physical camera feed and processes it so that we can integrate the virtual elements into the real image stream. Vuforia provides an asset called **AR Camera** that does this for us. Delete the existing Unity **Main Camera**, right-click on the **Hierarchy** window, and select **Vuforia Engine | AR Camera**:

Adding the AR Camera to the scene

8. Since it's the first time we're using Vuforia in the project, a message will appear asking us to import Vuforia's assets. Click **Import**:

Message to import Vuforia and its assets into the project

A new folder called `Vuforia` will appear in the **Project** window, inside the `Assets` folder.

9. Place the **Directional Light** inside the **AR Camera** so that the light moves along with the camera.

10. Now, we have to enable Vuforia in the **Player Settings** so that we can use it in the scene:

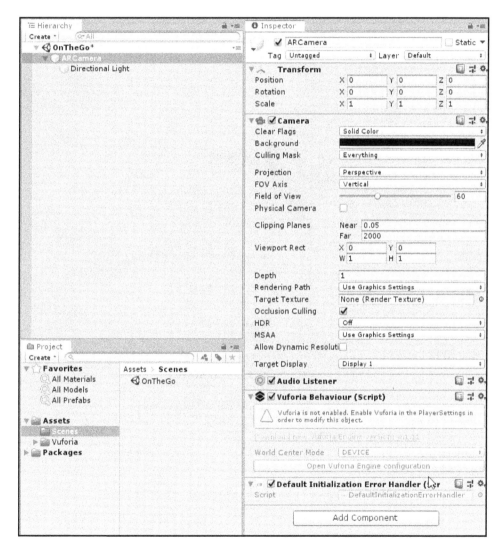

Vuforia Behaviour component detecting that Vuforia isn't enabled yet

11. Press *Ctrl + Shift + B* or go to **File**|**Build Settings...** to open the **Build Settings** window.

12. Before anything else, click on **Add Open Scenes** to include our scene in the building scenes list.

13. Then, switch platforms by clicking on **Android** and pressing **Switch Platform** in the bottom-right corner. With this, we will have configured our project so that it can be built on an Android device:

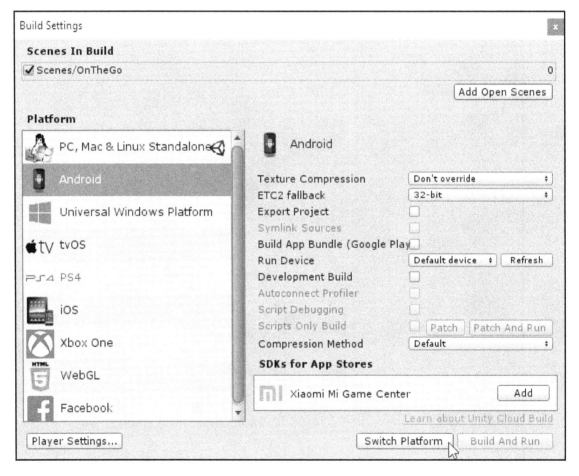

Build Settings panel, allowing us to add new scenes, switch platforms, and access Player Settings

14. Now, click on **Player Settings...** to open a new window.

15. Fill in the **Company Name** and **Product Name** (the name the app will have when we install it on a device).

16. In the last tab, **XR Settings**, enable **Vuforia Augmented Reality Supported** to allow the use of Vuforia in this project:

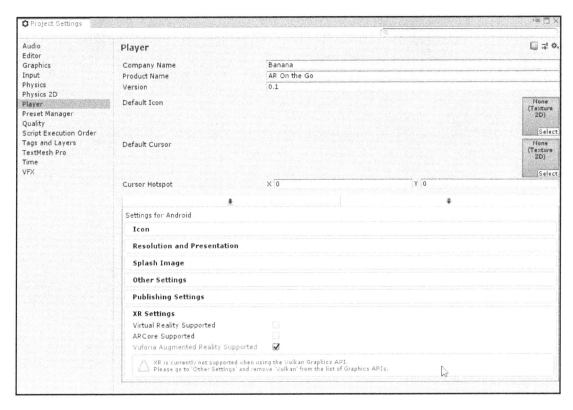

Player Settings with Company Name and Product Name filled and Vuforia activated in the XR Settings

17. A new message will appear indicating that XR is not supported by the Vulkan graphics API. To fix this, open the **Other Settings** tab and remove **Vulkan** from **Graphics APIs**:

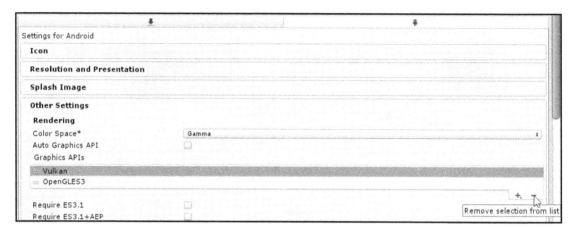

Removing Vulkan from the Graphics API under Other Settings|Rendering

18. Below this, fill in the **Identification** section's **Package Name** and minimum **API Level**:

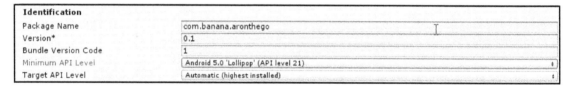

Updating the Package Name and Minimum API Level under Other Settings|Identification

 Currently, Vuforia supports Android 4.4 and above and iOS 11 and above. However, we recommend setting the **Minimum API Level** to 5 to ensure the devices running the apps are powerful enough to do so. You can check the minimum requirements for Vuforia here: `https://library.vuforia.com/articles/Solution/Vuforia-Supported-Versions`.

19. This step is not always required but it might be the case that the Vuforia version that's been installed with your Unity version is not the latest one. If so, when selecting the **ARCamera**, a message will appear on the **Vuforia Behaviour** component indicating that a new version is available:

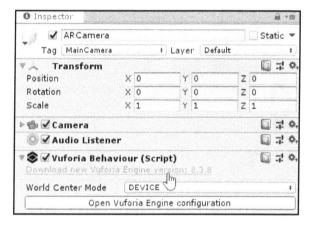

Link to the new Vuforia version in the Vuforia Behaviour component of the ARCamera

20. Click on the link to download the executable and follow the steps to install it:

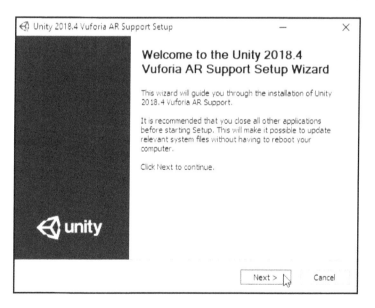

Vuforia AR Setup Wizard

21. When updating Vuforia, make sure you install it in your Unity root folder, usually in `C:/Program Files/Unity/Hub/Editor/{unity_version_name}`, and close your currently running Unity session if asked. If a message appears asking you to update your project, click **Update**. Vuforia will now be up to date in your project:

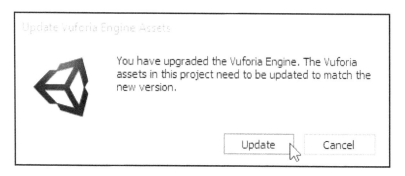

Update message from Vuforia Engine

Now that we know how to integrate Vuforia into a new project, we will start using its Ground Plane feature to create an app that detects flat surfaces and places 3D content on them.

AR on the go – using Ground Plane

Vuforia's main feature that's used to place virtual objects on the user's environment in real time is called **Ground Plane**. We are going to use this feature to create an app to place 3D content on horizontal surfaces of the real world, such as floors and tables.

Starting with Vuforia 7, the SDK introduced a new capability, called **Vuforia Fusion**, to improve the performance of spatial recognition according to each device's features, including cameras, sensors, chipsets, and internal AR frameworks. Vuforia Fusion tries to detect integrated frameworks such as ARKit (iOS) or ARCore (Android), which offer the best performance. If none are found, it tries to use VISLAM and SLAM, respectively.

Simultaneous localization and mapping (**SLAM**) algorithms estimate the pose of an object and the map of the surrounding environment at the same time. **visual-inertial simultaneous localization and mapping** (**VISLAM**) is Vuforia's algorithm that combines **visual odometry** (**VIO**) and SLAM to improve the latter's performance.

Although the list increases quickly, not all devices support Vuforia's Ground Plane yet. In general, if the running device supports ARCore or ARKit, it will work. If not, it will depend on internal AR-enabling technologies. Vuforia keeps a list of the currently supported devices on its web page: `https://library.vuforia.com/articles/Solution/vuforia-fusion-supported-devices.html`.

In the next subsection, we are going to learn how to enable ARCore in Vuforia. If your device doesn't support ARCore, you can directly skip to the next subsection. If you are planning to distribute your app among ARCore-supporting and -non-supporting devices, and want to test Vuforia's VISLAM performance first, skip this step and do this after testing the final app to see the difference.

Enabling ARCore in Vuforia

In this section, we're going to learn to enable ARCore for Vuforia; if your device supports ARCore, you will benefit from using it along with Vuforia, as the resulting app will detect flat surfaces faster and with more precision. To enable ARCore for Vuforia inside Unity, follow these steps:

1. Download the latest version of the ARCore library from Google's repository. The global link is `https://dl.google.com/dl/android/maven2/com/google/ar/core/<ARCORE_VERSION>/core-<ARCORE_VERSION>.aar`.
   You can check the latest version available at `https://github.com/google-ar/arcore-unity-sdk/releases`.

 At the time of writing this chapter, the current version is 1.9.0, so the link will be `https://dl.google.com/dl/android/maven2/com/google/ar/core/1.9.0/core-1.9.0.aar`.

2. In Unity, in the **Project** window, right-click on the `Assets` folder and press **Create|Folder**. Name it `Plugins` and create another one called `Android` inside it:

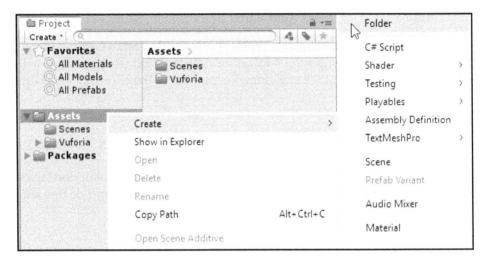

Creating a new folder inside Assets

3. Copy the downloaded `.aar` file inside the `Android` folder:

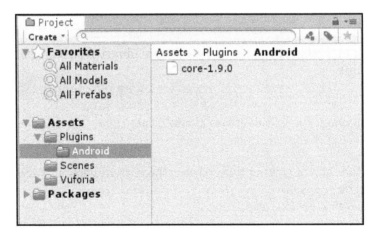

The ARCore plugin located inside the Android folder

4. Select the file and verify that **Android** is checked under **Select platforms for plugin** in the **Inspector** window:

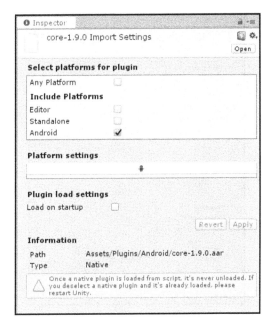

ARCore library's properties in the Inspector window

5. Select the **ARCamera** and click on the **Open Vuforia Engine configuration** button:

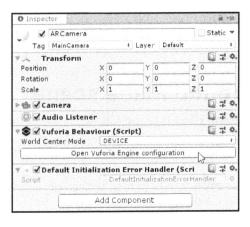

Opening Vuforia Engine configuration from the ARCamera

6. Under **Device Tracker**, set **ARCore Requirement** to **Optional** or **Required**, depending on your targeted user devices:

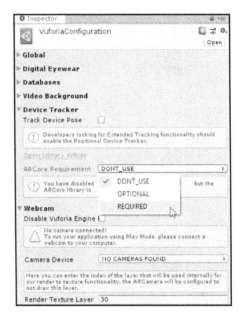

Setting ARCore to OPTIONAL or REQUIRED

If set to **OPTIONAL**, when using Ground Plane, Vuforia will try to make use of ARCore, and if the device doesn't support it, it will switch to Vuforia's internal algorithms. If set to **REQUIRED**, the app won't work on devices that don't support ARCore.

Now that we have configured ARCore, we'll create an AR scene to test the Ground Plane feature.

Creating the Ground Plane scene

The AR scene in this project will consist of the following elements:

- The **ARCamera**, which will retrieve the physical camera's feed and process each frame
- The **Ground Plane Finder**, which is in charge of searching for horizontal surfaces and placing objects on them when users tap on the screen

- The **Ground Plane Stage**, which is the parent GameObject where the virtual elements will go
- A test cube, which will appear on the ground when the user taps on the screen

We created the **ARCamera** element when we integrated Vuforia in Unity, so let's create the rest of the elements to make the Ground Plane features work:

1. Right-click on the **Hierarchy** window and select **Vuforia Engine | Ground Plane | Ground Plane Stage**. This will create the parent GameObject for the contents we want to show in AR. It's represented with a visual reference of a 100 cm square to help with the virtual objects' real-world scale. This reference is only visible inside the Unity editor:

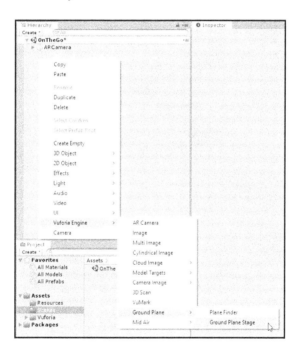

Creating a Ground Plane Stage element

2. The **Ground Plane Stage** GameObject has two scripts attached to it:

   - **Anchor Behaviour**, which determines whether the virtual objects appear attached to the ground or in mid-air
   - **Default Trackable Event Handler**, which is Vuforia's default script to show/hide elements when the target is found/lost

3. To create a virtual object to test, right-click **Ground Plane Stage** and create a **3D Object|Cube**. Make sure it appears as a child of the **Ground Plane Stage** so that it's shown/hidden when appropriate:

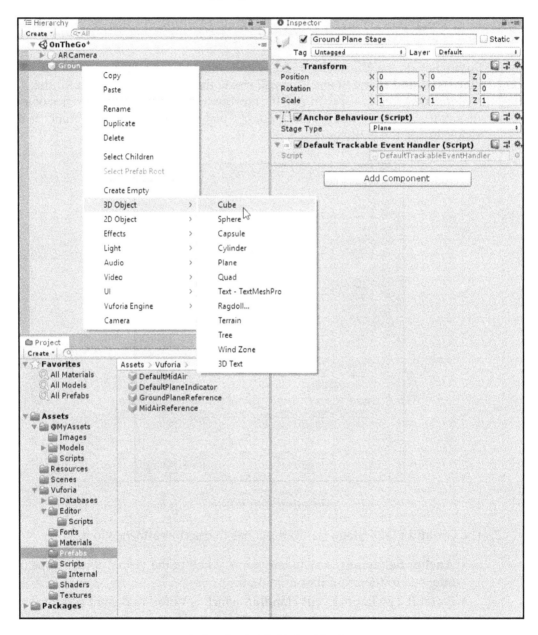

Creating a cube as the child of the Ground Plane Stage

4. Scale down the cube so that it's smaller than the visual reference of the **Ground Plane Stage**. Make sure it's visible from the **ARCamera** in the **Game** view (if not, move/rotate either the **ARCamera** or, preferably, the **Ground Plane Stage** until it's in view):

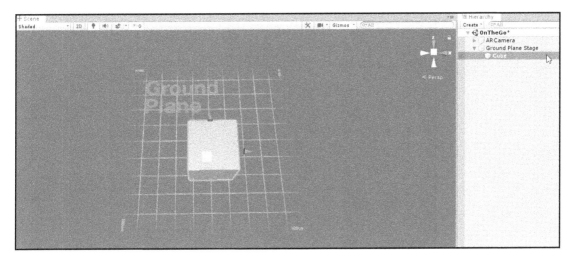

The cube placed over the reference grid of the Ground Plane stage

5. Right-click outside the **Hierarchy** window and select **Vuforia Engine** | **Ground Plane** | **Plane Finder**:

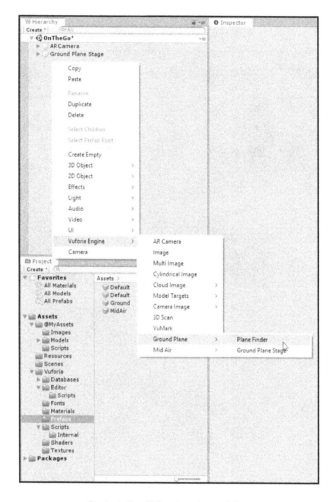

Creating the Plane Finder to detect the ground planes

6. This GameObject has three scripts attached to it:

- **Anchor Input Listener Behaviour**, which is in charge of listening for the user's input (tap on the screen)
- **Plane Finder Behaviour**, which is used to find horizontal surfaces to place the content

- **Content Positioning Behaviour**, which is used to position the content of the real world

7. On the **Content Positioning Behaviour** script, select (or drag from the **Hierarchy**) the **Ground Plane Stage** inside the **Anchor Stage** selection box:

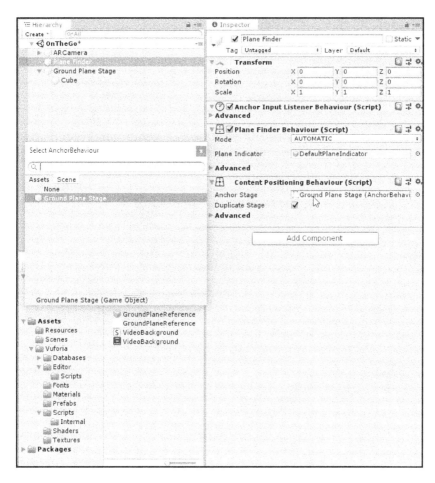

Linking the Ground Plane Stage to the Plane Finder

8. Before moving on, press *Ctrl + S to* save the current scene.

Now that we have our AR scene configured, we're going to add the Vuforia key, a necessary step that we need to take in order to build Vuforia on mobile devices.

Obtaining the key

Vuforia requires a development/deployment key for the app to work on a real device. To do this, follow these steps:

1. Go to Vuforia's developer page (`https://developer.vuforia.com/license-manager`), register, and log in.
2. On the **License Manager** tab, select **Get Development Key** to obtain a free key to use while developing.
3. Give it the name of your app, `AR On the Go`, read and accept the terms and conditions, and press **Confirm**.
4. Select your newly created license and copy the key numbers.
5. Go back to the Unity editor and select **ARCamera** from the scene.
6. Click on **Open Vuforia Engine Configuration** in the **Inspector** window to open the general Vuforia configuration:

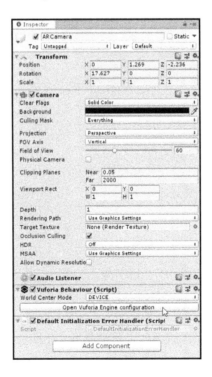

ARCamera GameObject in the Inspector window

7. Here, paste your key into the **App License Key** field:

Vuforia configuration options in the Inspector window

Now, we have included a Vuforia development key in our project that will let us build and install our app on a real device.

Keep in mind that when you want to upload an app to the store (Google or Apple), you will have to buy a deployment key according to Vuforia's plans. You can find the updated prices at `https://developer.vuforia.com/pricing`.

In the next section, we will test our app in Unity to make sure everything works as it should.

Testing the app

When developing a project in Unity, it's good practice to test it before building it since the building process takes time. This way, you can detect basic problems and errors and correct them quickly before actually trying the app on your phone.

Vuforia can't currently be built as a standalone application, but it has a script integrated with the ARCamera for testing purposes. When you are testing the app in Unity editor, it will use the computer's camera to simulate the AR. If it doesn't detect a camera, it will leave the background black and play the AR directly.

On the other hand, when you're working with a Ground Plane project and you want to test the app, Vuforia won't be able to use the device's sensors to detect a flat surface. Instead, it offers an image target reference to simulate Ground Plane recognition, and when the camera detects that image, it will behave like it's detecting a flat surface on the phone.

To test our app, follow these steps:

1. Locate the PDF called Emulator Ground
   Plane.pdf at **Vuforia|Databases|ForPrint|Emulator** from the **Project** window.
   Print it and place it on the ground (you can also open the PDF image directly on
   the computer, although the size reference might not be accurate).

2. Press the play button in the top Toolbar and point the webcam to the image. You
   will see a visual mark when the software detects a surface (the target, in this
   case). Before pressing the play button, you can click the **Maximize on
   Play** button in the **Game** view's top-right corner to see the image maximized on
   the screen:

Game view detecting the Ground Plane Emulator image

3. Click on the computer screen over the **Game** view to simulate a screen touch on the phone. The cube will appear over the target. Its size will depend on the size that you gave previously in the Unity editor (the **Ground Plane Stage** in Unity is 100 cm x 100 cm, while the printed emulator is 20 cm x 20 cm):

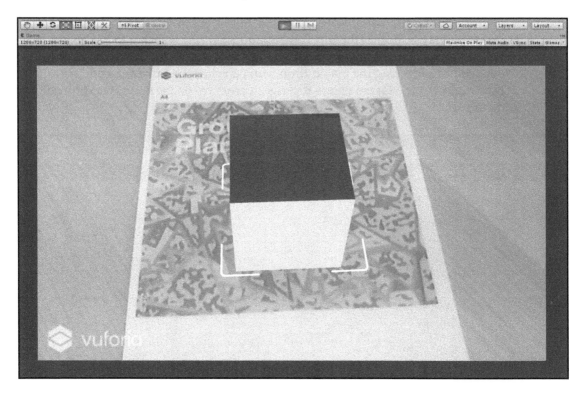

The cube appears on the floor when clicking the Game view

If everything works as expected, we can change the cube and start shaping our AR app to show furniture in the real world.

Creating an AR furniture viewer

Now that we have the main structure of the AR scene, we'll customize the app to create an AR furniture viewer that allows us to place chairs in the real world. The app will let us do the following:

- Place a single chair on the ground
- Duplicate the chair to create a cinema-like scene
- Rotate the chair to adjust it to the environment

Let's get started!

Adding elements to our project

We will start by adding new elements to our project and scene, including the 3D model and a user interface:

1. Create your own folder inside the Assets folder of the **Project** window and name it @MyAssets. Then, create three other folders called Images, Models, and Scripts inside it:

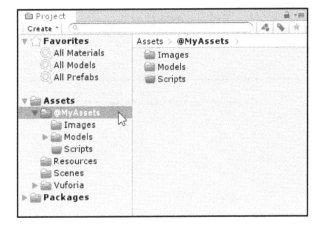

The new folders inside @MyAssets

2. Now, from the resources of the project, copy the models and images into their respective folders in the **Project** window.

3. In the **Inspector** window, change the `chair.png` and `cinema.png` images' **Texture Type** to **Sprite (2D and UI)** and click **Apply**. This will allow us to use them as UI elements later. The others will be used as regular textures on planes:

The chair.png image import settings in the Inspector window

4. Drag the **prince** model from the **Assets|Models|Prince** folder to the **Hierarchy** window as the child of **Ground Plane Stage**.

5. Delete the **Cube** since we don't need it anymore.

6. Scale it, rotate it, and move it until it's facing forward, over the **Ground Plane Stage** at a convenient size (you can adapt this later when you test the app):

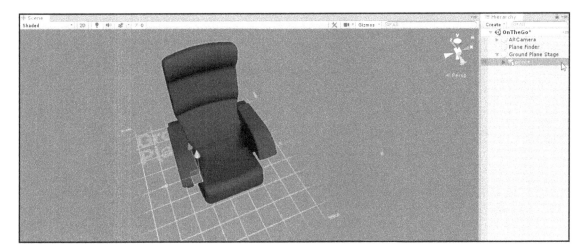

The prince model as the Ground Plane Stage object's child in the scene

7. To create the UI, right-click the **Hierarchy** window and select **UI** | **Button**. It will automatically encapsulate the **Button** in a new **Canvas** element and add the necessary **Event System** to the scene too:

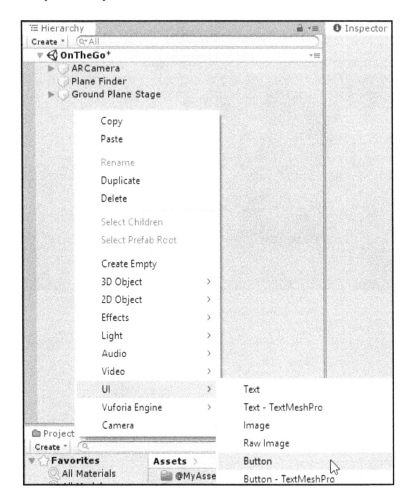

Creating a button in the Hierarchy window

8. Select the **Canvas** and change the parameters on the **Canvas Scaler** so that it scales up and down according to the device's screen size:

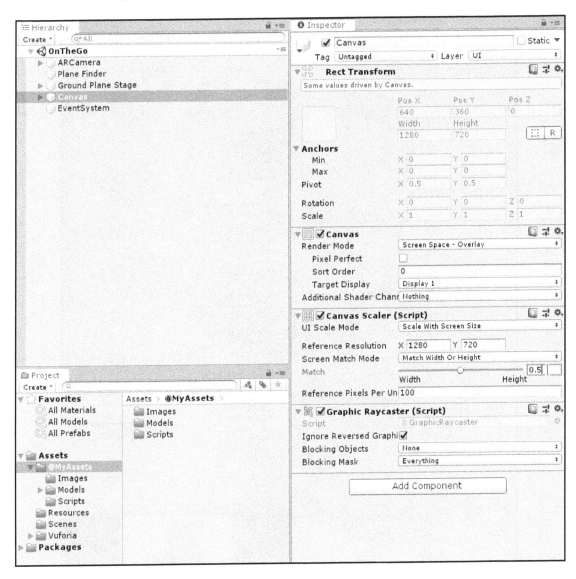

New Canvas Scaler parameters to adapt the UI's size to the screen size

9. Select the button and delete its **Text** GameObject.

10. In the **Inspector** window, change its name to chair_b to identify it, its position, and size using the **Rect Transform** component. Add the chair image to its **Source Image** in the **Image** component:

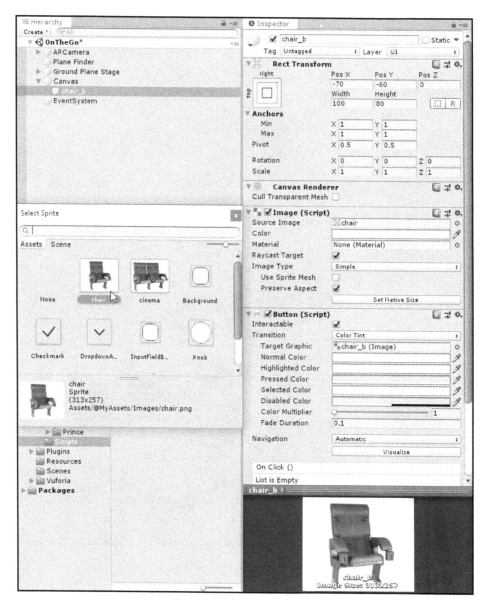

Customizing the created button

This is the button that will switch between moving a single chair and adding multiple chairs to form a cinema:

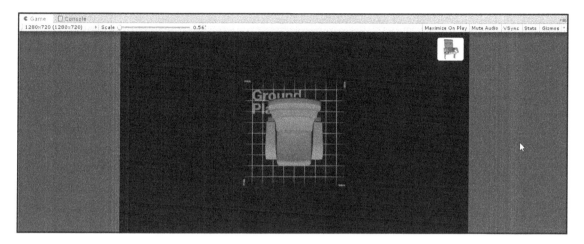

The view of the chair and button in the Game view

Now, we have to create a script that will contain the logic of the app.

Adding the logic of the app

Now, let's create the logic of the app by adding a new script to the project. This will be the script in charge of switching between one and multiple chairs:

1. In your **@MyAssets|Scripts** folder, in the **Project** window, right-click and select **Create|C# Script**. Call it `OnTheGoHandler.cs`:

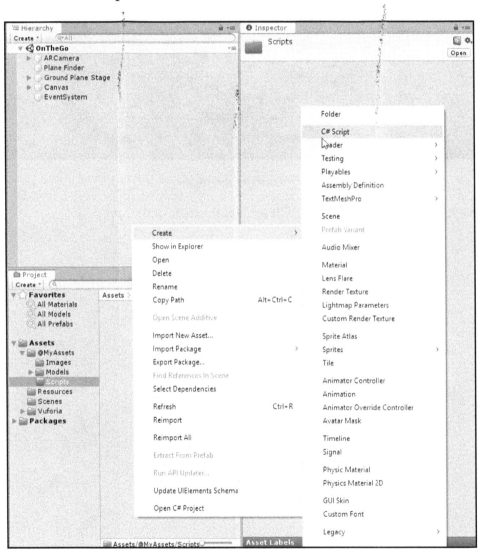

Adding a new script in the Project window

2. Double-click on it to open it in Visual Studio:

The OnTheGoHandler script in Visual Studio

3. Add the `Vuforia` library at the top of the script to use its features:

```
using Vuforia;
```

4. Inside the class, declare the following variables:

```
public GameObject chairButton;
public Sprite[] buttonSprites;
private ContentPositioningBehaviour contentPosBehaviour;
private bool multipleChairs = false;
```

The `chairButton` variable will correspond to the button we created in Unity. The `buttonSprites` array will contain the two background images for the button and we'll switch between them. The `contentPosBehaviour` variable comes from the `Vuforia` class, which is in charge of adding our virtual objects to the real world. We will use the `multipleChairs` Boolean to switch between the two states (one chair or multiple chairs). Public variables will be initialized in the Unity editor.

5. Inside the `Start()` method, add the following code:

```
contentPosBehaviour = GetComponent<ContentPositioningBehaviour>();
```

This will retrieve the `ContentPositioningBehaviour` component of the GameObject that contains the script.

6. After the `Update()` method, create a new method:

```
public void SwitchMultipleChairs()
  {
      if (!multipleChairs)
      {
          chairButton.GetComponent<UnityEngine.UI.Image>().sprite =
buttonSprites[1];
          contentPosBehaviour.DuplicateStage = true;
          multipleChairs = true;
      }
      else
      {
          chairButton.GetComponent<UnityEngine.UI.Image>().sprite =
buttonSprites[0];
          contentPosBehaviour.DuplicateStage = false;
          multipleChairs = false;
      }
  }
```

When this method is called, it checks whether the current state is a single chair or multiple chairs. It switches the image of the UI button accordingly and adjusts the `DuplicateStage` parameter of the `ContentPositioningBehaviour` class to allow one or multiple instances of the same chair. Then, it sets `multipleChairs` to `true` or `false` to keep track of the current state.

7. Back in the Unity editor, drag the script over the **Plane Finder**. Alternatively, in the **Inspector** window, click on **Add Component | On The Go Handler**:

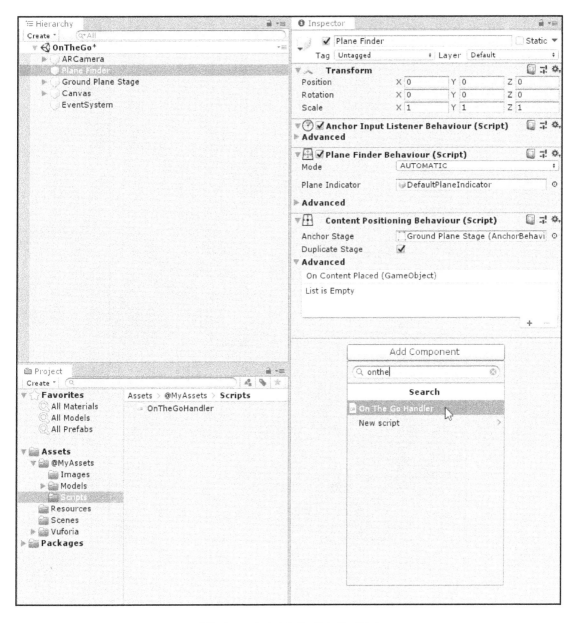

Adding the created script to the Plane Finder GameObject

8. In the **On The Go Handler** script, select or drag the button to the **Chair Button** field and select the two sprites, chair and cinema, from **@MyAssets|Images** in that order (see the following screenshot).

9. From the **Content Positioning Behaviour** drop-down, uncheck **Duplicate Stage** so that it starts with a single chair:

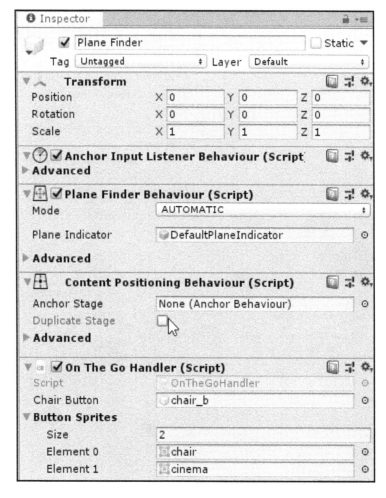

Assigning the corresponding elements to the OnTheGoHandler script in the Inspector window

10. Finally, select the button and, in the **On Click ()** method, at the bottom, choose the **Plane Finder** and select the **On The Go Handler|SwitchMultipleChairs** function:

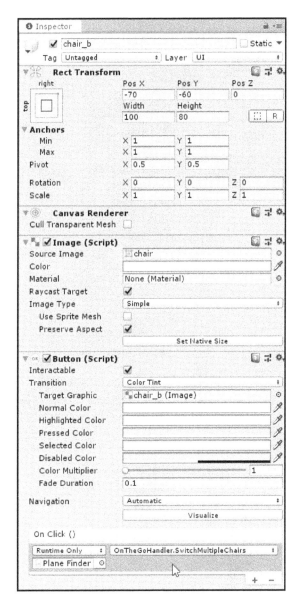

Selecting the OnClick() method behaviour for the button in the Inspector window

11. Before we add any new features, we need to build this app on a mobile device. Press *Ctrl + Shift + B* or go to **File** | **Build Settings...**:

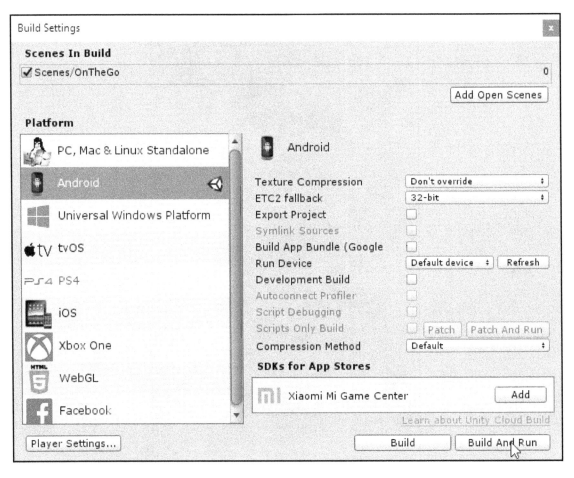

Build Settings panel to build and run the app on a mobile device

12. Press **Build And Run**, give your `.apk` file a name, and run it on the mobile device. Point the camera to the ground until a little icon appears, marking the ground level:

The white square shows the point of the ground where the virtual objects will be placed

13. Move around and tap on the screen to place a chair. Now, you can walk around the virtual chair to see it from different angles:

The virtual red chair placed in a real environment

14. Press the button to switch to multiple-chair mode, move the camera around, and place multiple chairs all over the room:

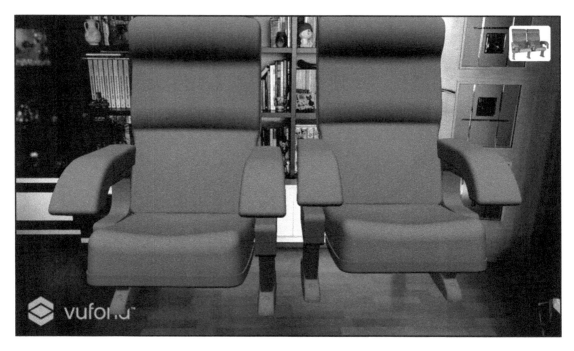

Two virtual chairs, one next to the other

It's probable that, on your first attempt, the chair won't have the desired size or the shadows won't correspond to the real ones. Furthermore, the chair will always be facing forward, so you'll have to move around the room before placing it in the desired place. Let's improve these little details to make the app more appealing.

Improving the app

Now, we are going to improve the current app to make it more appealing to the user:

1. First of all, try adding a new **Directional Light** (right-click on the existing one and press **Duplicate**) and play with its **Rotation**, **Intensity**, and/or **Shadow Type**. In this case, we have placed two lights, with **Rotation** values of (−30,−20,0) and (30,20,0) respectively and with **No Shadows**, creating a lighter-colored chair:

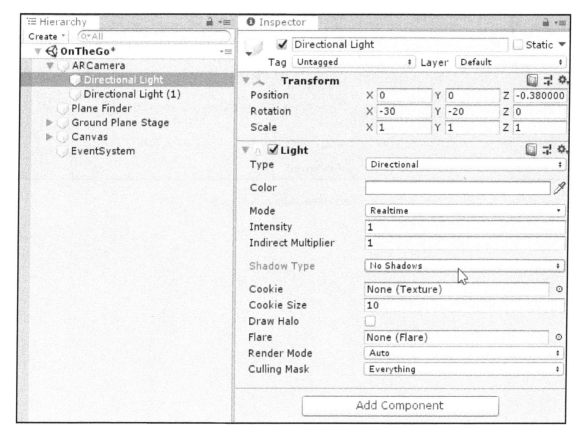

Values of one of the Directional Lights

2. Now, let's make the visual reference of the floor more visible: select the **Plane Finder** GameObject and, in the **Inspector** window, double-click on the **DefaultPlaneIndicator** element located in the **Plane Finder Behaviour** script. This will open the original element:

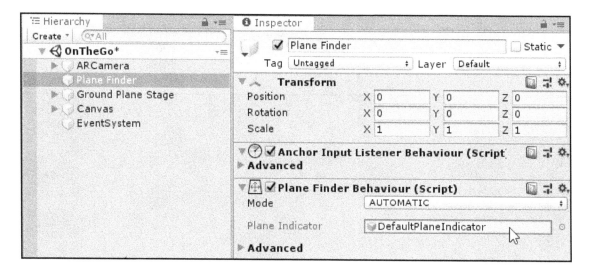

Selecting DefaultPlaneIndicator in the Inspector window

3. From the **Hierarchy** window, select the **DefaultIndicator** child. Then, in the **Inspector** window, increase its size to 0.05 and change the default image to **reticle_ground_surface**:

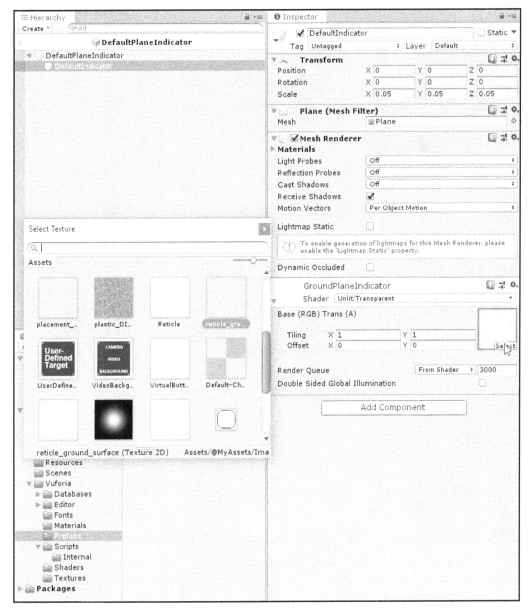

The DefaultIndicator GameObject's components in the Inspector window

4. Let's add a rotation indicator to the chair so that it appears when we use two fingers on the screen. Right-click on the **prince** GameObject in the **Hierarchy** window and select 3**D Object**|**Quad**:

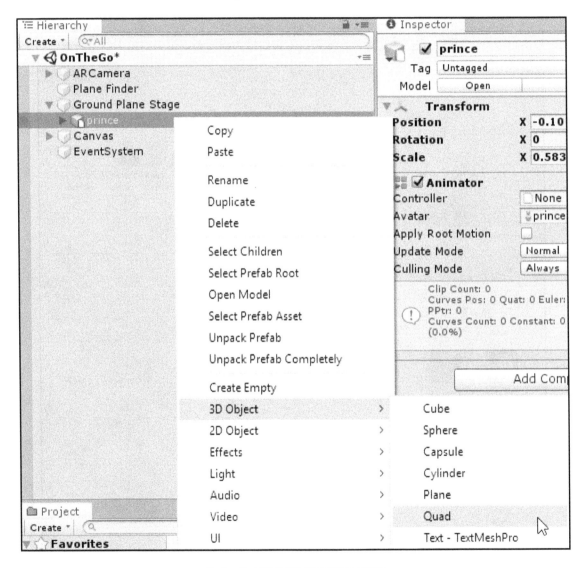

Creating a Quad element child of the prince GameObject

5. Drag the `placement_rotate` image from the **Project** window over the **rotate** GameObject in the **Hierarchy** window to convert it into its texture and set the material's **Rendering Mode** to **Cutout**:

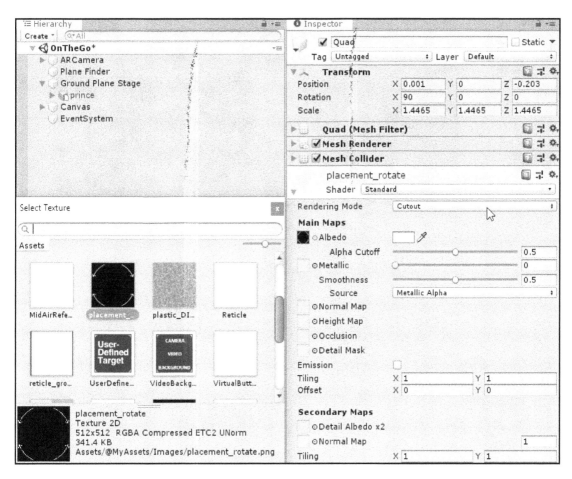

Quad's material's properties on the Inspector

6. Adjust its position and rotation so that it appears in the middle of the **Ground Plane Stage**:

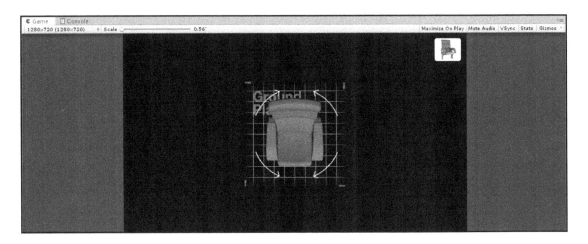

The Quad in the middle of the Ground Plane around the seat

7. Now, create another script in the **@MyAssets|Scripts** folder. Call it `ChairHandler.cs` and attach it to the **prince** GameObject:

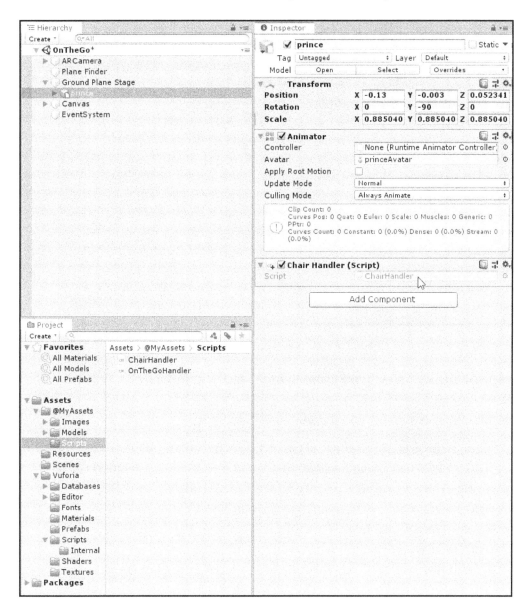

The prince GameObject with the newly created script attached to it

8. Double-click on the script to open it in Visual Studio:

ChairHandler script in Visual Studio

9. At the beginning of the class, add the following variables:

```
public GameObject rotateGO;
private float rotateSpeed = 0.8f;
```

The first variable refers to the **Quad** GameObject we created previously (with the rotation arrows image). The second variable controls the rotation speed of the chair.

10. Inside the `Start()` method, add the following code:

```
rotateGO.SetActive(false);
```

With this, we are hiding the rotate arrows until the chair is actually rotating.

11. Now, inside the `Update()` method, add the following code:

```
Touch[] touches = Input.touches;
if (Input.touchCount == 2 && (touches[0].phase == TouchPhase.Moved
|| touches[1].phase == TouchPhase.Moved))
{
 rotateGO.SetActive(true);

 Vector2 previousPosition= touches[1].position -
touches[1].deltaPosition - (touches[0].position -
touches[0].deltaPosition);
 Vector2 currentPosition = touches[1].position -
touches[0].position;
 float angleDelta = Vector2.Angle(previousPosition,
currentPosition);
 Vector3 cross = Vector3.Cross(previousPosition, currentPosition);

 Vector3 previousRotation = transform.localEulerAngles;
 if (cross.z > 0)
 {
 transform.localEulerAngles = previousRotation - new Vector3(0,
angleDelta * rotateSpeed, 0);
 }
 else if (cross.z < 0)
 {
 transform.localEulerAngles = previousRotation + new Vector3(0,
angleDelta * rotateSpeed, 0);
 }
}
else
{
 rotateGO.SetActive(false);
}
```

The preceding code retrieves the touches coming from the screen. If it's two touches (two fingers touching the screen) and at least one of them is moving, it does the following:

- Makes the rotation image visible.
- Retrieves the touches' positions.
- Calculates the angle between the last finger position and the current one, and rotates the chair accordingly. When the user stops rotating the chair, the rotation image is hidden again.

12. The final step is to drag the **Quad** GameObject from the **Hierarchy** to the **ChairHandler** script's **Rotate GO** field in the **Inspector** window.

13. Now, you can directly press *Ctrl + B* to build and run the project or do so through **File|Build And Run**. As you can see, the mark on the ground is much more visible now:

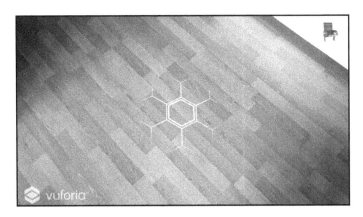

The new ground reference mark

14. Now, you can also rotate the chair to see how it would look in its place:

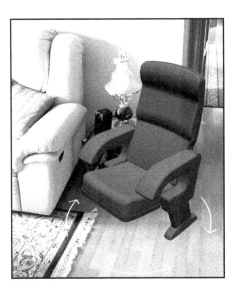

Rotation arrows appearing when the user rotates the chair with two fingers

With that, we have completed the AR furniture viewer.

Summary

In this chapter, we have learned about one of Vuforia's features: Ground Plane. We created a project that places virtual chairs in real-life scenarios and lets us manipulate them with touchscreens (rotate them) and through a simple UI button (multiply them).

By now, you will have a better understanding of how Vuforia works, how to create Vuforia elements inside Unity, and how to create a wholly functional Ground Plane example in it. With the skills that you've acquired through this project's development, you can improve it by adding new 3D models, new UI elements, or updating the current scripts to include more features in the app.

You also have better insight into how AR can work in the retail field so that you can adapt the current project to fill your personal or professional needs in this area. As we mentioned at the beginning of this chapter and seen throughout, the app can easily be changed to display other types of furniture, decorations, carpets, or any product that you want to show over a surface and observe from different angles.

In the next chapter, we will be exploring Vuforia's possibilities even further by looking at Image Targets and deploying the app inside Moverio AR glasses.

Further reading

From here, you can try to use Vuforia's **Mid Air** option, which, instead of placing the objects attached to the ground, places them at a distance from it. This can be useful for placing objects on walls, such as frames, pictures, and so on, or when working with flying objects such as drones. Their use is very similar; instead of creating a **Plane Finder** and **Ground Plane Stage**, you create a **Mid Air Positioner** and **Mid Air Stage**.

You can also download the Vuforia core samples from the Unity Asset Store (`https://assetstore.unity.com/packages/templates/packs/vuforia-core-samples-99026`), which includes a full example of the Ground Plane and its features.

7
AR for Automation with Vuforia and AR Glasses

In this chapter, we will go deeper into Vuforia, the SDK we introduced previously in Chapter 6, *AR for Retail with Vuforia*. You will learn how to use the framework along with AR glasses, more specifically, the Epson Moverio BT-350 model, and you will learn how to use the Vuforia image recognition features to create an app to guide operators, step by step, in industrial works, and how to modify a scene so that you can integrate it into your AR glasses.

 It's important to note that to complete this chapter, you will need to have the AR glasses to build upon them. Although we have structured the content so that you can follow most of the process using a mobile Android device, you will only be able to see the final result, the differences in the mobile device view, and the possibilities that the AR see-through devices offer if you can launch the project on the real glasses.

This chapter has three main goals: first of all, to acquire a fuller understanding of how Vuforia works so that you can extend and improve the current example beyond the scope of this book. The second goal is to understand the possibilities AR offers in the industrial field and, specifically, in automation. You will see that AR is not only a visually attractive technology but that it can guide operators in their work, reducing training time and possible errors during operations. The idea is to provide you with the necessary skills to reproduce and adapt the current project to your needs. The final goal is to introduce an AR headset, such as the Epson Moverio AR glasses, to explain how they work and to easily integrate Vuforia with them.

Using AR glasses instead of tablets can be a valuable asset in the industrial field as it allows operators to have both hands free while they are working. The following image shows a pair of AR glasses:

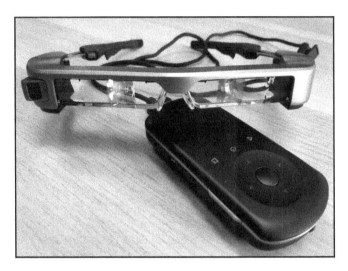

The Epson Moverio BT-350 AR glasses

In this chapter, we will be covering the following topics:

- Using AR in automation
- Exploring Vuforia
- Developing image-based AR in Vuforia
- Creating an industrial guide for AR glasses

Technical requirements

The technical requirements for this chapter are as follows:

- A Unity 3D supporting computer (see the latest requirements here: `https://unity3d.com/es/unity/system-requirements`). This chapter's example project has been developed on a Windows 10 x64 computer.
- Unity 3D (2019.1.2f1 in this book).
- Microsoft Visual Studio Community 2017 (included in the Unity installation).
- The latest version of Vuforia included with Unity 3D (8.3.8 in this book).
- Epson Moverio BT-350 AR glasses.

The resources and code files for this chapter can be found here: `https://github.com/PacktPublishing/Enterprise-Augmented-Reality-Projects/tree/master/Chapter07`.

 Other AR glasses (from Moverio and other companies) might work with this example. However, some points have to be taken into account, for example, their operating system must be Android 4.1 or above (required by Unity 3D v2019).

Let's get started with AR in automation.

Using AR in automation

The arrival of the fourth industrial revolution, also called **industry 4.0**, has boosted the use of AR in industrial environments. Industry 4.0 revolves around digitalization and interconnectivity, and technologies such as **Augmented Reality** (**AR**), **Virtual Reality** (**VR**), the **Internet of Things** (**IoT**), **Big Data Analytics** (**BDA**), **Additive Manufacturing** (**AM**), **Cyber-Physical Systems** (**CPS**), and **Artificial Intelligence** (**AI**) have become the base of this industrial revolution.

AR is the natural interface and connection to IoT and big data. It allows workers to visualize and interact with the data coming from the and sensors of a factory in an easy and attractive way, either using mobile devices or AR headsets.

AR use in automation can go from the facial recognition of an employee to getting access to a concrete machine, to real-time on-site surveillance of the production process or remote access to and control of the system through AR glasses.

Introducing the scenario and process

For this project, we will be creating a step-by-step guide that can be used in production, maintenance, and training. Users performing a task will receive guidance on how to do it correctly, as well as have access to useful information such as blueprints drawings, or pdf documents.

For that, we will use a Volkswagen Beetle (car) as an example. We will work with three pictures as targets (side, back view with the trunk closed, and back view with the trunk open) to simulate an operator that starts from the side of the car and then moves to check the state of the car engine, all while receiving information from the AR glasses. In a real environment, these pictures would correspond with the real car (or industrial equipment).

The images we are going to use in this project have been retrieved from the following link:

- A 3D model of the Beetle car: `https://sketchfab.com/3d-models/beetlefusca-version-2-2f3bea70178345c8b7cc4424886f9386`
- A blueprint: `https://getoutlines.com/blueprints/6826/1968-volkswagen-beetle-sedan-blueprints`
- An image in a PDF file: `https://getoutlines.com/blueprints/6943/1972-volkswagen-beetle-1500-sedan-blueprints`

In the next section, we will introduce Vuforia briefly before starting to develop the guide project.

Exploring Vuforia

As we discussed in `Chapter 6`, *AR for Retail with Vuforia*, Vuforia is one of the oldest and most well-known AR SDKs that has been integrated in Unity since its 2017.2 version. It provides multiple AR features such as image recognition, ground plane recognition, model detection, and so on. You can find all the available features at `https://engine.vuforia.com/features.html`. For this project, we will focus on image recognition.

In `Chapter 6`, *AR for Retail with Vuforia*, in the *Exploring Vuforia* section, we explained the steps to integrate Vuforia for the first time in a Unity project. Please follow *steps 1-7* in that section but change the following parameters:

- Unity project name (*step 3*): `AR_Automation`
- Scene name (*step 4*): `ARGuide`
- Product name (*step 6, player settings*): `AR Guide`

Finally, set the light's **Rotation** points or axes to **X**:20, **Y**:0, and Z:0 and place it inside the **ARCamera** (as a child) to maintain its directionality:

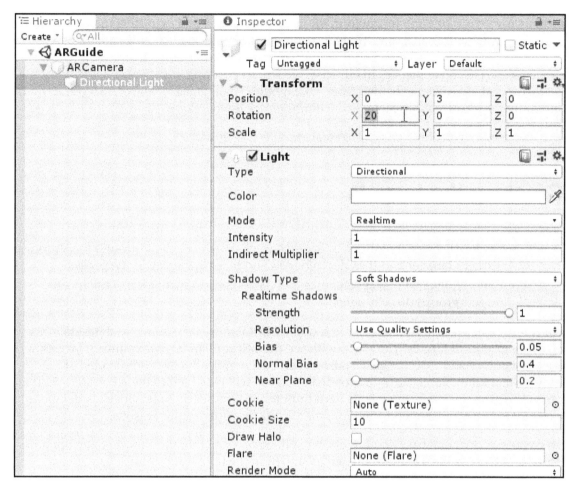

The Directional Light with its new values and child of the ARCamera

Now that we have the Vuforia engine ready in our project, let's start with the AR creation process.

Developing image-based AR in Vuforia

One of the most powerful features of Vuforia is image recognition. The Vuforia engine can process any `.jpeg` or `.png` image (our AR marker or target) and extract its main features. It will later compare those features to the real-time images coming from the camera of a mobile device or AR glasses to find that marker in the real world and overlap the virtual elements on it to create the AR. In our case, we will be working with three images of a Beetle car that have been extracted from a 3D model. The images, however, can come from any source, such as real-life pictures or computer designed images.

The next section will show us how to create targets in Vuforia.

Creating the targets

Vuforia offers two different options when working with images:

- *Device databases* are groups of image targets that are created through the Vuforia Target Manager and then downloaded and included *locally* in the project.
- *Cloud recognition* makes reference to the hosting and managing of the image targets groups directly *online*.

For this project, we will be using the first option. Databases, also known as **datasets** in the SDK, are groups of targets. They help with the classification of large amounts of targets, as well as memory and CPU usage. Databases can be dynamically loaded/unloaded at runtime and all the targets inside a loaded database will be added to the AR search. At the time of writing this book, there is no hard limit to the number of targets inside a database, although Vuforia recommends no more than 1,000 for performance reasons.

To create our own database and targets, we will have to log into the Vuforia development portal and head to the **Target Manager**, as shown in the following steps:

1. Go to the **Target Manager** page at `https://developer.vuforia.com/vui/develop/databases`.
2. **Log In** or **Register** (if you don't have an account) to enter the page:

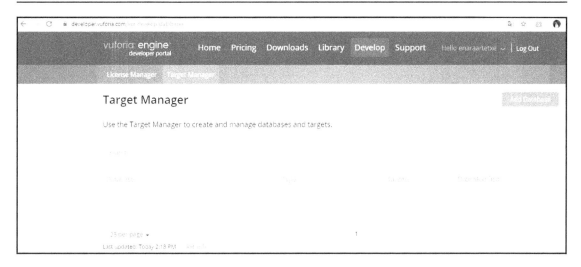

The Target Manager page

3. Click on **Add Database** at the top right to create a new database. Because we will be using the Beetle images as targets, give the database the name `Beetle`:

Creating a new database

4. Now, click on the created database and click on **Add Target**.

5. Click on the **Browse** button and select the `Side.jpg` image from the `Targets` folder of the project's resources. Once it's been uploaded, you will see that the **Name** field at the bottom will automatically be filled. Give it a **Width** value of 1 and click **Add**:

Creating a new target

6. The target will automatically be created, and next to it, you will see a number of stars, as depicted in the following screenshot. These stars indicate how recognizable the image will be by the AR software. Four or five stars are good targets.

> If you have any doubt or you want to know more about the other options that appear when you create a target, you can take a look at `https://library.vuforia.com/articles/Solution/How-To-Work-with-Device-Databases.html`.

7. Repeat *steps 4* and *step 5* with the `Back_closed.jpg` and `Back_open.jpg` images and with the same **Width** of 1 so that all of them will have a similar scale in the Unity editor:

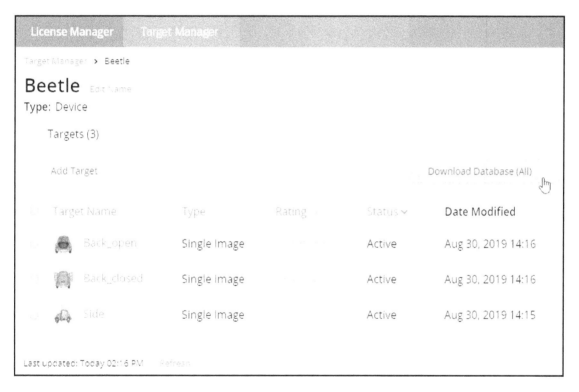

The Target Manager page with the Beetle database and its targets

8. Once the three targets have been created, click on **Download Database (All)**, select **Unity Editor,** and click **Download**. It will download a `Beetle.unitypackage` file that we will import into the project.

9. Double-click on the `Beetle.unitypackage` file to import it in Unity. You can also import it from the Unity editor by clicking on **Assets|Import Package|Custom Package...** and selecting the file:

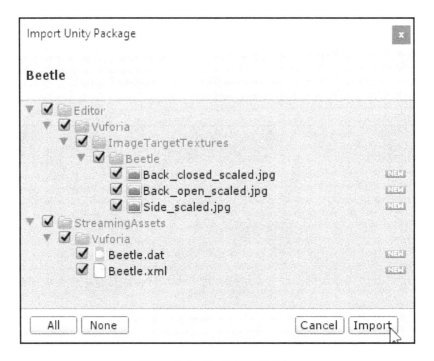

The target database files to be imported in Unity

10. This will add the database to a newly created `StreamingAssets/Vuforia` folder and the compressed images of the three targets to the `Editor/Vuforia/ImageTargetTextures/Beetle` folder.

Now that we have the database included in our project, we are going to add the three targets to the scene by following these steps:

1. Right-click on the **Hierarchy** window and click on **Vuforia Engine | Image**. This will create an **ImageTarget** object in our scene:

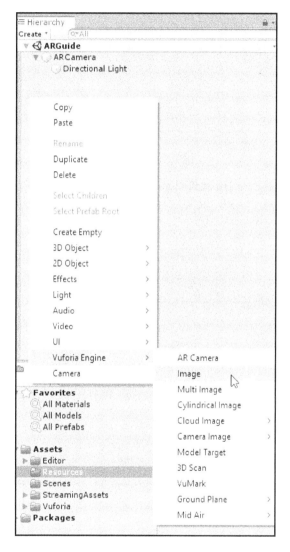

Adding a Vuforia ImageTarget to the scene

2. By default, the **ARCamera** and **ImageTarget** will be in the same position and nothing will appear on camera. Using the **Rotation** tab, rotate the camera by 90 in the **X** axis and move it upwards 3 units until the target is in view:

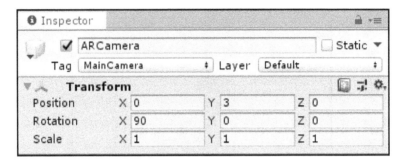

ARCamera Transform values

3. Create the other two **ImageTargets** and move them until the three are in view. Name them Target_Side, Target_Close, and Target_Open so that you can differentiate between them:

The three targets in the scene

4. By default, the **ImageTarget** represents the first target found in the first database, sorted alphabetically. To change it, select the **Target_Side** in the **Hierarchy** window, and in the **Inspector** window, under the **Image Target Behavior** component, select its image. Do the same with **Target_Open**. If you want, scale the targets up/down using the scale tab and move them until they look similar and take up all the camera width for a better view:

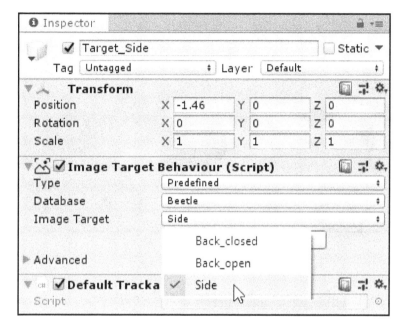

Changing the image reference for the targets

We'll learn how to add test cubes in the next section.

Adding some test cubes

To quickly test our scene, let's create three different objects to visualize on top of each target:

1. Right-click on **Target_Side** and select **3D Object | Cube**.
2. Scale it down so it doesn't hide the target completely.

3. For **Target_Close**, create a **3D Object | Sphere** instead of a cube, and for **Target_Open**, create a **3D Object | Capsule**.

4. Scale them down as well so that the targets are partially in view. As it's only for testing purposes, we are not going to add any material or texture to these objects:

Testing the 3D objects inside each target

Now, let's obtain our Vuforia key so that we can test the app.

Obtaining the key

In order to test the app or run it on a device, we need to provide a license key in the **VuforiaConfiguration** object. As we already logged into the Vuforia page to create the targets, we are now going to obtain the required key. Let's get started:

1. Go to the license manager page at `https://developer.vuforia.com/vui/develop/licenses`.

2. On the **License Manager** tab, select **Get Development Key** to obtain a free key to use while developing.

3. Give it the name of your app, `AR Guide`, read and accept the terms, and press **Confirm**.

4. Select your newly created license and copy the key.

5. Now, go to the Unity editor and select the **ARCamera** from the scene.

6. Click on the **Open Vuforia Engine configuration** button in the **Inspector** window to open the general Vuforia configuration:

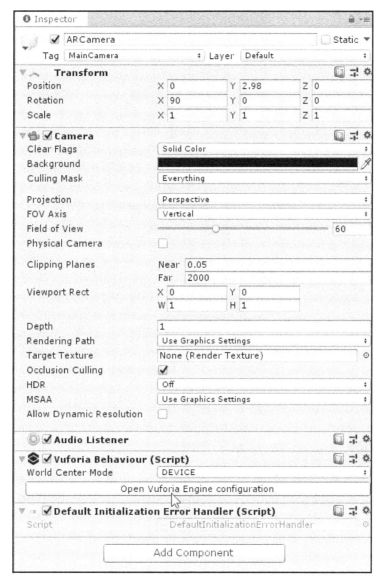

Opening the Vuforia Engine configuration button

7. Paste your key into the **App License Key** field:

Vuforia license key field in the Inspector window

Now, let's test the app to check that our AR scene has been set up properly.

Testing the app

Once the scene has been configured and the key has been added, click on the play button in the top Toolbar and point to the three target images with the webcam. You will see the different 3D objects appearing in each target when pointing at them.

 You will be able to see the scene better if you select **Maximize on Play** in the **Game** view's top-right corner.

The next image shows the cube appearing over the car side when the camera points at it:

In the Game view, the cube object appears over the Target_Side target

 You can find the pictures in the **Project** window inside the `Assets/ Editor/Vuforia/ImageTargetTextures/Beetle` folder. Double-click on them to open them in the computer, and either print them or directly point to them using the webcam.

Now that we have the basic functionality set up, let's create the full app.

Creating an industrial guide for AR glasses

Now that we have the basic setup ready, we are going to create a guide that will instruct workers on how to proceed, step by step, with the maintenance process of a car. The app will show them instructions with visual aids such as colored pictures and arrows that mark which part of the car they have to look at. It will also provide a help PDF file that they will be able to open to consult if needed.

The general working of the app will be as follows:

1. When the app starts, it will ask the worker to point at the car's side to start the process:

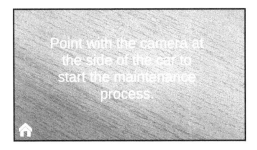

The initial message

2. When pointing with the camera at the side of the car (**Target_Side**), a blueprint of it will appear over the top of it, indicating a problem in the engine in red:

The blueprint over the marker with the engine in red

3. When the operator touches the red square, the app will instruct them to go to the back of the car:

The message when the user touches the engine

4. When pointing with the camera at the back of the car (**Target_Close**), the app will indicate to open the trunk via a blinking arrow:

The message to open the trunk

5. Once the worker has opened the trunk and is pointing at the engine (**Target_Open**), the app will indicate that the user needs to remove and change the top left spark plug.

6. On one side of the screen, a help PDF file with the instructions will be available in case the worker needs them.

7. When the operator has finished replacing the piece, they will press a button to confirm that they've completed the task:

The arrow pointing at the spark to replace and the UI buttons of this step

Note: The content we are going to use is just for demonstration purposes and doesn't correspond to the real instructions of this procedure.

In the following section, we are going to add the required material to our project.

Preparing the material

For this project, we are going to use some media content that has to be imported into the project and customized. We have to put it inside the project and then use it in our scene. For that, follow these steps:

1. Create your own folder inside the `Assets` folder on the **Project** window and name it `@MyAssets`. Then, create two other folders inside it called `Images` and `Scripts`:

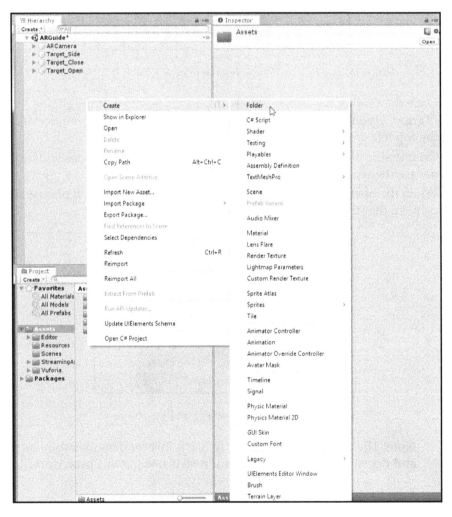

Creating a new folder in the Project window

2. From the resources of this chapter, drag the `arrow.png`, `blueprint.png`, `icon_file.png`, and `icon_home.png` image files into the `Images` folder you just created.

3. Select the images called icons and in the **Inspector** window, change their **Texture Type** to **Sprite (2D and UI)** so that we can use them inside the UI:

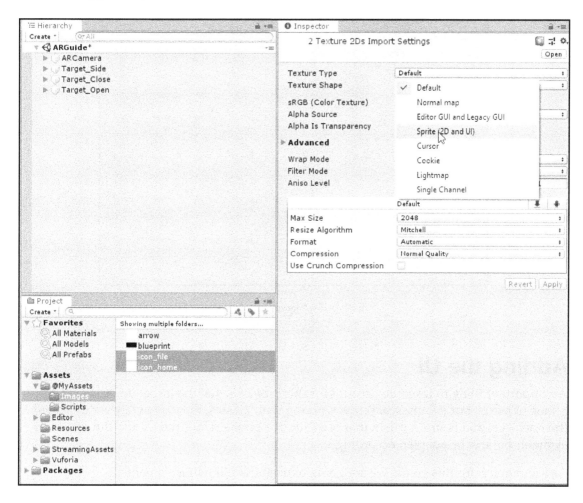

Changing the icon texture type

4. Create a new folder in the `Assets/StreamingAssets` folder of the **Project** window, call it `PDF`, and drag the `WorkOrder_0021.pdf` PDF file to it:

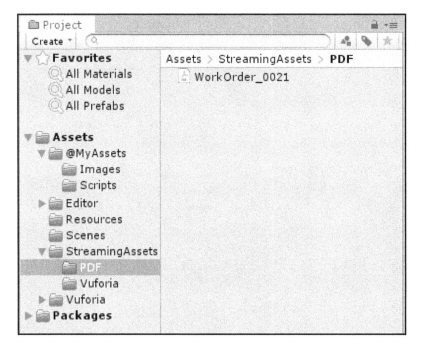

The PDF file in the StreamingAssets/PDF folder

Adding the UI

An important thing to take into account for this project is that the target device is not a phone or tablet, but AR glasses. When working with glasses, the scene view is duplicated (for each eye) and is smaller than that of a tablet or phone. Thus, the UI and the size of its elements have to be adapted accordingly.

As a summary, for this guide, we are going to need the following elements:

- **Main message**: Some text that occupies most of the screen to provide the main instructions (point at the side of the car, go to the back, and so on).
- **Bottom message**: Some indication text placed at the bottom of the screen to give secondary instructions combined with AR elements (touch the red elements to see instructions, open the trunk, replace a piece, and so on).

- **PDF button**: A button for the extra information in PDF format.
- **Home button**: To return to the initial screen.

Let's create all of them step by step:

1. Start by creating a **Canvas** object in the **Hierarchy** window:

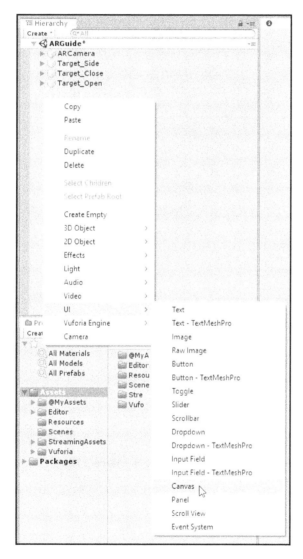

Adding a Canvas to the scene

When creating the **Canvas** object (parent to any other UI element), an **Event System** object, which is in charge of the user events that connect with the UI, is automatically created. If you try to create any UI component (for example, text, button, and so on) before creating the **Canvas**, Unity will create a **Canvas** element (with its **EventSystem** object) and make the new component a child of it.

2. In the **Inspector** window, change the **Canvas** component's **Render Mode** from **Screen Space - Overlay** to **World Space** and select the **ARCamera** as **Event Camera**. This way, the **Canvas** is placed in the 3D world instead of fixed and can be moved/scaled. In the **Rect Transform** component, enter the values of the image so that the **Canvas** is in front of the camera:

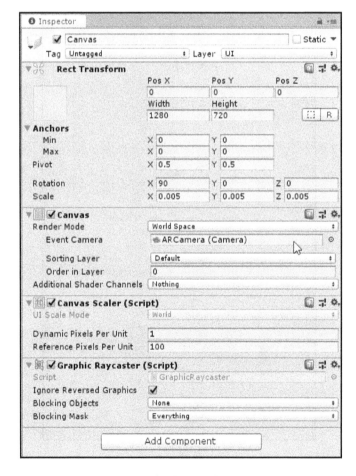

Values of the Canvas gameobject

3. Let's create the main message. Right-click on the **Canvas** element in the **Hierarchy** window and select **UI│Text**. Name it Main_message:

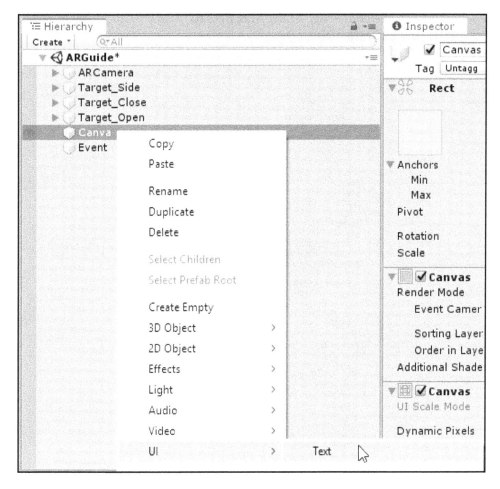

Creating new text inside the Canvas element

4. In the **Hierarchy** window, change the values on the **Rect Transform** component to match the following screenshot. Remove the default text, change the **Alignment** so it's centered in the screen, check the **Best Fit** checkbox so that the text fills the container, set the **Max Size** to 80 to ensure it's big enough, and change the **Color** to white:

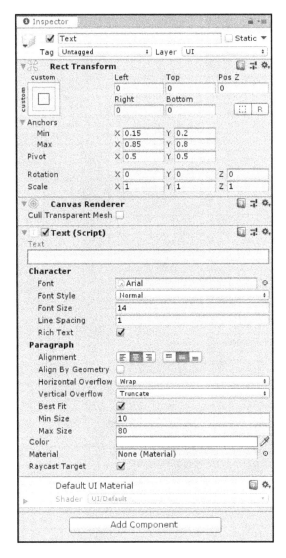

Values of the Rect Transform and Text components in the Main_message

5. We are now going to create a secondary message panel. As it's going to be very similar to the previous one, we can directly right-click on the previous and select **Duplicate**:

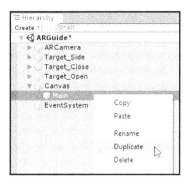

Duplicating the message

6. Change its name to `Bottom_message` and change its **Rect Transform** values so its place is at the bottom of the screen:

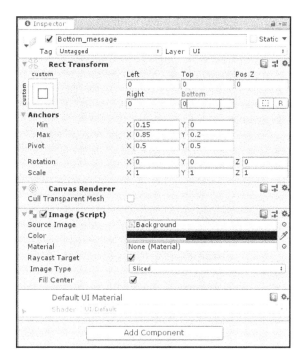

New message's values

7. To create the buttons, right-click on the **Canvas** element and select **UI** | **Button**:

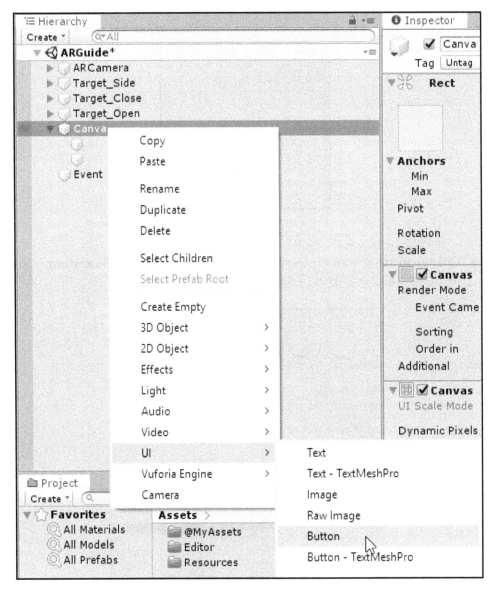

Creating a button element on the Canvas

8. Remove the text from it and change the button name to `Home_button`.

9. On the **Rect Transform,** select anchoring it to the bottom left and copy the values from the image to place it at the bottom left of the screen with an appropriate size for the glasses.

10. On the **Image** component, select the `icon_home` image as the **Source Image,** and on the **Button** component, change the **Pressed Color**. This way, when the button is clicked, it will change from white to blue:

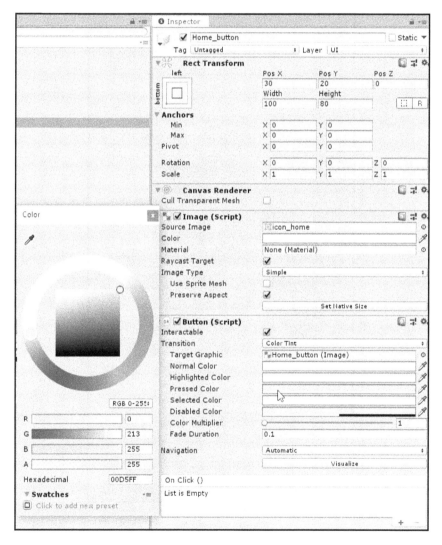

Home_button's values on the Inspector

11. Duplicate the button to create a copy of it and call it `File_button`. Change its **Rect Transform** so that you can locate it at the top-right corner of the screen and change its **Source Image** to **icon_file,** as follows:

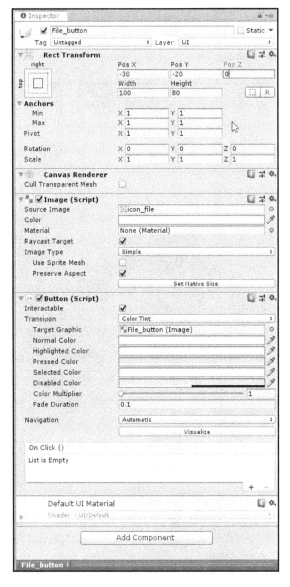

The values of the File_button

12. Now, create the last button from scratch, call it `OK_button`, and place it at the bottom-right corner of the screen. Change its **Normal Color** to light green:

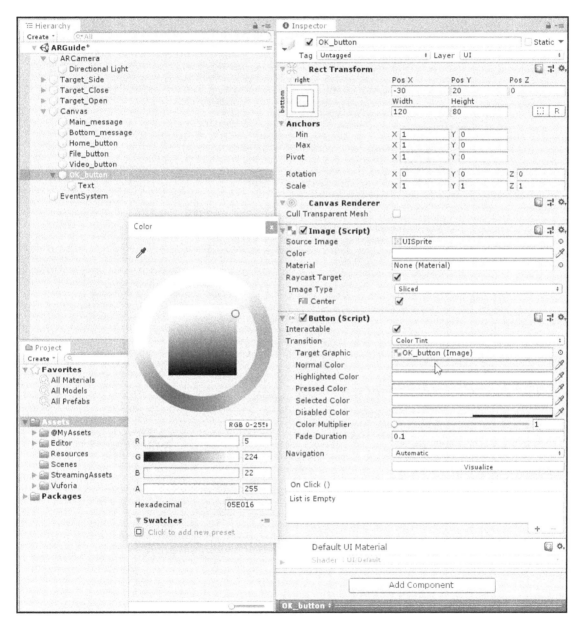

Values of the Ok_button element

13. Select the **Text** child on the button and change the **Rect Transform** and **Text** component parameters so that they match what's shown in the following screenshot:

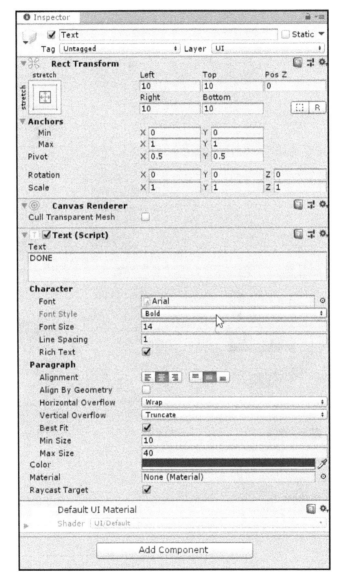

Values of the Text element inside the Ok_button

14. Your **Scene** and **Game** views should now look like this:

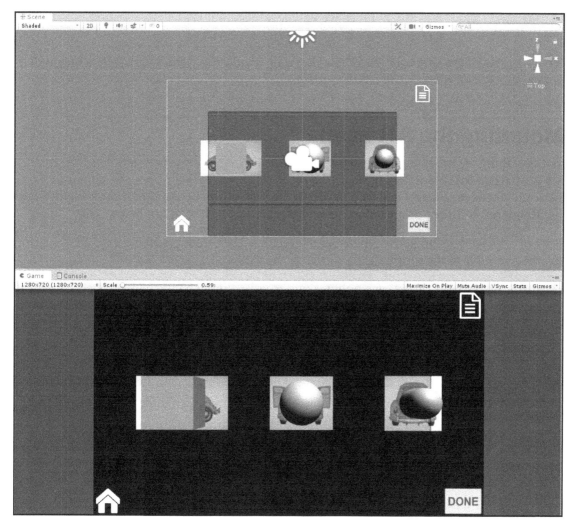

Scene and Game views with the created UI

Note that if you press the play button in the Toolbar, you will see that when the real camera feed is launched, the UI disappears. Don't worry about it at this point as we will be adjusting it later in this section.

Now that the UI elements are ready, we are going to add the virtual elements, which will appear in AR, and the logic attached to them.

Mounting the AR scene

The first thing we are going to do is modify the `DefaultTrackableEventHandler.cs` script attached to each of the targets in the scene. This script determines the actions to perform whenever a target is found or lost in the real world; by default, it shows and hides the **Renderer**, **Collider**, and **Canvas** elements attached to any child of that target.

For our app, we need to know whenever a target has been found, and for that, we are going to add a variable to the script.

For this project, we only need to make a slight change in the script. However, if you want to add more code to control when targets are found or lost, it's better to create a new class that inherits from `ITrackableEventHandler` like `DefaultTrackableEventHandler` does so that you always have a reference class to come back to in case anything fails in your code.

In the **Project** window, double-click on this script, which you can find in **Vuforia | Scripts**. When the Visual Studio window opens, we need to add the `public bool found = false;` variable to the variables:

Then, *inside* the `OnTrackingFound()` method, add `found = true;` at the end.

And *inside* the `OnTrackingLost()` method, add `found = false;` at the end.

This way, we can use this variable from any other class to know if a target has been found.

Back in Unity, let's start adding the AR elements. For that, first of all, remove the test 3D cube, sphere, and capsule.

Now, we are going to look at the first target:

1. Right-click on the **Target_Side** and create a **3D Object** | **Plane**:

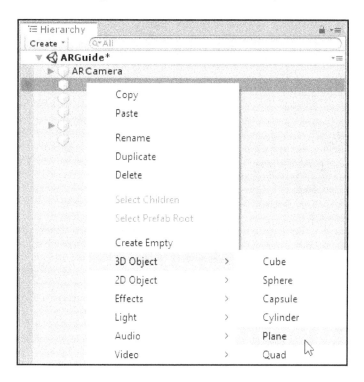

Creating a new plane

2. From the **Project** window, drag the blueprint image over the plane to make it its texture:

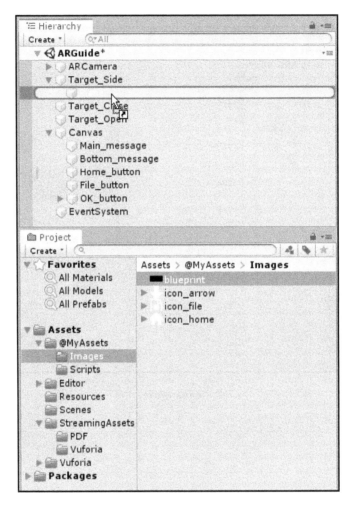

Assigning the blueprint image as texture of the plane

3. In the **Inspector** window, change its name to `Blueprint`. On the material panel at the bottom, change the **Rendering Mode** to **Fade** to make it transparent and smooth. Now rotate, scale, and move the plane until the blueprint matches the car beneath, as shown in the following screenshot:

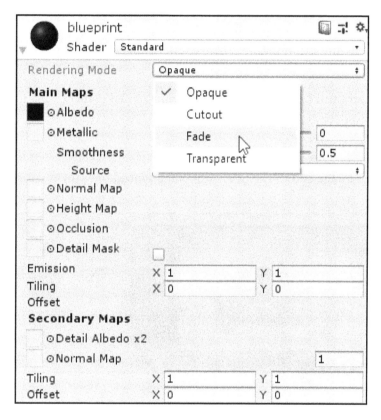

The blueprint over the target and its values in the Inspector window

Important! Keep the **Y** position value to `0.01` so the drawing is placed over the target but not too far away from it. This is to ensure the AR works correctly and the blueprint won't flicker for being too separated from the target.

4. Now, we have to create another plane that covers the engine area so that when the user touches it, it gives them directions. Create another plane child of the **Blueprint** and call it `Engine`. Move and resize it until it fits the engine area (marked in red in the blueprint):

Important! Keep it *on top* of the blueprint (**Y Position** `0.015` or `0.02`).

The next image shows the new grey plane placed over the engine area:

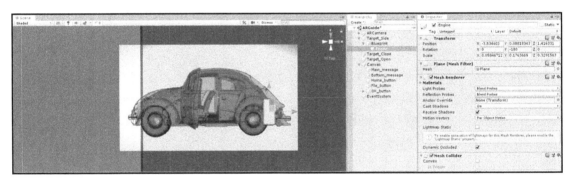

The new plane located over the engine area

Now, we have to make this plane invisible as it's only going to act as an activator. In the **Inspector** panel, remove its **Mesh Renderer** component by clicking on the gear at the top right and selecting **Remove Component**. Now, you will only see the plane if you select it:

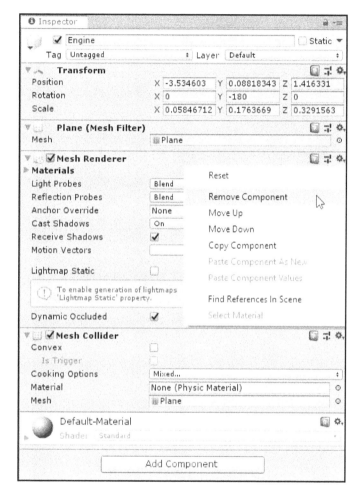

Removing the Mesh Renderer component from the plane

Let's move to the second target. This target will show an arrow to indicate to the user to open the trunk:

1. Right-click on **Target_Close**, create a new **3D Object|Plane,** and place it in the middle of the trunk.
2. Drag the arrow image to the plane to make it its texture.
3. In the **Inspector** window, call the plane `Arrow`. Remember to set the **Y Position** to 0.01. In the **Material** field, set **Rendering Mode** to **Fade** and change the **Albedo** color to a light blue:

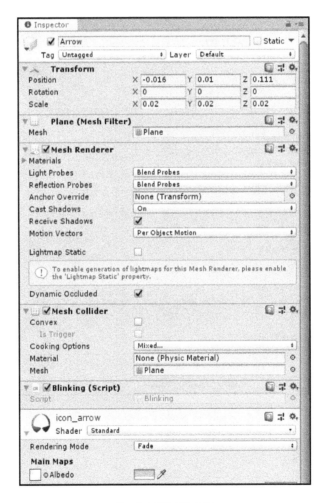

The values of the Arrow plane

4. To add the blinking effect of the arrow, create a new C# script in the @MyAssets/Script folder and call it Blinking.cs:

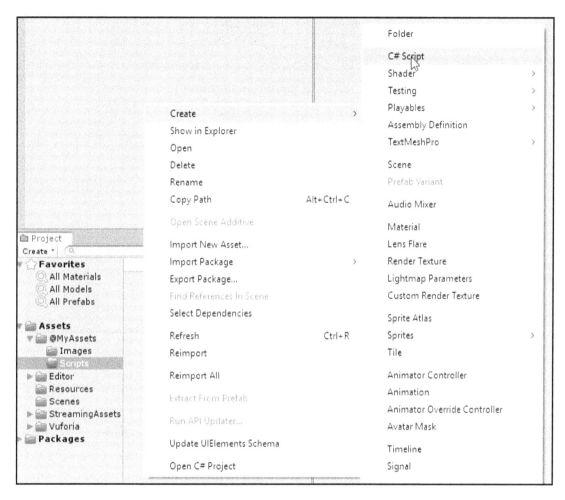

Adding a new script to the @MyAssets/Scripts folder

5. Double-click on it to open it in Visual Studio:

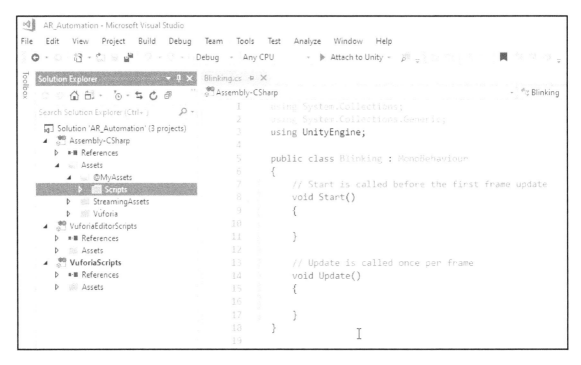

Blinking script in Visual Studio

6. Now, add the following lines to create the blinking effect. First, declare the following variables:

```
private IEnumerator coroutine;
private bool blinking;
```

`coroutine` is a special function in Unity that pauses the execution and gives control back to the calling method until a certain condition is completed, and then resumes the execution where it left off. We will use it to blink every half a second.

7. Now, *inside* the `Start()` method, include the following initialization lines:

```
coroutine = BlinkingArrow();
blinking = false;
```

8. Add the `coroutine` *after* the `Update()` method:

```
private IEnumerator BlinkingArrow()
{
    while (true)
    {
        GetComponent<MeshRenderer>().enabled = false;
        yield return new WaitForSeconds(0.5f);
        GetComponent<MeshRenderer>().enabled = true;
        yield return new WaitForSeconds(0.5f);
    }
}
```

The usual pausing command for a `coroutine` is `yield return null;`, which pauses the execution for a frame. For this `coroutine`, we have used `yield return new WaitForSeconds(0.5f);` to tell the `coroutine` to wait half a second before executing the following line. With this code, we are making the `MeshRenderer` component of the GameObject the script is attached to (the arrow) appear and disappear every half a second.

9. *Inside* the `Update()` method, we are going to use the `coroutine` so that the arrow blinks only while the target is being detected and is hidden otherwise. With the blinking Boolean, we will verify that the `coroutine` is only launched once:

```
if (GetComponentInParent<DefaultTrackableEventHandler>().found &&
!blinking)
{
    blinking = true;
    StartCoroutine(coroutine);
}
else if
(!GetComponentInParent<DefaultTrackableEventHandler>().found &&
blinking)
{
    blinking = false;
    StopAllCoroutines();
    GetComponent<MeshRenderer>().enabled = false;
}
```

10. Back in the Unity editor, go to the **Inspector** window, click on **Add Component**, and add the **Blinking** script to the **Arrow** plane:

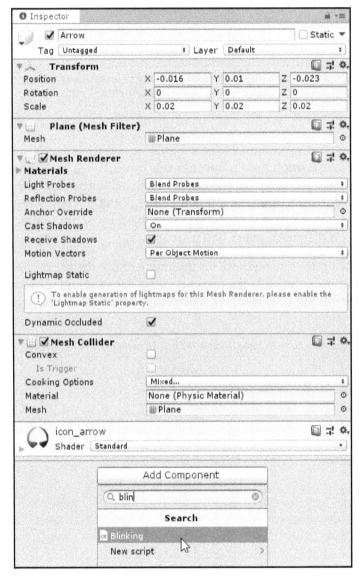

Adding the new script to the plane

To finish, let's go to the third target, which will have another arrow:

1. Right-click on the **Arrow** game object and press **Copy**.
2. Then, right-click on the **Target_Open** game object and paste it.
3. Move and rotate it until it's pointing at the top left of the trunk:

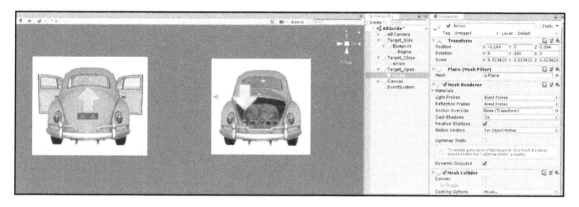

The two arrows pointing to different places on the trunk

At the moment, if we press the Play button on the top Toolbar, we will see the blueprint and arrows appearing when we point at each marker. However, we need to convert them into a step-by-step guide that will only show an instruction when the previous one is completed. We are going to add that logic in another script:

1. In the **Project** window, in the `@MyAssets/Scripts` folder, right-click and create another C# script.

2. Call it `MainHandler.cs` and double-click on it to open it in Visual Studio:

MainHandler script in VisualStudio

3. Start by adding Vuforia's `UnityEngine.UI` to the libraries:

```
using Vuforia;
using UnityEngine.UI;
```

4. Then, add the following variables:

```
public DefaultTrackableEventHandler targetSide;
public DefaultTrackableEventHandler targetClose;
public DefaultTrackableEventHandler targetOpen;

public GameObject mainMessage;
public GameObject bottomMessage;
public GameObject fileButton;
public GameObject okButton;
```

They are all `public` because we will initialize them from the Unity editor. They make references to the different scene elements we are going to play with, the targets, and the UI elements.

5. Now, add this property *after* the variables:

```
public bool Finished { get; set; }
```

It's also `public` because we are going to assign it from the editor as well when the user presses the **Done** button.

6. Finally, add the following private variable, which is an enumeration to control each of the states of the app:

```
private enum State
{
    Init = 0,
    Side = 1,
    Engine = 2,
    Close = 3,
    Open = 4,
    Plug = 5
}
private State state;
```

7. Now, let's add some methods *after* the `Update()` method. Create a new method called `ShowElements()`:

```
private void ShowElements()
{
}
```

It will be used privately inside the class to show or hide the different components, depending on the state the app is in. This method will also control which markers show information in each step.

8. We will create a `switch` call *inside* `ShowElements()`:

```
switch (state)
{
    case State.Init:
    break;
    case State.Side:
    break;
    case State.Engine:
    break;
    case State.Close:
```

```
    break;
    case State.Open:
    break;
    case State.Plug:
    break;
}
```

Here, we will tell the method to perform a different action, depending on which state the app is in at the time.

9. Inside the `State.Init` case, add the following:

```
targetSide.gameObject.SetActive(true);
targetOpen.gameObject.SetActive(false);
targetClose.gameObject.SetActive(false);

mainMessage.SetActive(true);
bottomMessage.SetActive(false);
fileButton.SetActive(false);
okButton.SetActive(false);

mainMessage.GetComponentInChildren<Text>().text = "Point with the
camera at the side of the car to start the maintenance process.";
```

Here, we are only showing the `targetSide` target. To ensure the user will not be able to see the instructions for the other two, we activate only the main message and add the text to it.

10. Inside the `State.Side` case, add the following:

```
mainMessage.SetActive(false);
bottomMessage.SetActive(true);

bottomMessage.GetComponentInChildren<Text>().text = "Touch the red
components to see instructions.";
```

When the user has found the `targetSide` with the camera, we enter this state, where we deactivate the main message and show the bottom message.

11. Inside the `State.Engine` case, add the following:

```
targetClose.gameObject.SetActive(true);

mainMessage.SetActive(true);
bottomMessage.SetActive(false);

mainMessage.GetComponentInChildren<Text>().text = "One of the spark
plugs is broken. Point at the trunk and follow the steps.";
```

If the user has touched the red component, we activate the next target and show the main message with instructions on how to find it.

12. Inside the `State.Close` case, add the following:

```
targetSide.gameObject.SetActive(false);
targetOpen.gameObject.SetActive(true);

mainMessage.SetActive(false);
bottomMessage.SetActive(true);

bottomMessage.GetComponentInChildren<Text>().text = "Open the trunk
to access the engine.";
```

The user has found `targetClose` so we deactivate the previous one and activate the next one. We also add a bottom message to open the trunk.

13. Inside the `State.Open` case, add the following:

```
targetClose.gameObject.SetActive(false);

fileButton.SetActive(true);
okButton.SetActive(true);

bottomMessage.GetComponentInChildren<Text>().text = "Take the spark
plug out and replace it. When you finish press 'Done'";
```

Here, we activate the two buttons: `fileButton` to see the PDF, and `okButton` to finish the process.

14. Inside the `State.Plug` case, add the following:

```
targetOpen.gameObject.SetActive(false);

mainMessage.SetActive(true);
bottomMessage.SetActive(false);
fileButton.SetActive(false);
```

```
okButton.SetActive(false);

mainMessage.GetComponentInChildren<Text>().text = "Well done, you
can take a coffee now :)";
```

This is the final step, so we will hide the buttons and targets and only leave the end message visible.

15. Now, create another method called `NextStep()`:

```
private void NextStep()
{
    state++;
    ShowElements();
}
```

We will call this method to change from one step to the next one.

16. Add another method called `ResetInstructions()`:

```
public void ResetInstructions()
{
    state = 0;
    ShowElements();
}
```

This method is `public` because it will be called from the editor by the **Home** button. It will go to the initial state of the app.

17. Now, let's modify the `Start()` method to convert it into a `coroutine` that waits until Vuforia is initialized before hiding the second and third targets with `ShowElements()`. Otherwise, it might not recognize them:

```
IEnumerator Start()
{
    while (!VuforiaARController.Instance.HasStarted) //waits until
Vuforia has instanciated the three markers
        yield return null;
    state = State.Init;
    ShowElements();
}
```

18. Finally, inside the `Update()` method, enter the logic to change from one step to the next one. Thus, the app will jump from one step to the next when the following happens:

   - In the `Init`, `Engine`, and `Close` states, the app detects the corresponding target (side, close, open)
   - In the `Side` state, the user touches the screen over the engine area of the car
   - In the `Open` state, the user has touched the **Done** button:

```
if ((state == State.Init && targetSide.found) || (state ==
State.Engine && targetClose.found) || (state == State.Close &&
targetOpen.found))
{
    NextStep();
}
else if (state == State.Side)
{
    if (Input.GetMouseButtonDown(0))
    {
        RaycastHit hit;
        Ray ray =
Camera.main.ScreenPointToRay(Input.mousePosition);
        if (Physics.Raycast(ray, out hit))
            if (hit.transform.name == "Engine")
                NextStep();
    }
}
else if (state == State.Open && Finished)
{
    Finished = false;
    NextStep();
}
```

Once we have finished with the script, go back to Unity:

1. Drag the script from the **Project** window to the **ARCamera** game object in the **Hierarchy** window. Alternatively, click on the **ARCamera** and in the **Inspector** window, click **Add Component** and select the script. Fill in each of the fields in the **Main Handler** script with the elements from our scene:

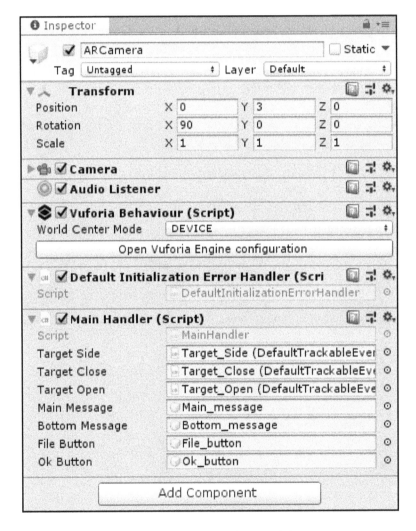

Main Handler with its fields in the ARCamera GameObject

2. Select the **Home_button**. Then, in the **Inspector** window, in the **On Click ()** panel, add a new event, select the **ARCamera,** and then select the **ResetInstructions()** method:

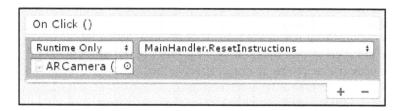

On Click () event in the Home_button

3. Select the **OK_button**. Then, in the **Inspector** window, in the **On Click ()** panel, add a new event, select the **ARCamera,** and then the **Finished** property. Mark the checkbox so that whenever the button is pressed, the **Finished** property will be set to **true**:

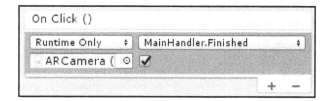

On Click () event in the OK_button

Now that we have the main functionalities ready, let's configure the scene so that we can build it in the glasses.

Configuring the AR for glasses

This step is an important one so that we understand how the glasses work.

If, at this point, we compile the app in the Moverio glasses, we will see the video feed over the glasses screens, as if we were using a phone. This is not the best way of working with AR; what we want is for the background to remain transparent and only the UI elements and AR elements appear over the screens.

However, to see the effect and some characteristics of the AR in the glasses, we are going to compile the app and then make the relevant modifications.

Turn on the Moverio glasses and connect them to your computer via USB.

As you have already defined the settings, switched the platform to Android, and added the current scene to the building list in the introduction, just click *Ctrl + B* or click on **File**|**Build And Run** (if you skipped any of these steps, or if you are not sure, go to **File**|**Build Settings...** and check if everything is correct). Give the .apk file a name and build it.

As we've discussed, you will see the video feed on your glasses, and the UI will be larger than expected. For now, forget about the UI and take a look at the video feed. If you compare the video feed to the real-world image behind it, you will see that the video feed is smaller and slightly displaced compared to the real world (take into account that the camera is placed on one side of the glasses). The following image shows this displacement (take into account the picture is taken only from the left screen of the glasses, so the displacement is even greater than when the left- and right-hand sides are combined):

The AR view from the glasses

We have to take this into account because when we take the video feed out, the AR elements will look smaller and displaced on the targets.

So, first of all, let's take the video feedback. This is a very easy step in Vuforia as in the latest versions, they have taken it out from the code and placed it as a checkbox in the Vuforia Engine configuration. Follow these steps to do so:

1. Select the **ARCamera** and in the **Inspector** window, click on **Open Vuforia Engine configuration**.
2. In the **Video Background** component, uncheck **Enable video background**:

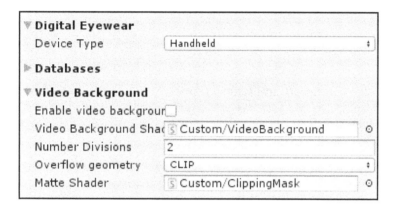

Disabling the video feed in the Vuforia Engine configuration

3. And that's it! Build the app again by pressing *Ctrl + B* and you will see how the video doesn't appear this time and that when you point at the side target with the glasses, only the AR element is shown. You will also see how, without the video feed, the UI will be of the correct size.

Before the **Video Background** component, there is also a **Digital Eyewear** component. In the beginning, when Vuforia first enabled the AR glasses, the configuration of the scene went through this component. However, now, it is only valuable for HoloLens users to select the configuration for those glasses.

4. Finally, let's make the AR elements match the real elements that can be seen through the glasses. Unfortunately, at the moment, there is not an exact method to do this. Therefore, we will take the displacement and size parameters out by trial and error and apply them to the rest of the elements. For this project, those values are as follows:

   - Displacement: +0.5f in the x axis
   - Scale: *2.5 in all axes

Instead of applying them one by one, create a new script called `GlassesHandler.cs` in your `@MyAssets/Scripts` folder and open it in Visual Studio. Add the following lines *inside* the `Start()` method:

```
foreach (Transform child in transform)
{
   Vector3 scale = child.localScale;
    scale *= 2.5f;
    child.localScale = scale;
    Vector3 position = child.position;
    position += new Vector3(0.5f, 0, 0);
    child.position = position;
}
```

Position, rotation, and scale parameters can't be added directly; an intermediate variable has to be used instead.

Your code should look like this:

GlassesHandler script in Visual Studio

5. Drag this script to the three targets or add it by selecting each target, pressing **Add Component** in the **Inspector** window, and selecting the script.

6. Press *Ctrl + B* to build your app and see how the elements now appear over the real elements.

To finish our app, we will add the PDF functionality to help the operator with their work.

Adding the PDF file

PDF files are a slightly difficult task; since Unity doesn't open them internally, an external application must be used. In this section, we are going to learn about a simple call that we can use for opening the PDF files but that can also be used for other types of extensions (such as videos) and opening server files through a URL.

 Important! First, you must install an app in the glasses that can open PDF files, such as Adobe Reader. Please head to the Moverio website to learn where to find and how to install these kinds of applications.

As you may remember, we have not placed the video and PDF files inside the `@MyAssets` folder but in the `StreamingAssets/PDF` folder. This folder is a special folder inside Unity, and all the files in it are copied verbatim to the destination device, meaning they are not processed by Unity at all. We can't load them directly from this path, so we will copy them to an accessible path first.

Go to Visual Studio and in the `MainHandler.cs` script, let's add some code to handle these files. Follow these steps to do so:

1. Add the `System.IO` library:

   ```
   using System.IO;
   ```

2. Add the following variables at the beginning to indicate the paths of the PDF file inside the device:

   ```
   private string originalPath;
   private string savePath;
   ```

3. Initialize them *inside* the `Start()` method:

   ```
   originalPath = Application.streamingAssetsPath +
   "/PDF/WorkOrder_0021.pdf";
   savePath = Application.persistentDataPath + "/WorkOrder_0021.pdf";
   ```

4. Add the following `coroutine`, which copies the PDF file from the `StreamingAssets` location to an accessible path and opens it:

```
private IEnumerator OpenFileCoroutine()
{
    WWW www = new WWW(originalPath);
    yield return www;
    if (www.error != null)
        Debug.Log("Error loading: " + www.error);
    else
    {
        byte[] bytes = www.bytes;
        File.WriteAllBytes(savePath, bytes);
        Application.OpenURL(savePath);
    }
}
```

5. Finally, add the following `public` method to open the PDF file:

```
public void OpenPDFFile()
{
    if (File.Exists(savePath))
        Application.OpenURL(savePath);
    else
        StartCoroutine(OpenFileCoroutine());
}
```

If the file already exists in an accessible location, it opens it. Otherwise, it copies first and opens it from the coroutine.

`Application.OpenURL()` opens the given path, regardless of whether it's a URL or an internal path.

Back in Unity editor, select the **File_button**, and in the **Inspector** window, add the **OpenPDFfile()** call to its **On Click ()** event:

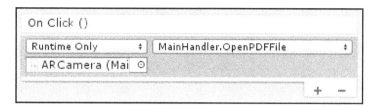

On Click () event in the File_button

Press *Ctrl* + *B* one last time to see the full app in the glasses.

Summary

In this chapter, you have learned about another of Vuforia's features, `ImageTargets`, and how to create your own image target and add virtual content to it. You have also learned about how to work with the Unity interface and scripts in order to create messages and buttons, as well as sequenced instructions.

With all this, you have acquired the skills you need to use Vuforia to create an industrial AR guide that can be implemented in mounting, maintenance, or training processes. You have also learned how to customize a step with extra PDF or even video and data files that have been taken either locally (like in this project) or from a remote server by using the OpenURL method with a URL inside it.

Now, you can use this knowledge to create your own guide for your processes and use the current project as a template for it. You can also improve and extend it by using real-life pictures, linking some of the steps to your instruction PDF files or triggering the change from one step to another using signals or information coming from your servers.

As you have seen, the project is also easily deployed in mobile devices, and from here, you can try to migrate it to other types of glasses and see the results. You have also acquired the skills to try the rest of the Vuforia examples, which can be found in the Unity Asset Store, which has been published by PTC: `https://assetstore.unity.com/publishers/24484`.

In the next chapter, we will completely change the scope and learn how to create an AR portal to transport the user into a virtual 3D world with ARKit for the tourism sector.

8
AR for Tourism with ARKit

In this chapter, we will explore ARKit, Apple's own AR SDK, which offers many features such as spatial tracking, image tracking, collaborative AR, and more. We will also learn how to exploit world tracking in order to create a different AR experience for the tourism sector.

The main goals of this chapter are to introduce you to ARKit and how it works by searching and tracking flat surfaces in the real world. Then, you will learn how to use these features to place elements in AR and anchor them in order to create a dimensional portal that will introduce the user to a 3D world. The second goal of this chapter is to present a different way of viewing tourism. You will learn how to take advantage of AR to create unique experiences that can be implemented in museums, landscapes, points of interest, and so on. By doing this, you will be able to modify and apply this project to your own interests.

In this chapter, we will cover the following topics:

- Using AR for tourism
- Exploring ARKit
- Developing an ARKit app
- Creating an AR portal

Technical requirements

The technical requirements for this chapter are as follows:

- A Mac computer with macOS Sierra 10.12.4 or above (we used a Mac mini, Intel Core i5, 4 GB memory, with macOS Mojave in this book)
- The latest version of Xcode (10.3 in this book)
- An ARKit-compatible iPhone/iPad with iOS 11+ (we tested the project on an iPad Pro 10.5 with iOS 13.1.1)

The code files and resources for this chapter can be found here: `https://github.com/PacktPublishing/Enterprise-Augmented-Reality-Projects/tree/master/Chapter08`

You can view the compatible devices at `https://developer.apple.com/library/archive/documentation/DeviceInformation/Reference/iOSDeviceCompatibility/DeviceCompatibilityMatrix/DeviceCompatibilityMatrix.html`

When we explore ARKit, we will explain the device requirements you'll need, depending on the ARKit features that you want to use, since not all devices can use them.

Finally, take into account that this chapter is dedicated to iOS devices. Therefore, you will need an Apple account (free or developer account) to compile the project on your iOS device. You can find more information here: `https://developer.apple.com/support/compare-memberships/`

Using AR for tourism

AR is mainly a visual technology. Although it can combine other effects such as sounds to make the experience more realistic or vibrations on the phone when we are playing a game, its main attraction is the visual content it displays over the real world. That makes this technology perfect for enhancing traveling experiences, from showing skyline information to making animals in a museum come to life or even translating signs and guides in real time.

Back in the late 2000s/early 2010s, when smartphones started to become popular, some of the first AR apps that appeared were tourism-oriented. In 2010, for example, the Museum of London released an iPhone app that showed historical photos of the city over the real places. This example has also been carried to other cities and scopes, such as in Navarra, Spain, where users can replay scenes of famous films shot in different locations of the region in AR by pointing their mobile devices to the panels that had been placed in said locations. In this case, the mobile devices use image recognition (the panel) to launch the AR experience. However, back in the early 2010s, the most stable and widespread AR technology was location-based and used a device's GPS, accelerometer, and compass. AR engines and apps such as Layar and Wikitude were mostly used as they allowed developers to generate routes, gymkhanas, and even games based on **points of interest (POIs)** across cities.

Nowadays, some of the most common uses of AR in tourism are as follows:

- To serve as a live guide in the streets of a new city, where a user can go around the city while the AR app is showing them where the most interesting points to see are through the use of arrows.

- To show attractions and POIs over a map. Here, when a user points at a map with the camera, the POIs pop up from it and they can interact with them to find out more.
- To provide extra information about paintings, sculptures, or monuments. Here, when a user points at a painting, it can show a video about the artist and the place and time where it was painted, or even make it come to life as a 3D simulation.

Apart from all these experiences, when AR is combined with other immersive technologies such as virtual worlds or 360º videos, the experience goes one step ahead, allowing users to visit several places at the same time (for example, in a museum network, while visiting one of them, to be able to virtually visit the others).

In this chapter, we will learn about how to mix these experiences using Apple's ARKit SDK to create an art experience. We will create an AR portal, and when users go through it, they will land on a painting represented in 3D. In our case, we will use a painting from Van Gogh (Bedroom in Arles) that's been downloaded from Sketchfab to give the users the illusion of being inside a 3D Van Gogh painting: `https://sketchfab.com/3d-models/van-gogh-room-311d052a9f034ba8bce55a1a8296b6f9`.

To implement this, we will create an app oriented to the tourism field that can be displayed in museums, galleries, and more. Regarding the tool we are going to use, in the next section, we will explain how ARKit works and its main features.

Exploring ARKit

Apple launched the first version of ARKit in 2017 along with Xcode 9 and iOS 11 to bring AR to iOS devices. The framework, which is included in Xcode, offered developers the possibility to produce AR experiences in their apps or games with software that's combined with an iOS device's motion features and camera tracking. It allows users to place virtual content in the real world. Months after its official release, it added new features such as 2D image detection and face detection. The main features that are available for iOS 11 and above are as follows:

- Tracking and visualizing planes (iOS 11.3+), such as a table or the ground, in the physical environment
- Tracking known 2D images (iOS 11.3+) in the real world and placing AR content over them (image recognition)

- Tracking faces (iOS 11.0+) in the camera feed and laying virtual content over them (for example, a virtual avatar face) that react to facial expressions in real-time

Apart from these features, the AR experience can also be enhanced by using sound effects attached to virtual objects or integrating other frameworks such as vision to add computer vision algorithms to the app, or Core ML, for machine learning models.

In 2018, with the iOS 12 release, ARKit 2 was launched with new features:

- 3D object tracking, where real-world objects are the ones that trigger the AR elements
- Multiuser AR experiences, allowing users near each other to share the same AR environment
- Adding realistic reflections to the AR objects to make the experience more realistic
- Saving the world-mapping data so that when a user places a virtual element in the real world, the next time the app restarts, the virtual elements will appear in the same place

At the time of writing this book, iOS 13 with ARKit 3 has just been launched and promises a huge improvement to the current state since it's added a new way of interacting with virtual elements, such as hiding virtual objects when a person is detected in front of them. It also allows users to interact with 3D objects by gestures and captures not only facial expressions but the motions of a person.

Because of the changes that are made in each iOS launch, not all the features that we mentioned here are available on all devices. The developers' page at `https://developer.apple.com/documentation/arkit` enumerates the current ARKit features and required minimum Xcode and iOS versions to develop and test with.

For this project, we will be using plane detection, which is a basic feature that can be run on iOS 11 and above. We will look at this in the next section.

Developing an ARKit app

To start developing an app with ARKit, make sure you have the required hardware we discussed in the *Technical requirements* section, including an iOS device, since it's necessary to run the app.

You will also need an Apple account to build your project on a real device. If you don't have a paid account, you can also sign in with your regular free Apple ID. The current limits when using a free account are as follows: up to three installed apps on your device at the same time and the ability to create up to 10 different apps every seven days.

In this section, we will create an AR project using Xcode's template and go through its main components. Then, we will modify the basic app to visualize the detected surfaces and display important messages to users.

Creating a new AR project

Let's create a new AR application using ARKit. We will start by creating the project in Xcode, the developer toolset for macOS that we can download freely from the Mac App Store, by following these steps:

1. Create a new project, select **Augmented Reality App**, and click **Next**. This will give us the basic frame so that we can start working with AR:

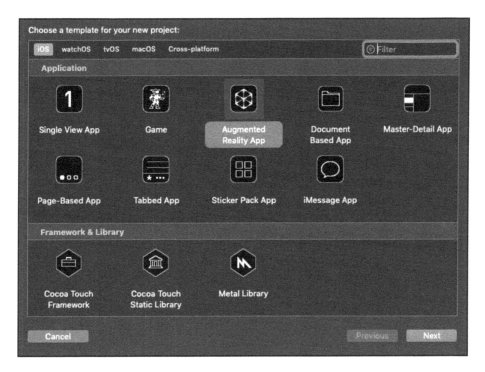

Selecting the Augmented Reality App template

2. Fill in the **Product Name**, **Team** (here, you have to enter your Apple ID, and although you can leave it as **None** (as shown in the following screenshot), you will have to fill it in later to deploy the project onto the device), and **Organization Name**:

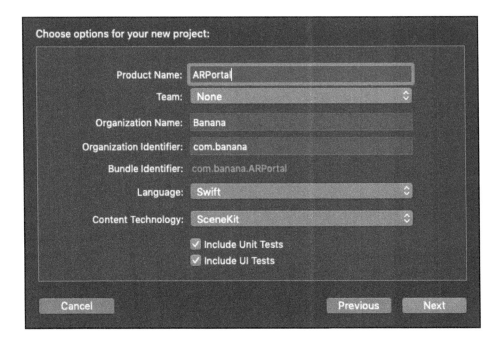

Filling in the main values of our project

3. Press **Next**, select a location for the project, and press **Create.**

4. If you didn't enter your developer ID in *step 2*, the project's general window for the **Signing** tab will show an error that will prevent the app from building on a device, as shown in the following screenshot. Fix it now to be able to run the app:

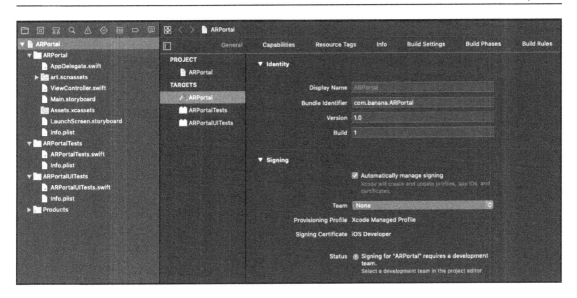

The signing tab of the project shows an error when a team hasn't been selected

5. We already have an AR app ready to be executed. To test it, connect your device and select it from the top-left corner of the window, as shown in the following screenshot:

Selecting the device to run the app

6. Run the app by clicking on the play button in the top-left corner of the window (see the preceding screenshot). The first time you launch it, it will ask for the camera's permission, and as soon as the camera feed appears, it will anchor a spaceship to the middle of your environment:

The ship appears anchored to the real environment

7. Since ARKit will be tracking your environment, try to move around the ship and get close to it or look at it from different angles, as shown in the following screenshot:

Now, let's take a look at the main parts that form this project, that is, `Main.storyboard`, where the UI elements are, and `ViewController.swift`, where the logic of the app resides.

Main.storyboard

Open the `Main.storyboard` file by clicking on it. This file contains the UI elements. At the moment, it only contains an **ARSCNView**, which occupies the whole screen.

If you right-click on the scene view, you will see the **Referencing Outlets** that are linked to the **View Controller** with the **sceneView** variable, as shown in the following screenshot:

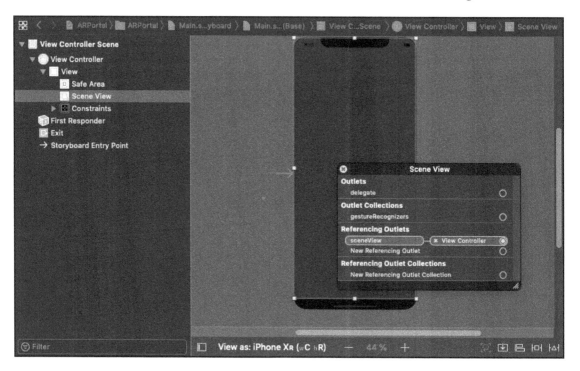

The UI element ScenView and its Referencing Outlets

Let's take a closer look at the view controller element.

ViewController.swift

Now, click on `ViewController.swift`, which is where the main logic of our application lies.

The first thing you will see is that the class requires the `ARKit` library for the AR, the `UIKit` library for the interface, and the `SceneKit` library. This last one is a high-level 3D framework that Apple offers so that you can create, import, and manipulate 3D objects and scenes. We will be using it later in this chapter to import our external 3D models into the scene.

Our only variable at the moment is as follows:

```
@IBOUtlet var sceneView: ARSCNView!
```

This is the `ARSCNView` element from `Main.storyboard`. It will allow us to control the AR scene.

Our `ViewController` class inherits from `UIViewController`. From here, we have three `override` methods. The first one is `viewDidLoad`:

```
override func viewDidLoad() {
    super.viewDidLoad()

    sceneView.delegate = self
    sceneView.showsStatistics = true

    let scene = SCNScene(named: "art.scnassets/ship.scn")!
    sceneView.scene = scene
}
```

This method is called when the view is loaded in memory and is used to initialize elements. In this case, we attach the `sceneView` element's delegate to the class itself, we activate the statistics that will appear at the bottom of the app, we create a scene with the ship model, and we assign that scene to the scene from the `scenView` element. This will make the battleship appear as soon as the app is launched.

The second method is `viewWillAppear`:

```
override func viewWillAppear(_ animated: Bool) {
    super.viewWillAppear(animated)
    let configuration = ARWorldTrackingConfiguration()
    sceneView.session.run(configuration)
}
```

This method is called when the device is ready to show the interface to the user. The AR session is launched from here. The `ARSession` is the main element that controls the AR experience; it reads the data from the sensors of your device, controls the device's camera, and analyzes the image coming from it to create a correspondence between the real world and a virtual space where you place the AR objects.

Before running the session, we need to make use of the `ARConfiguration` class, which will determine the ARKit features that have been enabled for the session. In this case, it will track the device's position and orientation in relation to surfaces, people, images, or objects using the device's back camera and then run the session with that configuration. We could use a different configuration if we wanted to track only people's faces or only images, for example. (See `https://developer.apple.com/documentation/arkit/arconfiguration` for more information.)

The third override method is `viewWillDisappear`:

```
override func viewWillDisappear(_ animated: Bool) {
    super.viewWillDisappear(animated)
    sceneView.session.pause()
}
```

This method is called when the view is about to be removed. When that happens, the view's session is paused.

These are the methods we have implemented at the moment. Now, we are going to start changing and adding code to see how ARKit tracks planes and find out about the different state changes.

Modifying the basic app

Starting from the current code in `ViewController.swift`, we are going to modify it so that it only detects horizontal surfaces (not verticals, faces, or known images) and displays those horizontal surfaces as they are being detected to show extra information about the `ARSession`, such as whenever `ARTracking` is ready or if a new horizontal surface has been detected.

Before we do this, though, we will delete the ship model as we no longer need it. Follow these steps to delete the ship model:

1. Delete the `art.scnassets` folder from the project.
2. In the `viewDidLoad()` method of `ViewController.swift`, delete the reference to the ship from the scene, leaving the `scene` line like so:

```
let scene = SCNScene()
```

We are also going to enable an AR debug option that will let us see the feature points of our environment. As we have seen already in this book, feature points are unique points of an image that make it possible for that image to be identified and tracked. The more features we have, the more stable the tracking will be. We will activate this option for now so that we can see how well our environment is detected, and deactivate it for our final app. For that, in the `viewDidLoad()` method, after the `sceneView.showStatistics = true` line, add the following code:

```
sceneView.debugOptions = ARSCNDebugOptions.showFeaturePoints
```

And with this, we can proceed to plane detection.

Detecting and showing horizontal planes

As we mentioned previously, `ARSession` is the main element of the AR app. Another essential element of ARKit is `ARAnchor`, which is the representation of an interesting point in the real world, along with its position and orientation. We can use anchors to place and track virtual elements in the real world that are relative to the camera. When we add those anchors to the session, ARKit optimizes the world-tracking accuracy around that anchor, meaning that we can walk around the virtual objects as if they were placed in the real world.

Apart from adding anchors manually, some ARKit features can automatically add their own special anchors to a session. For example, when we activate the plane detection feature in the `ARConfiguration` class, the `ARPlaneAnchor` elements are created automatically whenever a new plane is detected.

Let's make these plane anchors visible so that we can see how ARKit works. Let's get to it:

1. In the `viewWillAppear` method, *after* the `configuration` definition, add the following code:

```
let configuration = ARWorldTrackingConfiguration()
configuration.planeDetection = .horizontal
```

Now, ARKit will only look for horizontal surfaces to track.

2. Uncomment the `renderer` method that's already present in the class:

```
func renderer(_ renderer: SCNSceneRenderer, nodeFor anchor:
ARAnchor) -> SCNNode? {
    let node = SCNNode()
    return node
}
```

This method is called when a new `ARAnchor` is added to the scene. It helps us create a `SceneKit` node called `SCNNode` for that anchor.

3. Now, to paint the planes, *between* the creation of the node and the `return` statement, add the following:

```
guard let planeAnchor = anchor as? ARPlaneAnchor else {return nil}

let plane = SCNPlane(width: CGFloat(planeAnchor.extent.x), height:
CGFloat(planeAnchor.extent.z))
plane.firstMaterial?.diffuse.contents = UIColor.orange
plane.firstMaterial?.transparency = 0.4

let planeNode = SCNNode(geometry: plane)
planeNode.position = SCNVector3(x: planeAnchor.center.x, y:
planeAnchor.center.y, z: planeAnchor.center.z)
planeNode.eulerAngles.x = -Float.pi/2

node.addChildNode(planeNode)
```

Here, if our anchor is an `ARPlaneAnchor`, we create a new semi-transparent orange plane that's the same size as the `planeAnchor`. Then, we create a `SCNNode` with that plane and add it to the empty node that was already created. Finally, we return this parent node so that it's related to our current anchor and displayed in the scene.

Instead of this method, we could also implement another method from `ARSCNViewDelegate`: func renderer(_ renderer: SCNSceneRenderer, didAdd node: SCNNode, for anchor: ARAnchor){}. Here, the empty node has already been created, so we would only have to add the same preceding code extract.

4. If you test the app now, you will see how it paints orange planes whenever it detects a flat surface. However, you will see that once a plane is painted, even if ARKit detects more points around it, the plane's size is not updated, as shown in the following screenshot:

ARKit detecting a flat surface and placing a plane

Let's add some more code to make the displayed plane change its size and position when more points are detected.

5. At the beginning of the class, after `sceneView`, create an array to save all the planes in the scene and their respective anchors:

```
var planes = [ARPlaneAnchor: SCNPlane]()
```

6. Now, in the `renderer` method, *after* creating the plane, and *before* the `return` statement, add the following code:

```
planes[planeAnchor] = plane
```

This will save our plane node and anchor for later.

7. Let's add a new method:

```
func renderer(_ renderer: SCNSceneRenderer, didUpdate node:
SCNNode, for anchor: ARAnchor)
{
    guard let planeAnchor = anchor as? ARPlaneAnchor else {return}

    if let plane = planes[planeAnchor]
    {
        plane.width = CGFloat(planeAnchor.extent.x)
        plane.height = CGFloat(planeAnchor.extent.z)

        node.childNodes.first?.position =
SCNVector3(planeAnchor.center.x, planeAnchor.center.y,
planeAnchor.center.z)
    }
}
```

This method is called when the anchor is updated. First, we check that the anchor is an `ARPlaneAnchor`. Then, we take the plane that corresponds to that anchor from the array and change its `width` and `height`. Finally, we update the `position` of the `child` node (remember that we added our plane node to an empty node; we want to update our plane's position, not the empty node's position).

8. Run the app to see how the more you move the device around, the bigger the planes will become:

The detected plane becomes bigger as ARKit detects more of its points

In this section, we have learned how plane anchors are created and how to visualize them.

When testing the app, you may have noticed that the device needs a little time before it starts showing the plane anchors. That's the time when ARKit is initializing. In the next section, we are going to create a track for the ARKit state changes so that the user knows when the app is ready.

Adding ARSessionDelegate to track state changes

In our class, we already have three methods that can be used to notify session changes to the user when the session fails or is interrupted. We are also going to add two new methods, that is, for when an anchor is added to the session and when the camera changes its tracking state. But before we do any of this, we need to create a label in our UI to display all the messages.

Adding a label UI element

Let's add a new UI element, that is, a label, to show notifications to users. For that, follow these steps:

1. Open `Main.storyboard` and open the library button located in the top-right corner of the screen (the first button of its set, with a square inside a circle):

Library button

2. Find and drag a **Label** onto the view:

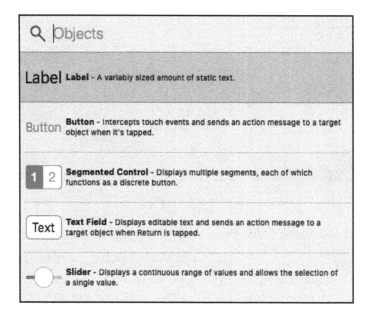

Selecting the Label from the library

3. With the label selected, use *Ctrl* + mouse drag to create constraints for the label regarding the view, or in the toolbar *below* the phone view, click on the **Add New Constraints** button. Constraints help us fix the elements on the screen so that they appear properly on any device screen and in any orientation.

4. Then, modify the values of the left, right, and bottom constraints to 20, 20, and 0, respectively (the icon of the constraint will turn a bright red). Check the **Height** constraint box and set it to 60, as follows:

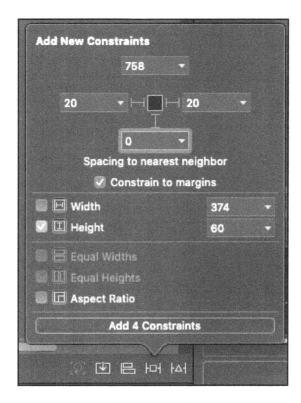

Adding constraints to the label

5. The new constraints will appear on the right-hand side window, under the Show the Size **Inspector** tab, as follows:

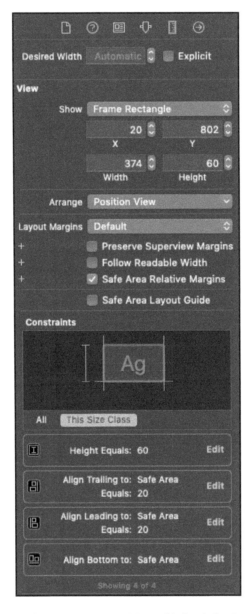

The four new constraints added at the bottom of the Show the Size tab

6. In the Show the Attributes **Inspector** tab, *delete* the default **Text**, set the label **Color** to *green*, check the **Dynamic Type** checkbox, and set the **Alignment** of the text to centered, as follows:

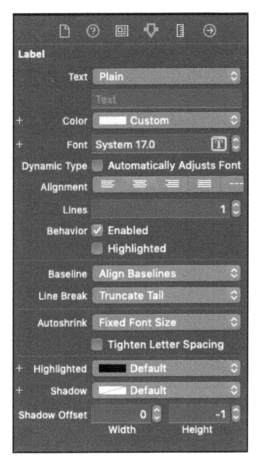

Changing the properties of the label

7. To connect the label to our `ViewController.swift` script and use it in our methods, click on the Show the Assistant Editor button in the top-right corner (two circles intersecting) to open the script:

Selecting the Assistant Editor

8. Press *Ctrl* + drag the label (you will see a blue line as you drag the mouse) from the hierarchical view to the code, below the `sceneView` variable. Release the mouse. Then, on the pop-up window shown in the following screenshot, enter the **Name** of the variable, which will be `infoLabel` in this case, and click **Connect**:

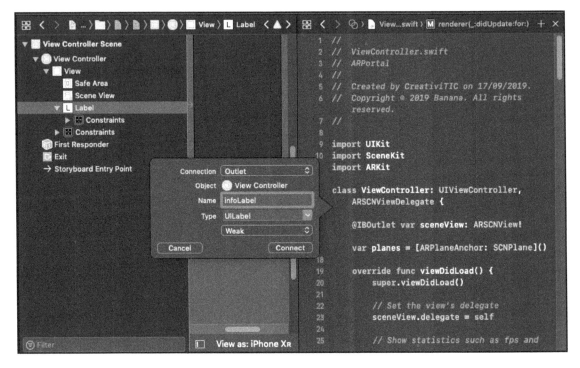

The label from the UI will be attached to the infoLabel variable

9. Open the `ViewController.swift` file to check that the new variable has been added correctly, as follows:

```
@IBOutlet weak var infoLabel: UILabel!
```

Now, we can start sending messages to the user through the interface.

Sending notifications to the user

Now that we have our label to display messages to the user, let's use the `session` methods we already have in our `ViewController` class and create new ones to display useful information, as shown in the following steps:

1. In the `ViewController.swift` file, within the `didFailWithError` session, add a new message:

```
func session(_ session: ARSession, didFailWithError error: Error) {
    infoLabel.text = "Session failed :
\(error.localizedDescription)."
}
```

This message will appear when there is an error in the `ARSession`.

2. In the `sessionWasInterrupted` method, add the following message:

```
func sessionWasInterrupted(_ session: ARSession) {
    infoLabel.text = "Session was interrupted."
}
```

This will be executed when the session is interrupted; for example, when the app is minimized.

3. In the `sessioInterruptionEnded` method, add the following message and code:

```
func sessionInterruptionEnded(_ session: ARSession) {
    infoLabel.text = "Session interruption ended."
    let configuration = ARWorldTrackingConfiguration()
    configuration.planeDetection = .horizontal
    sceneView.session.run(configuration, options: [.resetTracking,
.removeExistingAnchors])
}
```

When the session interruption finishes, we have to reset the tracking. For that, we will create the configuration parameter again and run the session by removing the previously existing anchors.

4. Now, let's create a new method that will detect whenever the tracking state has changed:

```
func session(_ session: ARSession, cameraDidChangeTrackingState
camera: ARCamera) {
    let message: String
    switch camera.trackingState {
```

```
        case .normal where session.currentFrame!.anchors.isEmpty:
            message = "Move the device around to detect horizontal
surfaces."
        case .notAvailable:
            message = "Tracking unavailable."
        case .limited(.excessiveMotion):
            message = "Tracking limited - Move the device more
slowly."
        case .limited(.insufficientFeatures):
            message = "Tracking limited - Point the device at an area
with visible surface detail, or improve lighting conditions."
        case .limited(.initializing):
            message = "Initializing AR session."
        default:
            message = ""
        }
        infoLabel.text = message
    }
```

Your Xcode window will look like the following screenshot:

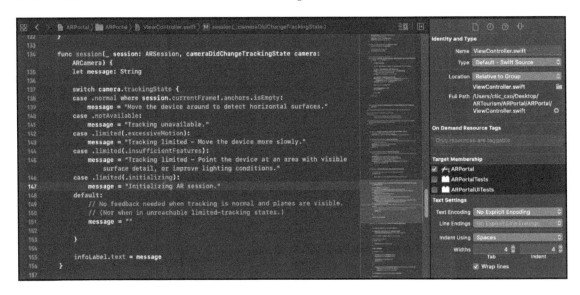

The new method in ViewController

This method checks the tracking state and displays messages when the session is initializing or there are problems. We also display a message when the tracking state is normal, but we haven't found a plane anchor yet, so the user keeps looking around.

5. Now, we have to notify the user when an anchor has been added so that they don't have to look around anymore. For that, we are going to use `ARSessionDelegateProtocol`. The first thing we will do is add the delegate to the class, as shown in the following code:

```
class ViewController: UIViewController, ARSCNViewDelegate,
ARSessionDelegate {
```

The class declaration will look as follows:

```
13  class ViewController: UIViewController, ARSCNViewDelegate, ARSessionDelegate {
14
O       @IBOutlet var sceneView: ARSCNView!
O       @IBOutlet weak var infoLabel: UILabel!
```

The ViewController class with the added delegate

6. In the `viewWillAppear` method, just after the `sceneView.session.run(configuration)` line, add the following code:

```
sceneView.session.delegate = self
```

With this line, we assign the delegate to the class. The `viewWillAppear` method will now look as follows:

```
41      override func viewWillAppear(_ animated: Bool) {
42          super.viewWillAppear(animated)
43
44          // Create a session configuration
45          let configuration = ARWorldTrackingConfiguration()
46          configuration.planeDetection = .horizontal
47          // Run the view's session
48          sceneView.session.run(configuration)
49          sceneView.session.delegate = self
50      }
```

The viewWillAppear method

7. Now, create the new method to show the message when an anchor has been added:

```
func session(_ session: ARSession, didAdd anchors: [ARAnchor])
{
    infoLabel.text= "New anchor added."
}
```

8. Run the app to see how the label changes according to the state of the camera, as follows:

The label notifying the user that the AR session is initializing

After the AR has been initialized, the label changes to detecting the **horizontal surfaces** message, as shown in the following screenshot:

The label asking the user to move the device to detect horizontal surfaces

 The debugging messages of the `cameraDidChangeTrackingState` session method come from the *Tracking and Visualizing Planes* example, which is available at `https://developer.apple.com/documentation/arkit/tracking_and_visualizing_planes`. This example project uses more methods to show planes and messages that we won't need for this project. You can download and test it if you want to learn about them.

Now that we have our app's base, let's create an AR portal where we will display a *door* to a virtual 3D painting. Once we physically go through that door, we will find ourselves immersed in that virtual painting.

Creating an AR portal

Currently, we have an app that detects horizontal planes and notifies us about the state of the tracking system. Now, we want to create an AR experience where users will tap on the screen to create a portal and, when going through it, see themselves inside a 3D representation of Van Gogh's *Bedroom in Arles* painting. The following diagram depicts the scene in SceneKit's coordinate system:

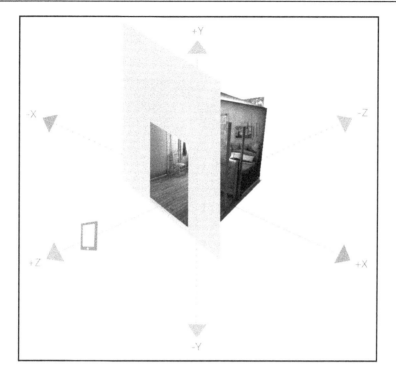

The scene in the XYZ coordinates

From the user's perspective, we will have a portal with a hole in it, as shown in the previous diagram. The hole will let us see the model in the background, that is, the 3D painting. The portal will not be gray; it will be transparent so that we can see the camera feed instead of the whole 3D painting scene that hides behind it. In this section, we will learn how to make this possible.

For that, we need to add the 3D model, create the screen-tapping functionality, and create the actual portal, which only shows part of the painting from the outside.

 From this point on, you can specify whether you want the **showFeaturePoints** option and the two `renderer` methods showing the planes. We will leave them until the end of the project because it's best if we understand how ARKit works first.

In the following subsections, we will do the following:

- Import a 3D model into our project and scene
- Add the user interaction so that when a user touches the screen, the 3D model will appear over the touched anchor plane

- Add the walls to the portal to make the model invisible from the outside, except for the door
- Improve the app by adding textures to the walls and a compass image to help users find out where the portal will appear

Now, let's start by adding the 3D model we want to show.

Importing the 3D model

SceneKit's preferred 3D model type is Collada (`.dae` files). However, it can also read OBJ (`.obj`) files, and in this case, the downloaded model is in the latter format. We have slightly modified it using a 3D modeling program and put the pivot point on the floor, in the nearest edge away from us. This way, when we place it in the real world, we will see the model in front of us, instead of surrounding us. If you try this with another model or you don't know how to modify a pivot point, you can adjust the transform's position directly in the code (we will explain how later).

Adding the model to the project

To import the model and show it in our scene, download it from the resources of this project and follow these steps:

1. Right-click on the project and select **New Group**, as shown in the following screenshot. Call it `Models`:

Creating a New Group to contain our model

2. Right-click on the `Models` folder and select **Add Files to "ARPortal"...**, as follows:

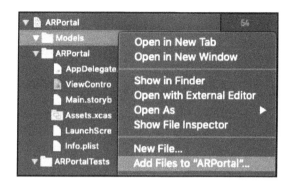

Adding files to our folder

3. Navigate to the `vangogh_room` folder, which contains the model, material, and textures. Select it, make sure that it's added to our app in **Add to targets**, and click **Add**, as shown in the following screenshot:

Selecting the folder and adding it to the target app

4. If you unfold the `vangogh_room` folder, you will see all the files inside it. Click on the `vangogh_room.obj` file to visualize the 3D model on the screen. When we create the portal, we will enter the model from the open wall, as shown in the following screenshot:

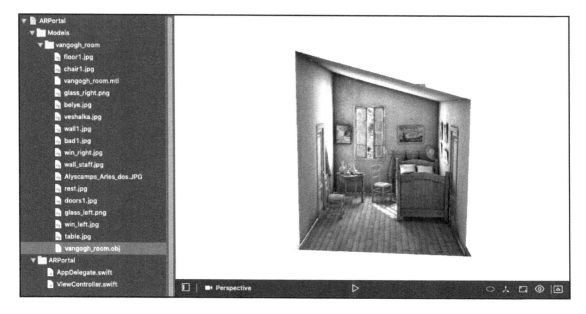

The .obj file displayed in 3D

Now, we can use our model in our code.

Adding the model to our scene

Now that we have imported the model into our project, let's add it to our scene using code, as follows:

1. Create a new file by right-clicking on the `ARPortal` folder and selecting **New File...**, as follows:

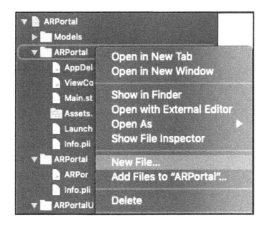

Creating a new file

2. Select **Swift File** and click **Next**:

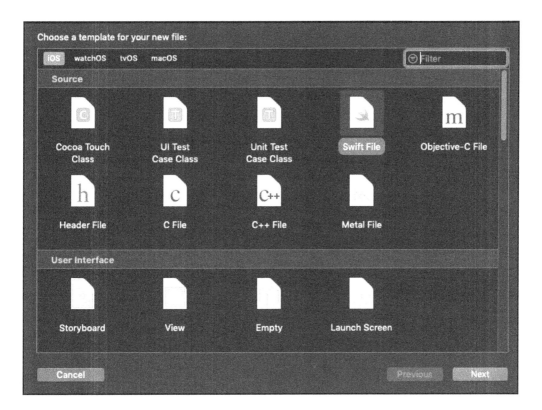

Selecting Swift File

3. Call it `Portal.swift` and click **Create**. This will be the class where we will create our full portal, including the 3D model we imported previously.

4. Delete the code and add the `ARKit` library:

```
import ARKit
```

5. Create a `class`:

```
class Portal: SCNNode {
}
```

Our portal will be of the `SCNNode` type.

6. Now, inside the class, we'll create a new method to load the 3D model. Add the following code:

```
func add3DModel() {
    let modelScene = SCNScene(named: "vangogh_room.obj")!
    let modelNode: SCNNode = modelScene.rootNode.childNodes[0]
    self.addChildNode(modelNode)
}
```

Here, we load the scene from the `.obj` file and take the node out of it. Then, we attach the node as a child of our portal.

 If you use another model and it doesn't appear where you want it to be (displaced in one or more axes), you can adjust its position inside this method by adding the following before the `self.addChildNode(modelNode)` line: `modelNode.position = SCNVector3(x: YourValue, y: YourValue, z: YourValue)`. You can check how coordinates work in SceneKit by looking at the diagram at the beginning of this section.

7. Now, `override` the `init` method, as follows:

```
override init() {
    super.init()
    add3DModel()
}

required init?(coder aDecoder: NSCoder) {
    fatalError("init(coder:) has not been implemented")
}
```

In the first method, we initialize our portal by adding the 3D model. The second method is required for a subclass of SCNNode.

Now that we have added our 3D model, we want to show it in our scene.

We could just open ViewController.swift and add the following at the end of the viewDidLoad() method, as follows:

```
portal = Portal()
self.sceneView.scene.rootNode.addChildNode(portal!)
```

The viewDidLoad method will now look as follows:

```
21    override func viewDidLoad() {
22        super.viewDidLoad()
23
24        // Set the view's delegate
25        sceneView.delegate = self
26
27        // Show statistics such as fps and timing information
28        sceneView.showsStatistics = true
29        // Uncomment to see the feature points
30        //sceneView.debugOptions = ARSCNDebugOptions.showFeaturePoints
31
32        // Create a new scene
33        let scene = SCNScene()
34
35        // Set the scene to the view
36        sceneView.scene = scene
37        portal = Portal()
38        self.sceneView.scene.rootNode.addChildNode(portal!)
39
40    }
```

The viewDidLoad method with the Portal added

In this case, the 3D model will appear like the ship we saw at the beginning of this chapter, from the start of the session and in the middle of the screen (we would have to translate it downward for a better view). However, we want to add a twist and attach it to one of the plane anchors when the user taps on the screen, so delete those two lines. We'll learn how to do this in the next section.

Including user interaction

Let's add some user interaction to the app. Instead of just making the virtual content appear in the scene from the beginning, we will make it appear when the user taps the screen. For that, follow these steps:

1. In `Main.storyboard`, click on the library button (the square inside a circle button) and look for **Tap Gesture Recognizer**. Drag it onto the view:

Selecting Tap Gesture Recognizer from the library

2. It will appear on the hierarchy, as shown in the following screenshot:

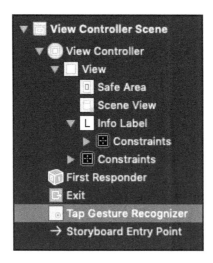

Tap Gesture Recognizer in the View Controller Scene hierarchy

3. Show the Assistant Editor (two circles intersecting button) and open `ViewController.swift` on the right-hand side. *Ctrl* + drag the **Tap Gesture Recognizer** over to the code, as shown in the following screenshot:

Dragging the Tap Gesture Recognizer to the code to create the connection

4. Fill in the box that appears with the following parameters:

- **Connection:** Action
- **Object:** View Controller
- **Name:** didTapOnScreen
- **Type:** UITapGestureRecognizer

5. Open the ViewController.swift file to ensure the method has been created:

```
@IBAction func didTapOnScreen(_ sender: UITapGestureRecognizer){
}
```

6. Now, include the following variable at the beginning of the class, after the planes variable:

```
var portal: SCNNode? = nil
```

We will use this variable to make sure we only have one portal in the view.

7. Modify the text of the session's `didAdd` method to instruct the user to place the portal when an anchor is detected, but no portal has been added yet. For that, modify `infoLabel.text`, as follows:

```
func session(_ session: ARSession, didAdd anchors: [ARAnchor]) {
    if portal == nil
    {
        infoLabel.text = "Tap on the floor to create the portal."
    }
}
```

8. Now, go to the `didTapOnScreen` method and add the following code:

```
let location = sender.location(in: sceneView)
let hitResults = sceneView.hitTest(location, types:
ARHitTestResult.ResultType.existingPlaneUsingExtent)
guard let result = hitResults.first else {return}
if portal != nil {
    portal?.removeFromParentNode()
}
portal = Portal()
portal?.position = SCNVector3(x: result.worldTransform.columns.3.x,
y: result.worldTransform.columns.3.y, z:
result.worldTransform.columns.3.z)
self.sceneView.scene.rootNode.addChildNode(portal!)
infoLabel.text = ""
```

Here, we are taking out the location of the tap and checking whether the tap is hitting an existing plane. (You can check the options for the `ARHitTestResult` here: https://developer.apple.com/documentation/arkit/arhittestresult.) We take the first plane of the hit results. If the portal already exists, we delete it to ensure we only have one portal in view. If the user taps in different places on the screen, the portal will appear to move from one place to the other. Then, we will apply the position from the plane to our portal object. Finally, we will add the portal to our scene and we'll clear the information label as we no longer need to tell our users to tap on the screen. The resulting method will look like this:

```
      @IBAction func didTapOnScreen(_ sender: UITapGestureRecognizer)
167   {
168
169       let location = sender.location(in: sceneView)
170
171       let hitResults = sceneView.hitTest(location, types:
              ARHitTestResult.ResultType.existingPlaneUsingExtent)
172
173       guard let result = hitResults.first else {return}
174
175       //delete previous portal
176       if portal != nil
177       {
178           portal?.removeFromParentNode()
179       }
180
181       portal = Portal()
182       portal?.position = SCNVector3(x: result.worldTransform.columns.3.x, y:
              result.worldTransform.columns.3.y, z: result.worldTransform.columns.3.z)
183
184       self.sceneView.scene.rootNode.addChildNode(portal!)
185
186       infoLabel.text = ""
187   }
```

The didTapOnScreen method

9. In the `sessionWasInterrupted` method, after `infoLabel.text`, we are going to delete the portal so that it doesn't appear when the session is recovered. For that, add the following code:

```
func sessionWasInterrupted(_ session: ARSession) {
    infoLabel.text = "Session was interrupted."
    portal?.removeFromParentNode()
    portal = nil
}
```

The `sessionWasInterrupted` method should look as follows:

```
109       func sessionWasInterrupted(_ session: ARSession) {
110           infoLabel.text = "Session was interrupted."
111           portal?.removeFromParentNode()
112           portal = nil
113       }
```

The sessionWasInterrupted method

10. Run the app and tap the screen to place the 3D model. It will appear over the orange planes, as shown in the following screenshot:

The 3D painting appearing in AR when tapping on the screen

If you enter the model and look back, you will see the real world from the open wall in the 3D model, as shown in the following screenshot:

The opening to the real world from the 3D room

Move around the room and explore the 3D space from different angles. You will see how you are immersed in the virtual environment while the real world is still on the other side.

Now, it's time to actually create a portal that hides most of the model until the *door* is crossed. For that, we are going to create transparent walls and play with the rendering order property.

Adding the walls of the portal

The main trick of an AR portal is based on two things: the transparency and the rendering order. We are going to create a wall with an opening (we will call it the *door*) in the middle, through which we will see the 3D painting. Open the `Portal.swift` file and follow these steps:

1. Create a new method called `createWall` with the following code:

```
func createWall(width: CGFloat, height: CGFloat, length:
CGFloat)->SCNNode {
    let node = SCNNode()
    let wall = SCNBox(width: width, height: height, length: length,
chamferRadius: 0)
    wall.firstMaterial?.diffuse.contents = UIColor.white
    let wallNode = SCNNode(geometry: wall)
    node.addChildNode(wallNode)
    return node
}
```

Here, we created a parent node. Then, we created a box with the given size and set its material to white. We created a node with the box geometry that we attached to the parent node and returned it. This will be our base to create the portal walls:

```
33    func createWall(width: CGFloat, height: CGFloat, length: CGFloat)->SCNNode
34    {
35        let node = SCNNode()
36
37        let wall = SCNBox(width: width, height: height, length: length,
            chamferRadius: 0)
38        wall.firstMaterial?.diffuse.contents = UIColor.white
39        let wallNode = SCNNode(geometry: wall)
40
41        node.addChildNode(wallNode)
42
43        return node
44    }
```

The new createWall method

2. Let's create another method called `createPortal`:

```
func createPortal() {
}
```

3. Inside it, let's define the variables for the sizes of the walls. Add the following code:

```
let wallWidth: CGFloat = 2
let doorWidth: CGFloat = 0.8
let topWidth = 2 * wallWidth + doorWidth
let height: CGFloat = 2
let length: CGFloat = 0.05
```

We will have four walls, that is, on the left, right, top, and bottom of our portal door. The first three have to be big enough to hide the model from being displayed behind the portal. Their length will be the only thing that's displayed (thereby simulating a door to another dimension). The bottom wall will close that opening.

4. Now, create the main node and the four walls using the previous method `createWall`:

```
let portal = SCNNode()
let leftWall = createWall(width: wallWidth, height: height, length:
length)
leftWall.position = SCNVector3(x: Float(-(wallWidth +
doorWidth)/2), y: Float(height/2), z: 0)
let rightWall = createWall(width: wallWidth, height: height,
length: length)
rightWall.position = SCNVector3(x: Float((wallWidth +
doorWidth)/2), y: Float(height/2), z: 0)
let topWall = createWall(width: topWidth, height: height, length:
length)
topWall.position = SCNVector3(x: 0, y: Float(height*3/2), z: 0)
let bottomWall = createWall(width: topWidth, height: length,
length: length)
bottomWall.position = SCNVector3(x: 0, y: Float(-length/2), z: 0)
```

5. Add the walls to the portal node and then the portal itself to the class' node, as shown in the following code:

```
portal.addChildNode(leftWall)
portal.addChildNode(rightWall)
portal.addChildNode(topWall)
portal.addChildNode(bottomWall)
self.addChildNode(portal)
```

Our 3D portal is ready. Your code should appear as follows:

```
 <   >    ARPortal >  ARPortal >  Portal.swift > No Selection
46       func createPortal()
47       {
48           let wallWidth: CGFloat = 2
49           let doorWidth: CGFloat = 0.8
50           let topWidth = 2 * wallWidth + doorWidth
51           let height: CGFloat = 2
52           let length: CGFloat = 0.05
53
54           let portal = SCNNode()
55
56           let leftWall = createWall(width: wallWidth, height: height, length: length)
57           leftWall.position = SCNVector3(x: Float(-(wallWidth + doorWidth)/2), y: Float(height/2), z: 0)
58
59           let rightWall = createWall(width: wallWidth, height: height, length: length)
60           rightWall.position = SCNVector3(x: Float((wallWidth + doorWidth)/2), y: Float(height/2), z: 0)
61
62           let topWall = createWall(width: topWidth, height: height, length: length)
63           topWall.position = SCNVector3(x: 0, y: Float(height*3/2), z: 0)
64
65           let bottomWall = createWall(width: topWidth, height: length, length: length)
66
67
68           portal.addChildNode(leftWall)
69           portal.addChildNode(rightWall)
70           portal.addChildNode(topWall)
71           portal.addChildNode(bottomWall)
72
73           self.addChildNode(portal)
74       }
```

The createPortal method

6. Now, let's call this method from `init`. After adding the 3D model, add the following code:

```
createPortal()
```

7. If we run the app, when we tap on the floor, we will see a white wall, and through its gap, the 3D model. When we cross it, we will find ourselves in the 3D painting, as shown in the following screenshot:

The white wall covering most of the 3D painting

We can also see the walls so that we can go back to the real world:

The view from inside the 3D painting

8. However, from the outside, we don't want to see a white wall; the portal should just be an opening in the air (the gap on the wall). To get that effect, let's add another box to the `createWall` method before the `return node` call. Add the following code:

```
let maskedWall = SCNBox(width: width, height: height, length:
length, chamferRadius: 0)
maskedWall.firstMaterial?.diffuse.contents = UIColor.white
maskedWall.firstMaterial?.transparency = 0.000000001
let maskedWallNode = SCNNode(geometry: maskedWall)
maskedWallNode.position = SCNVector3.init(0, 0, length)
node.addChildNode(maskedWallNode)
```

This new wall, located before the other one, has a transparency of near 0 (if set to 0, it is painted black) so that we can see the background. But this alone won't work.

9. Add a rendering order of `100` to `wallNode` and a rendering order of `10` to `maskedWallNode`, but leave the final code for the `createWall` method like this:

```
func createWall(width: CGFloat, height: CGFloat, length:
CGFloat)->SCNNode {
    . . .
    wallNode.renderingOrder = 100
    node.addChildNode(wallNode)
    . . .
    maskedWallNode.renderingOrder = 10
    node.addChildNode(maskedWallNode)
    return node
}
```

The `createWall` method should now look as follows:

```
33    func createWall(width: CGFloat, height: CGFloat, length: CGFloat)->SCNNode
34    {
35        let node = SCNNode()
36
37        //Visible wall
38        let wall = SCNBox(width: width, height: height, length: length, chamferRadius: 0)
39        wall.firstMaterial?.diffuse.contents = UIColor.white
40        let wallNode = SCNNode(geometry: wall)
41        wallNode.renderingOrder = 100 //Last to render (inside)
42
43        node.addChildNode(wallNode)
44
45        //Masked wall
46        let maskedWall = SCNBox(width: width, height: height, length: length, chamferRadius: 0)
47        maskedWall.firstMaterial?.diffuse.contents = UIColor.white
48        maskedWall.firstMaterial?.transparency = 0.000000001
49
50        let maskedWallNode = SCNNode(geometry: maskedWall)
51        maskedWallNode.renderingOrder = 10 //First to render (outside)
52        maskedWallNode.position = SCNVector3.init(0, 0, length)
53
54        node.addChildNode(maskedWallNode)
55
56        return node
57    }
```

The createWall method with the final code

10. To finish this, add a rendering order of `200` to `modelNode`, which we created in the `add3DModel` method:

```
func add3DModel() {
    ...
    modelNode.renderingOrder = 200
    self.addChildNode(modelNode)
}
```

The lower the rendering order, the faster the object will be rendered in the scene. This means that we will see `maskedWallNode` first, then `wallNode`, and finally `modelNode`. This way, whenever the masked wall is in view, the 3D elements behind its surface won't be rendered, leaving us with a transparent surface that will show the camera feed directly. The only part of the 3D painting that will be rendered will be the one that's not covered by the walls, that is, our portal door. Once we go through the portal, we will see the 3D painting in full, and when we look back, we will see our white wall.

11. Run the app to see how the portal appears by touching the screen. In the following screenshot, we can see how the masked wall shows us the camera feed hiding the rest of the elements. Here, we can only see the opening from the wall (since we have placed it behind the masked wall in the *z* axis) and the painting through the opening:

You can comment on the `showFeaturePoints` line and the `renderer` methods so that the feature points and anchor planes don't interfere with our 3D scene.

The portal appearing in AR

Once inside the painting, if we look back, we will still see the white walls and the opening to go back to the real world, like before.

Now that the scene is ready, let's improve it by adding some texture to the walls.

Improving the portal

We are going to improve our portal by adding some texture to the walls and a compass image that will show where the portal will appear. For that, we have to add the texture image and the compass image to our project. To do this, follow these steps:

1. Right-click on the **ARPortal** project and select **New File...** In this case, select **SceneKit Catalog** from the **Resource** tab, as shown in the following screenshot:

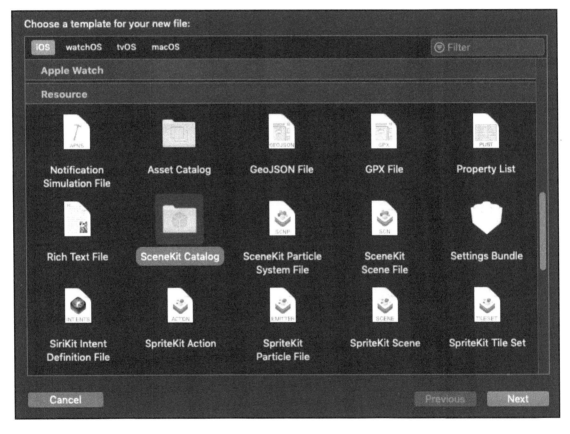

Selecting a new SceneKit Catalog

2. Name it `Media.scnassets` and create it, as follows:

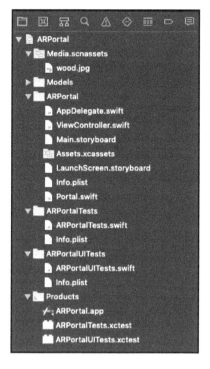

The SceneKit catalog has been successfully created

3. Right-click on the newly created `Media.scnassets` and select **Add Files to "Media.scnassets"**.... Now, select the `wood.jpg` image from the resources of this project and accept it. Our image is ready to be used.

4. Repeat *step 3* with the `compass.png` image.

5. Open `Portal.swift` and, in the `createWall` method, find the following line:

```
wall.firstMaterial?.diffuse.contents = UIColor.white
```

Change it so that it reads like so:

```
wall.firstMaterial?.diffuse.contents = UIImage(named:
"Media.scnassets/wood.jpg")
```

Here, we have added the wooden texture to our portal.

6. Now, we will paint the compass in `ViewController.swift`. For that, create the following variable after the portal variable:

```
var compass: SCNNode? = nil
```

7. Now, uncomment the first `renderer` method, which is where the anchor planes are added (if you had it commented), and substitute the code inside it with the following:

```
if portal == nil && compass == nil
{
    let node = SCNNode()
    guard let planeAnchor = anchor as? ARPlaneAnchor else {return nil}

    let plane = SCNPlane(width: 0.8, height: 0.8)
    plane.firstMaterial?.diffuse.contents = UIImage(named:
"Media.scnassets/compass.png")
    plane.firstMaterial?.transparency = 0.8

    let planeNode = SCNNode(geometry: plane)
    planeNode.position = SCNVector3(x: planeAnchor.center.x, y:
planeAnchor.center.y, z: planeAnchor.center.z)
    planeNode.eulerAngles.x = -Float.pi/2

    node.addChildNode(planeNode)

    planes[planeAnchor] = plane
    compass = node

    return node
}
return nil
```

Here, when a plane anchor is detected, if there is no portal or compass in view (the first time a plane is detected), we will paint a semitransparent compass showing the user the place and orientation of the future portal. Then, we'll save the node as the anchor so that we can use it in *step 9*.

8. Comment the `didUpdate` renderer method if you haven't. We won't need it anymore.

9. In the `didTapOnScreen` method, remove the code between `portal = Portal()` and `self.sceneView.scene.rootNode.addChildNode(portal!)` and include the following code instead:

```
if (compass != nil)
{
    portal?.position = compass!.position
    portal?.rotation = compass!.rotation
```

```
    compass?.removeFromParentNode()
    compass = nil
}
else
{
    portal?.position = SCNVector3(x:
result.worldTransform.columns.3.x, y:
result.worldTransform.columns.3.y, z:
result.worldTransform.columns.3.z)
}
```

Here, when the user taps on the screen for the first time (the compass is in view), we place the portal using the compass position and rotation, and we delete the compass as we no longer need it. From that moment on, if the user keeps tapping on the screen, the portal will move according to the taps and anchor plane position, like before.

10. Run the app to see how the compass appears as soon as the device detects an anchor plane:

The compass appearing on the screen, signaling the place and orientation of the future portal

11. Now, tap the screen to see how the portal has a wooden frame. This can be seen in the following screenshot:

The portal now has a wooden frame

12. From the inside, the texture of the walls has changed too, as shown in the following screenshot:

The view from the inside of the 3D painting

And that's it. Now, you can place the portal wherever you want and play with different options such as changing the 3D painting or creating more than one portal at the same time. It's up to you!

Summary

In this chapter, we have learned what ARKit is and how it works. We have seen how the camera recognizes the feature points and how it creates anchor planes where you can place virtual elements. We have also learned to use SceneKit to insert 3D models into the scene and manipulate them to create an AR portal that leads the user to a 3D environment.

By now, you should have the basic skills to continue improving the current project and adapt it to your personal needs in the tourism sector or even other sectors. You could try to add buttons to the interface to change the 3D content of the portal, add particle effects when the portal first appears, or even try to use 360º videos instead of 3D models. AR is a transversal tool that can be used in several ways and applied to many different needs, so you could also create this portal for fields such as marketing or retail.

This is the last chapter of this book and it is dedicated to the use of AR in enterprises. By now, you should have a broader idea of how AR can be useful for many purposes, including tourism. Now, all you need to do is start playing around with the different frameworks and tools you have learned about and adapt them to your own needs and projects. Have fun!

Further reading

If you want to explore ARKit, either to push the current project further or to try out new things, we recommend Apple's example projects, which can be found at `https://developer.apple.com/documentation/arkit`. Some of these projects are as follows:

- The mentioned `https://developer.apple.com/documentation/arkit/tracking_and_visualizing_planes` project, which you can use to track and visualize the plane anchors
- The `https://developer.apple.com/documentation/arkit/detecting_images_in_an_ar_experience` project, which you can use to detect 2D images (the portal could appear over a real painting instead of in the middle of the street, for example)
- The `https://developer.apple.com/documentation/arkit/tracking_and_visualizing_faces` project, which you can use to track faces and animate virtual avatars through real expressions

With the launch of iOS 13, there are even more features and projects you can try out, such as occluding virtual objects when people move in front of them or interacting with the virtual content by using gestures.

Other Books You May Enjoy

If you enjoyed this book, you may be interested in these other books by Packt:

Hands-On Game Development Patterns with Unity 2019
David Baron

ISBN: 978-1-78934-933-7

- Discover the core architectural pillars of the Unity game engine
- Learn about software design patterns while building gameplay systems
- Acquire the skills to recognize anti-patterns and how to avoid their adverse effect in your codebase
- Enrich your design vocabulary so you can better articulate your ideas on how to better your game's architecture
- Gain some mastery over Unity's API by writing well-designed code
- Get some game industry insider tips and tricks that will help you in your career

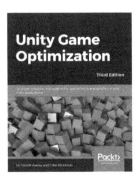

Unity Game Optimization - Third Edition
Chris Dickinson, Dr. Davide Aversa

ISBN: 978-1-83855-651-8

- Apply the Unity Profiler to find bottlenecks in your app, and discover how to resolve them
- Discover performance problems that are critical for VR projects and learn how to tackle them
- Enhance shaders in an accessible way, optimizing them with subtle yet effective performance tweaks
- Use the physics engine to keep scenes as dynamic as possible
- Organize, filter, and compress art assets to maximize performance while maintaining high quality
- Use the Mono framework and C# to implement low-level enhancements that maximize memory usage and prevent garbage collection

Leave a review - let other readers know what you think

Please share your thoughts on this book with others by leaving a review on the site that you bought it from. If you purchased the book from Amazon, please leave us an honest review on this book's Amazon page. This is vital so that other potential readers can see and use your unbiased opinion to make purchasing decisions, we can understand what our customers think about our products, and our authors can see your feedback on the title that they have worked with Packt to create. It will only take a few minutes of your time, but is valuable to other potential customers, our authors, and Packt. Thank you!

Index